Brought up in a happy family environment Peter developed a love of nature by bringing home and nursing a constant stream of abandoned animals including baby Jackdaws and squirrels. But as a young adult he became fascinated by Spain, embracing its culture of the 'Fiesta Brava' and Flamenco, a passion which still burns today, together with his love of antiques.

FROM CASTANETS TO CONSCRIPTION

To my wife, who has endured my pursuit of the passion for the Fiesta, the Flamenco and the bulls.

Marcus, J. (1998) 'The peaks and valleys of ancient states: an extension of the dynamic model', in G.M. Feinman and J. Marcus (eds) *Archaic States*. Sante Fe, NM: School of American Research Press, pp. 59–94.

Marcus, J. and G.M. Feinman (1998) 'Introduction', in G.M. Feinman and J. Marcus (eds) *Archaic States*. Sante Fe, NM: School of American Research Press, pp. 3–14.

Marozzi, J. (2004) *Tamerlane: Sword of Islam, Conqueror of the World*. London: Harper Perennial.

Marshall, A. (1890) *Principles of Economics*. London: Macmillan.

Martin, H-P. and Schumann, H. (1997) *The Global Trap: Globalization and the Assault on Democracy and Prosperity*. London: Zed Books.

Mattessich, R. (2000) *The Beginnings of Accounting and Accounting Thought*. New York: Garland.

McCormack, M. (2001) *Origins of the European Economy: Communications and Commerce AD 300–900*. Cambridge: Cambridge University Press.

McDonald, J.F. (1997) *Fundamentals of Urban Economics*. New York: Prentice Hall.

McIntoch, R.J. and S.K. McIntoch, (2003) 'Early urban configurations on the Middle Niger', in M.L. Smith (ed.) *The Social Construction of Ancient Cities*. Washington, DC: Smithsonian Books, pp. 103–20.

McNeill, J.R. and W.H. McNeill (2003) *The Human Web: A Bird's-eye View of World History*. New York: Norton.

Meier, R. (1962) *Communications Theory and Urban Growth*. Cambridge, MA: MIT Press.

Mellaart, J. (1964) 'A neolithic city in Turkey', *Scientific American*, April, 94–104.

Mellaart, J. (1965a) *Earliest Civilisations of The Near East*. London: Thames & Hudson.

Mellaart, J. (1965b) 'Çatal Hüyük: a neolithic city in Anatolia', *Proceedings of the British Academy* 51, 201–13.

Merrington, J. (1976) 'Town and country in the transition to capitalism', in R. Hilton (ed.) *The Transition from Feudalism to Capitalism*. London: Verso, pp. 170–95.

Mithen, S. (2003) *After the Ice: A Global Human History 20,000–5000 BC*. Cambridge, MA: Harvard University Press.

Modelski, G. (2003) *World Cities: -3000 to 2000*. Washington, DC: Faros 2000.

Moore, J.D. (2003) 'Life behind walls: patterns in the urban landscape on the prehistoric north coast of Peru', in M.L. Smith (ed.) *The Social Construction of Ancient Cities*. Washington, DC: Smithsonian Books, pp. 81–120.

Morris, I. (1997) 'An archaeology of equalities? The Greek city-states', in

Peter E. Mardle

FROM CASTANETS TO CONSCRIPTION

AUSTIN MACAULEY
PUBLISHERS LTD.

A CIP catalogue record for this title is available from the British Library.

ISBN 978 184963 548 6

www.austinmacauley.com

First Published (2014)
Austin Macauley Publishers Ltd.
25 Canada Square
Canary Wharf
London
E14 5LB

Printed and bound in Great Britain

Preface

Living in an age in which travel agents struggle to cater to the more extremes of holidaymakers' demands, the world in which we now live continues to grow increasingly smaller due to the advent of cheaper and faster travel. It is because of such changes that it is difficult to imagine Spain as it was in the nineteen fifties.

Unbelievably, less than seventy years ago, people living throughout the length and breadth of Spain struggled to survive in a country which was still being ruled by an army general whose secret police wielded the same inexorable power as that of his more recent counterpart, General Augusto Pinochet of Chile.

General Franco, or El Caudillo as he liked to be called, was an autocratic ruler who, just a few years earlier, had forced brother to fight against brother and father to fight against son in a bloody civil war. With merciless deliberation he had led thousands of Fascist troops in an attempt to crush communism and the legendary International Brigade, a dedicated body of volunteers consisting of men and women who came from all over the world to answer a call to arms in an attempt to put a stop to his bloody form of dictatorship.

It was only after his death in 1975 that Spain became a very different place following the accession to the Spanish throne of King Juan Carlos I. Gradually under the king's leadership, the country became much more liberated. Initially magazines began to feature photographs of women exposing a small amount of cleavage, something which was unheard of during Franco's tyrannical reign; this being gradually followed by even more risqué photographs which showed bare breasted women until inevitably full fronted nudity also became much in evidence.

Today, despite its economic uncertainty, Spain continues to enjoy one of the highest standards of living in Europe, a country that has become a second home to many thousands of foreign nationals. British, Americans, Germans, Swedes and even Russians have descended on this cosmopolitan refuge, setting up home to enjoy the many benefits that life in Spain has on offer.

Even life in rural Spain today is in sharp contrast to the days when young men risked their lives by leaping into a bull ring, 'protected' only by home-made wooden swords and capes. Although against the law, these desperately poor and heroic young men known as *espontaneos* would jump into the ring hoping to catch the eye of an *empresario* or bullfight promoter who, if the young man showed promise, would take him under his mercenary wing and provide him with sufficient funds to enable him to overcome the hardship and poverty imposed by the harsh and restrictive practices put in place by the jack-booted dictator.

This then is the story of a simple and naïve young man who set out on his own voyage of discovery in the early days of tourism, hell bent on discovering the delights of Spain in the early fifties, armed only with a British passport, a pitiful amount of pesetas and the same arrogance of youth that accompanied voyages of discovery which set sail to conquer the new world over four hundred years earlier.

Came the Fateful Day...

The rattling of the letter box announced the arrival of the postman and, with it, came the same awful sinking feeling in the pit of my stomach that had accompanied that relatively cheerful sound on a daily basis for the last few weeks.

With a cheery shout of 'I'll get it' emanating from the kitchen, my mother stomped down the hallway to retrieve whatever mail had arrived, the promptness of her action leaving me poised half standing and half sitting at the breakfast table.

As the door to the dining room swung open, my mother appeared wiping one hand on her apron while the other remained embalmed in a sticky coating of flour and jam, sufficient in quantity to make several more of whatever she was in the process of baking, while her marginally cleaner hand clutched the morning post.

Holding two letters which were now also liberally coated with flour and traces of jam, she uttered the words I had been dreading to hear for the last few weeks.

'I think it's arrived,' she said. 'This one has got OHMS stamped on the envelope so it looks like the one you've been waiting for.'

Holding the second letter at arm's length she peered at the envelope before dropping them both on to the dining table.

'This other letter will cheer you up though; it looks like it might be from Pam and Nick.'

Wiping her hands on her apron she headed back into the kitchen.

'I'll just finish what I'm doing and then I'll come back and you can tell me what it's all about.'

Working as an apprentice in a local coach painting and motor body repair business, I had discovered very early on that, as well as gaining limited experience in the more intricate and constructive practices of that noble profession, I was also being treated as a source of cheap labour, being constantly reminded that if I ever considered resigning I would immediately be called upon to do my National Service, a threat which continually hung over me like the proverbial Sword of Damocles.

One day when being ordered to perform a particularly onerous task, my bad mood had overcome common sense sending the blood coursing through my veins like a surging tsunami. This rush of hot blood had resulted in me suggesting that my employer might like to take his paint and other associated materials and put them in a place where the sun wasn't known to shine. The result of this ill-considered outburst was having been handed a pitifully small brown envelope containing my wages together with a further amount of money which was to serve in lieu of holidays, this monetary insult being followed several days later by a letter from the MOD telling me that I was now required to render myself available to serve Queen and country.

Reluctantly obeying the carefully worded instructions contained in the letter, I attended what was laughingly referred to as an 'aptitude entrance examination', where, with thirty or so other assorted melancholy individuals, we had grudgingly sat down at small school room style desks to attempt to answer a series of questions clearly designed to assess the mental aptitude of ten year olds or younger.

The object of this exercise we had been told was to determine which branch of the armed forces would be better served by an assessment of our intelligence which would result in us being placed in an environment where such intelligence would be fully utilised. As I appeared to be one of the few persons present who had the capability of 'doing joined up writing', I was duly selected to reinforce the ranks of other such unfortunates currently serving in the RAF, and this was almost certainly the letter which would tell me when and where to report for duty.

Realising that it was pointless to simply stick the letter behind the clock on the mantelshelf to be opened later, I picked up the long brown envelope and sliced open its end with my unused butter knife. I groaned, as leaping from the page, in what appeared to be inch high letters were the words, 'You will report to RAF Cardington in Bedfordshire for the purpose of medical assessment and to receive the necessary clothing and equipment required for a period of two years National Service to be served in this country or abroad'.

In addition to a short list of items I was advised to take with me was the date I was ordered to report to this establishment for the start of my obligatory removal from society, July 24th 1957.

Although the expectations of receiving such a letter since my dismissal by my former employer had invariably been uppermost in my mind, the dispassionate wording of its contents did nothing to alleviate the overwhelming feeling of gloom I was now feeling. Why hadn't I gritted my teeth and kept my big mouth shut rather than succumb to the hot blood of my youth? In hindsight, perhaps if I had just held my tongue and served out my so-called apprenticeship, National Service may have been abolished and I wouldn't now be in this sorry situation. (As it transpired, National Service was abolished two years later.)

Walking back into the room, still wiping her floury hands on her apron, my mother asked, 'Well, is that it then? Is that the letter you've been dreading?'

I nodded glumly. 'I've got to report at Cardington on the 24th of July.'

She sat down and picked up the letter, quickly scanning its contents. Sensing my despondency she placed her hand reassuringly on my knee.

'Don't upset yourself,' she said. 'When you get settled in you'll probably love it. Your father was in the army for over twelve years and he thought it was wonderful.'

Now, why is it that all parents seem to have that inborn philosophical penchant for seeing the best side of everything?

I scoffed at her optimistic attempt to cheer me up.

'Dad enjoyed it because of his love of music and his wish to play in a decent band, so he got everything he wanted from the army. Apart from his music, he always wanted to travel and to see India so he couldn't have wished for anything more.

He played in the regimental band and spent years in a country he would never have got to see if it wasn't for being in the army, so I think he was lucky. With my luck, I'll probably end up in a cookhouse somewhere in the Outer Hebrides.'

Seeing that there was no way she was going to console me she tried a different approach.

'I think you're worrying too much, you're good at sport and your father has always said that there are lots of opportunities to do things like that in the forces. I remember him telling you once that if you showed any sort of promise you get out of doing rotten jobs so you can train properly to represent your regiment or whatever it's called in the RAF. Look how he loved boxing, when he took it up in the army he never looked back and it's probably the same in the RAF, anyway I can't stand here talking to you all day I've got a lot to do before your father gets home. Why don't you read your other letter, it might cheer you up a bit?'

The other letter I mused, that's all I needed, today of all days, a letter from my cousin Pam living in Spain, telling me once again what a wonderful time she was having and how life couldn't be better. Oh yes, that was bound to cheer me up!

My cousin was someone who, in the forties and fifties, fell into the category of being referred to as 'a yankee basher', a term cruelly applied to women who 'fraternised' with American service personnel stationed over here, but in my cousin's case, she was, as they say in the best American tradition, 'a one man woman'.

Despite repeated chastisement and threats from my uncle and aunt, she had met and fallen desperately in love with an American Air Force sergeant stationed at the nearby non-operational air base at RAF Chicksands. Although essentially an English RAF base, it was manned by both English and American servicemen. This 'foreigner', to whom she had willingly given her heart, answered to the poetically sounding name of Clyde Graves Dumas, but to his friends and work colleagues he was always affectionately referred to as 'Nick'.

It appeared to those that knew them that this Anglo-American relationship was one which was destined to stand the test of time, a relationship which ultimately would last for the rest of their lives, but despite demonstrating their sincere love for each other, there were two overriding issues which my uncle and aunt weren't happy about. Firstly was the difference in their ages, Pam was only seventeen and Nick was twenty seven, but equally important was the fact that he was still a 'foreigner'.

Despite the fact that America's entry into the Second World War had been this country's saviour, there was still a great degree of smouldering animosity shown to American servicemen who were stationed in Britain. This animosity was due in no small part to the obvious difference between 'those who had, and those who had not'.

American servicemen wore smart tailored uniforms, had money in their pockets, and by and large oozed an appeal which the poverty stricken British could only envy.

It was thought by a great number of women in this country that America was the 'promised land' and after years of struggling to make do and mend, an American man was considered by some to be a great catch, offering a potentially more exciting and glamorous lifestyle.

In addition to the term 'yankee basher' being applied to women, American servicemen in this country were also labelled with an even more dubious epithet, that of 'being overpaid, oversexed and over here' a term which did little to endear Nick as a future son-in-law, but despite objections raised by them in a futile attempt to end the relationship, Pam and Nick duly married, a marriage which was later blessed with two children and one which was to flourish throughout the remainder of their lives.

Picking up the letter, I looked at the stamp on the envelope where the face of General Franco stared impassively back at me. Here was I about to endure untold horrors in the service of Her Majesty while others appeared to be living the life of film stars in a hot and sunny land, how could life be so cruel?

Anything vaguely associated with either Nick or America was something to be kept and treasured, so I carefully opened the envelope to avoid damaging any of its contents, and pulling out the letter I saw it also contained a black and white photograph. Eagerly scanning the photograph I stared at an image of a scene that did little to make my own circumstances appear any more uplifting.

Squinting against the glare of the sun, Pam and Nick were seated at a table in a tree-lined square raising half-filled glasses in a silent toast, while hordes of snow white doves pecked at crumbs both on the table at which they sat and also around their feet.

Turning the photograph over, I read the message written in pencil on the back. It read quite simply in Nick's sloping scrawl, 'You see that other bottle and glass on the table Pete, that one's for you. Why don't you come on over?'

Looking again at the photograph, I noticed a half-filled glass, beside which, stood a bottle containing the remainder of the beer, a bottle on which an exotic sounding label proudly proclaimed it to be a foreign elixir named San Miguel.

Drooling over the photograph I gazed enviously at the rest of their surroundings. Leafy avenues of trees were made even more seductive by shadows cast by the bright sunlight, while fluttering pigeons and doves completed a picture of sublime happiness being enjoyed by my happy looking relations.

Putting the photograph down on to the table I picked up the letter and began to read, its content carrying me away like a fabled magic carpet to a place where it clearly seldom rained, the sun appeared never to set, and life consisted only of days of pleasure interspersed with nights of dreamless sleep, all of those things being romantically accompanied by wild gypsies strumming vibrant melodies on flamenco guitars which lasted long into the early hours of the morning.

Finally, putting down the letter, I leaned back in my chair, its final sentence burning into my brain like a red hot branding iron... 'Why don't you pack a bag and come out and see us, we've got plenty of room and we would love to see you?'

Staring hard at the letter, I re-read the final sentence. Did it really say that or was I imagining it? Yes, there it was, boldly underlined... 'Why don't you come out and see us, we've got plenty of room and we would love to see you?'

I dropped the letter back on to the table and sat back in my chair.

I couldn't believe it, one letter was telling me that I must report in a few weeks' time to do my National Service and in the same post I had just received an invitation to visit what I considered to be the next thing to paradise, unbelievable.

My heart sank, how could life be so cruel and unjust?

I picked up the letter for a third time; it was as if a light bulb had been switched on in my head.

What was to stop me? I had some of my wages left and some money saved, surely it wouldn't alter the overall scheme of things if I arrived at Cardington a few days late, after all there were probably a few other blokes already there who were more than capable of holding the fort until I arrived. What was the worst they could do to me; smack my wrist and send me home again for being late? Tell me that I had missed the boat and they didn't want me any more? I didn't think so.

My mother's voice broke my train of thought as I stared at the letter.

'Well, tell me all about it, are Pam and Nick ok, what have they been getting up to?'

Pushing my chair back away from the table, I handed her the letter.

'Yes, they're fine,' I answered. 'Here, you can read it if you like, there's also a photograph.'

As I walked from the room my mind was in turmoil as I tried to get things into some sort of perspective.

Supposing I did decide to take the plunge and go, what would I need? I would certainly need a passport, and as I didn't have one, the first thing I needed to know was how you went about getting one. Thinking about it, I suddenly remembered that friends of mine had recently returned from France so they would know what to do. They had proudly shown off their newly acquired passports, telling me that they were valid for five years, so perhaps if I could get one that lasted just for this trip it would probably be cheaper which would certainly help towards my overall costs.

Leaving my mother reading the letter, I raced up the stairs to my bedroom and pulled open the dressing table drawer in which my building society passbook was kept. As I thumbed through its pages, a sense of disappointment swept over me as I stared at the figures at the bottom of last page, £84-16s-10d. A worthy enough amount when there's nothing in particular that you want to spend it on, but hardly enough to take me to Seville and back in a grand manner, and definitely not enough to ensure limitless funds for sightseeing and weeks of riotous fun.

Flopping full length down on the bed I optimistically flicked over the pages in the forlorn hope that there might be some undiscovered interest payment lurking there. Perhaps a previously unnoticed amount which might swell the balance to a point where I didn't need to search for other means of raising some extra capital, but it was not to be. Interest for the year had already been calculated and added to the total so I could expect no further help from those exceedingly nice people at the Woolwich.

Staring at the book, I wondered about the cost of flying to Spain and the likelihood of flying directly to Seville, or would Madrid be the only option? The more I thought about it the more I became convinced that if there were no airlines which flew directly to Seville, there were sure to be flights to Madrid, and once I arrived there, surely it would be easy enough to get on a train that would take me the rest of the way.

With my mind bursting with unanswered questions, I jumped up from the bed and took down my jacket which hung from a peg attached to the back of the bedroom door. There was only one way to find out I told myself, and that was to go to a travel agent and ask.

Thrusting my precious building society book into my pocket I rushed down the stairs, narrowly avoiding my mother who had just emerged from the dining room.

'Where are you off to in such an all fired hurry?' she asked, stepping back against the wall as I pushed past her.

'Sorry mum, I'm just going to pop into town, I've just thought of something that I need to do, I won't be very long.'

Kissing her lightly on the cheek, I opened the front door.

'Don't be late, your father will be coming home for his lunch today and he'll want it on the table at his usual time so he won't be best pleased if he has to sit and wait for you, otherwise he'll be late back to work.'

Cheerfully agreeing to be back on time, I gave her another peck on the cheek before slamming the front door behind me.

The Man in the Dark Blue Suit...

With my heart beating at twice its normal rate I stared into the window of Thomas Cook's travel agency. Stepping on to the bus which would take me into town, I could hardly contain my excitement at the prospect of what might lay ahead, and now having reached this point I was feeling incredibly nervous.

Looking out of the window from the top of the bus I was oblivious to everything that flashed past as I tried to weigh up all the pros and cons of what I was about to do. The pros were happily obvious but it was the uncertainty of the cons which were worrying me.

On one hand there was the exciting prospect of travelling by a means of transport which, to my young mind, was solely the prerogative of only the rich and famous, and secondly and more importantly, was the mouth-watering prospect of spending time in a foreign country with the two people, apart from my parents, whom I admired most in the world. These were the obvious delights which beckoned enticingly, but looming large were also the objections my parents would undoubtedly raise in view of my imminent conscription into the RAF, but overwhelmingly was the most important problem of all, my possible shortage of the necessary funds.

Pushing these thoughts to the back of my mind, I pushed open the travel agent's door and stepped inside to be greeted by the creamy sweet smell of colourful and carefully arranged holiday brochures. Looking around, my gaze lingered over the glossy posters which showed nubile young women stretched out on white sandy beaches while palm trees swayed enticingly in the background, and it was these seductive images which immediately strengthened my resolve; come hell or high water, I was going to Spain even if I had to work my passage on a cargo boat or something similar to get there.

With a small voice in my head telling me that I could do this, I closed the door.

'Can I help you, sir?'

The voice came from an immaculately attired man dressed in a dark blue suit and matching tie sitting behind a low counter, and in the buttonhole of his beautifully cut jacket, a crisp white carnation added to his aura of elegance and authority. I looked around but with no-one else in the room it was clearly me that he was addressing. Was this epitome of suave elegance actually talking to me?

Nobody had ever addressed me as sir before and I felt myself growing in stature. Why hadn't I spruced myself up a bit? My grey flannel trousers and the jacket with the leather patches on the elbows were clearly out of place here, it was obvious that, in this man's presence, I had severely underestimated the necessary dress code.

Again the question.

'May I be of help, sir?'

'Sorry,' I muttered, feeling my face taking on a slightly pinker hue, but in addressing me as 'sir' he had clearly recognised the fact that he was about to deal with someone who was used to being addressed in such a manner.

'Yes,' I said, regaining a degree of composure, 'I hope so.'

Taking a deep breath I heard myself say in a slightly hesitant manner, 'I want to go to Seville in Spain and I would like to know the best way of getting there.'

'Yes sir, I am aware that Seville is in Spain, and in answer to your question, it is my considered opinion that the most direct way of getting there is by air.'

In that brief moment the man behind the desk had recognised me for what I was, someone extremely naïve in the ways of the world and of travel in particular, and he was taking pleasure in putting me firmly in my place with just a single sentence.

Aware that I had been recognised as someone unfamiliar with this environment, I decided to throw myself on his mercy, blurting out that all of this was new to me and I needed to establish the likelihood of flying directly to Seville and of the cost involved.

With a look of barely concealed haughtiness on his smooth pampered face he said, 'I assume that "sir" is already in possession of a passport?'

I shook my head, immediately wishing that I had gone somewhere more down to earth where I might have been treated with more courtesy and respect.

'Ah, just so sir,' he said. 'Unfortunately that's the first thing "sir" will require, and then of course "sir" will require a visa.'

'A visa,' I spluttered, 'I thought that you only needed a visa if you were travelling to America or somewhere like that?'

'Oh, indeed not sir, I'm afraid that "sir" will also require a visa.'

It seemed to me, that in answering, he appeared to be putting even greater emphasis on the use of the word 'sir'.

Looking him straight in the eye I began to feel angry at his pseudo superior attitude and felt that the time was quickly approaching when I would need to point out the error of his ways. He was clearly taking pleasure at my discomfort and enjoying his role of authoritarian superiority, but he was now becoming dangerously close to seeing a different side of 'sir'.

Sitting back with his fingers clasped in front of him he awaited my next question.

Telling myself that he was just a man who sold tickets and offered travel advice, I decided that I was no longer going to be intimidated by this stuffed shirt and the time had now come for him to re-assess his role in all of this.

'I need to know how to go about obtaining a passport and visa and obtaining all the relevant tickets I might need in the shortest possible time?' I snapped tersely. 'It's important that I get this sorted out quickly. I don't have the time to spend messing about making phone calls or writing letters to people.'

Sensing that he had overstepped the mark and that I was no longer overawed by his supercilious air of authority, his attitude quickly changed. Unbuttoning his jacket he gave a loud theatrical sniff and took out an expensive looking fountain pen from the pocket of his waistcoat, placing it on the desk in front of him before asking in a slightly edgy, but more reasonable and polite manner, when I intended to travel.

It was now my turn. By nature I am not an aggressive person, but my father had instilled in me that if I ever found myself face to face with someone who was by definition not necessarily my friend, I must exploit any weakness he might show to its fullest extent, emphasising that if I didn't I might not get a second chance.

My father had joined the army at the age of eighteen and had become an accomplished musician, but in addition to that he had proved himself to be a formidable opponent in the boxing ring, fearlessly taking the blows to become regimental lightweight boxing champion for three consecutive years. His quiet courage and self-discipline had always been an inspiration to me and his steadying influence was now going to be put to the test as I prepared to end this charade.

'I want to be able to leave as quickly as possible and, if for some reason you feel that you're unable to help with my travel arrangements, I'll go somewhere else and find someone who can.'

For someone who ten minutes earlier had timidly entered the travel agent's feeling like a lost soul with very little idea of what the real world was all about, I now felt far more comfortable in this new role, so much so that I showed my new found confidence by leaning back in my chair as I awaited his reaction.

An uneasy and worried smile flickered briefly across his face.

'Yes of course, sir. I'm sure that we at Thomas Cook will be able to help you.'

I was now listening to a very different kind of 'sir'. This time I felt that he almost meant it, but despite the thin smile that hovered about his lips, there still remained a haughty look in his pale grey eyes.

'Firstly you will need to apply for a passport from the British Consulate in London. As this will be your first passport it will only be valid for five years, but once you have it, you can renew it annually. Alternatively, you can renew it for a further five years, but after ten years you will have to re-apply for a new one. If you decide to renew it annually it will cost you two shillings (10p) per year, but the majority of people renew it for a further five years. On applying, one simply goes to the post office for the necessary form; one fills it in and sends it with a current photograph of oneself together with a cheque to the consulate.'

'What is the cost a five year passport?' I asked, ignoring the emphasis placed on the word 'one', sensing that 'one' was now being taken very much more seriously.

'It's currently twenty shillings (£1.00), sir. Of course it's possible that there may well be an increase in the near future so I would advocate a degree of haste'

'What about applying for a visa? What do I need to do and what sort of costs are involved?'

'Well, once you have your passport,' he replied, 'it needs to be sent to the Spanish Consulate in London together with the appropriate fee.'

The man leaned across his desk and reached into a drawer, pulling out a plastic-covered folder which he flicked open. Running his finger down a list on one of the pages, he muttered to himself as he looked at each entry… 'Spain… Spain… Spain, where are we? Oh yes, here we are, an entry visa to Spain costs a further twenty shillings.'

'Once your application has been sanctioned,' he continued, 'your passport will be stamped with a relevant visa stamp. It will carry the appropriate number on the top and will be returned to you. It doesn't usually take any longer than two weeks, but under normal circumstances it could take less than that.'

This was beginning to look better than I had first imagined. The cost of a passport and visa weren't going to hurt my budget that much and the timescale involved wasn't bad either. I wished that it could be sooner rather than later but the dream I had carried with me into the travel agent's was now looking more like a reality.

Putting a lid on my mounting excitement I quickly realised that all I had discovered so far was that a passport would cost me less than I had at first anticipated, and that the price of a Spanish visa was also well within my budget.

Looking him straight in the eye I heard myself say, 'That's about what I imagined it might be.'

If he had told me that those two items were going to cost twenty times that amount I would have said exactly the same thing. Taking a deep breath, I prepared to take the plunge and ask the all important question.

'That's fine,' I said. 'What about the cost of the air fare, can I fly directly into Seville?'

'Of course, sir. The airport is only a few miles from the city and a taxi will take you to wherever you want to go. May I ask if you have made enquiries in respect of accommodation? We at Thomas Cook pride ourselves on choosing the right hotels for our customers and it would be a pleasure to arrange this for you if you so wish?'

Attempting to appear casual, I airily waved my hand before answering. 'That won't be necessary. I have relatives who live in Seville who I haven't seen for some years, and I thought that this would be an ideal time for me to spend a few weeks with them.'

I had visited the local library when Pam and Nick had first moved to Spain and had eagerly devoured everything the library had on offer with regard to both the country and its history, but apart from the festival of San Fermin, I had absolutely no idea of dates of possible forthcoming festivals, but I felt that the manner in which I had casually trotted this time thing out made the whole thing sound fairly convincing.

Looking suitably impressed on hearing my comments, the man sitting opposite answered in what I felt was an altogether different tone of voice.

'Yes,' he mused, 'you are quite right. I have visited Spain at this time of the year on numerous occasions and it is indeed a good time to go. There are many religious festivals held in and around Andalucia and most are quite spectacular.'

Turning in his chair, the travel agent plucked a brochure from a small rack of shelves which sat beside his desk, thumbing through its pages he finally came to the page he was seeking. Holding my breath I waited on tenterhooks as he ran his finger down the list of entries, which from where I sat, appeared to be a detailed schedule of air fares to various destinations in Spain.

'Ah yes, here we are,' he said. 'Flying with Iberia Airlines which depart from Heathrow on Tuesdays and Thursdays, the return air fare will be £38.16s.0p.'

I gulped, although not as much as I had anticipated, I didn't need a degree in in mathematics to tell me that spending that amount on just the air fare was going to leave me short if I wanted to contribute in some small way towards my keep. Not only would the air fare leave a large hole in my budget, I also needed to take into account the cost of getting from Luton to London as well.

Perhaps detecting a look of disappointment on my face, the travel agent asked, 'Is that the sort of figure you had anticipated sir?' before placing both hands on the folder in front of him.

I realised that if I was to stand any chance of getting things sorted out while I was there, the time had come to be honest and again throw myself on his mercy.

'I have to admit that it's about what I thought it might be,' I answered, 'but as I have no pressing engagements for the foreseeable future, I was hoping to stretch my budget to enable me to stay for perhaps a couple of months or even more.'

'I see sir, then if one has no deadlines to meet which govern the length of time one is out of the country, may I suggest an alternative?'

My mind went back to the brown envelope marked OHMS which I had left on the breakfast table earlier containing the letter that said quite categorically what my options were with regard to me making myself available on a specific date.

'Yes, please do. I have no pressing reasons to bring me back on any given date,' I lied. 'If you could suggest some interesting alternative I might well be interested.'

Putting to one side the brochure containing the air fares, the man opposite opened a desk drawer and pulled out what looked like a huge bus timetable, opening it up and flicking through its pages as he answered.

'Flying is fine if you need to get from point A to point B in a hurry but it can be relatively expensive, but for someone like yourself who isn't governed by the length of time he's away or isn't bothered by the amount of time he spends travelling, there are far more satisfying alternatives which can be considerably cheaper.'

At the mention of the word 'cheaper' my heart leaped. This man to whom I had taken such a dislike earlier was now going up in leaps and bounds in my estimation, and there was now a distinct possibility that we may well become friends for life.

Like a drowning man desperately reaching out for a life line, I leaned forward in my chair in hopeful expectation.

'What sort of alternatives do you have in mind?' I asked eagerly.

'Well sir, one can always travel by train and by boat, obviously it takes a great deal longer, but on the other hand it is a far more interesting and satisfying option. I also think that one could save a considerable amount of money as a result.'

'Purely as an example you understand, should one feel so inclined, one could travel to Portsmouth by train and board a cargo vessel that has cabin accommodation for passengers wishing to sail to Bilbao.'

Bilbao, at the mention of the name my mind shifted up into overdrive. I hadn't the vaguest idea where Bilbao might be, but in my mind it conjured up visions of a hot and steamy city where dusky maidens wearing huge straw hats on their heads and flaunting beautifully bronzed bodies wandered the streets singing exotic love songs. I knew in an instant that Bilbao was where I wanted to spend the rest of my life.

Forgetting all about trying to appear worldly, I excitedly plunged straight in, swept up with the idea that I was about to embark on the greatest adventure of my life.

'Where exactly is Bilbao?' I asked.

The man in the blue suit smiled, now fully aware that all previous pretence had been swept aside and that he was now once again in charge, but this time there was a more understanding look in his eyes, a look that indicated that he might be recalling times past when he too had started out on a life changing adventure of his own.

'Bilbao is in northern Spain. It lies just across the border from France and is not very far from San Sebastián and Santander.'

'It's a most pleasant way to get to Spain and although one has to cross the Bay of Biscay which can sometimes be a bit choppy, at this time of the year it should be reasonably calm.'

He leaned back in his chair as he continued.

'I first travelled there in this manner when probably not much older than you, but I went later in the year when we encountered some really bad storms. It takes around twenty hours to reach Bilbao and I remember that there were some pretty ill people on board who were extremely happy when they finally stepped ashore.'

I didn't much like the thought of being seasick and the vision that I had in my head of looking like a young and virile Noël Coward, casually leaning over the ship's rail smoking a cigarette, quickly vanished.

'If I choose not to go by that route, surely I would still need to travel by boat to cross the channel wouldn't I, how does that work?'

He smiled. 'Obviously one has to cross the channel to reach Europe sir, but with the short crossing from Dover to Calais on the boat train, one would spend less time at sea and far more time travelling by an alternative means of transport.'

In my wildest dreams I would never have envisaged me travelling on a boat train.

This was getting more exciting by the minute as the image I had in my mind of me emulating Noël Coward quickly changed to a more dangerous and manly one of me playing the role portrayed by Humphrey Bogart in the film *Casablanca*.

The man's voice became a distant and blurred hum as I imagined myself stepping down from the train, the escaping steam from the pistons swirling around my legs as I casually lit a cigarette and looked around from beneath the turned down brim of my trilby hat, my face obscured by the turned up collar of my raincoat.

This was more like it, now we were getting somewhere. This was obviously what I had been born to do, travelling from country to country carrying secret documents to the heads of various governments, or carrying out daring rescues while being pursued by armed foreign agents. Not for me the mundane tasks of re-spraying people's rusting vehicles or repairing a broken lorry chassis, this was obviously to be my destiny.

I was jolted back from my reverie by the travel agent's voice as he repeated his question.

'Would you like me to work out some sort of itinerary to see if the dates and times suit your requirements sir, then if these prove to be acceptable we can then tailor the whole thing to precisely the dates you wish to travel. If you apply for your passport and visa immediately you will probably receive your passport in just over a week's time and your visa in a further week or so, and if you find that the dates and times are in fact convenient, you could be on your way in about three weeks' time.'

I thought about the date I was to report for duty at RAF Cardington. If I got my skates on and did as he suggested I could be out of the country by then, and that being the case there would be very little that could be done until my return. What was likely to happen to me when I did report? Surely just being late for duty wasn't a hanging offence, if it consisted of a few minor punishments for a week or so I could put up with that, at least I would have had some wonderful times to look back on which would certainly make any punishment they chose to throw at me a risk worth taking.

As I thought about my options I began to worry about the likely cost involved. What if he were to come up with a figure that was still too much, could I go to my parents and ask to borrow the money knowing that I couldn't begin to pay them back until I had finished my National Service, probably not? In addition I couldn't imagine either of them being inclined to lend me any money anyway knowing that I shouldn't be going to Spain but reporting for duty instead, particularly my father who was very proud of his army career and a stickler for doing the right thing at all times.

Oh, the hell with it I thought, you're a long time dead.

Feeling less confident than I sounded, I heard myself saying, 'Yes, I think that's a good idea, at least I'll know what's involved and what the total cost is likely to be.'

Somewhat relieved now that I had reached this point, I leaned back in my chair and watched the travel agent as he put on his spectacles and bent to his task, studying book after book as he scanned their pages searching for any relevant information. Every now and then he would pause to jot things down, his brow furrowing periodically as his finger traced lines along pages of dates, times and destinations, flicking back over pages as he checked and double checked what he had written.

Finally sitting back in his chair he sighed, screwing back the top of his fountain pen before carefully studying what he had written. I held my breath as he slowly took off his glasses and placed them on the desk in front of him.

'I've covered several options which are available to you and considered various routes one might use and happily most are cheaper than I had first anticipated.'

I breathed a sigh of relief at his news; I liked the sound of it being 'cheaper' than he had first anticipated. At least it now appeared fairly 'do-able' but his idea of cheap and my idea of cheap might be vastly different and I waited anxiously for his results.

'If one travels by boat and train without the additional cost of a couchette, I think we can get you to Seville and back for £23.18s.6d.'

My heart soared, with that figure in mind there would be no need to ask anyone for a loan and it would leave me with a fairly decent amount of money left in hand for 'spends', enough I felt to last me for three or four weeks at least. In the past, Nick had written on numerous occasions saying that the cost of living in Spain was incredibly cheap, and if that was indeed the case, with a little judicious spending and not going too mad on frivolities I would hopefully be able to manage.

'As I previously mentioned,' he continued, 'I've worked out the cost of rail fares without having a couchette, but to compensate for that I've included travelling on a very special train called the Talgo Express.'

'Not only is this train an express, it is without doubt a very luxurious express. It has leather reclining seats, full waiter and bar service and is really quite superb. The other benefits are that it travels directly from Irun to Madrid, so by travelling in greater comfort, one almost certainly feels far more relaxed on arrival.'

Picking up his spectacles once again, the travel agent thoughtfully polished them with a snow white handkerchief which dangled foppishly from the top pocket of his jacket, before placing them precisely on the bridge of his nose.

'I'll run through the details to give you some idea of what the journey entails.'

'Firstly, one catches the train from Luton to St Pancras, and once there one simply crosses to Waterloo to connect with the boat train to Dover. On your arrival in Dover you will find that the cross channel ferry is already there waiting for you.'

He smiled, 'Once at sea I'm sure that you will be more than ready for lunch, after which you can enjoy a relaxed voyage to Calais where I'm confident you will be eager for the next leg of your journey which will take you to the wonderful city of Paris.'

He looked into my eyes as he continued.

'I appreciate that you might think that it all sounds a little involved, but believe me it really is quite straight forward. The only slightly complicated part is actually crossing Paris to get to the Gare du Nord where you catch your next train to Hendaye, but if you simply take a taxi from the rank outside the station, the driver will whisk you across the city with no problems whatsoever.'

'Please don't try to memorise all of this, I'll write it down for you with all the arrival and departure times and then when you receive your printed itinerary and tickets, it will contain any additional information you might need.'

I inwardly winced at the thought of having to catch so many trains. I had rather stupidly imagined that all I had to do was to step straight from one train and on to the next. Neither had it occurred to me that I might have to travel from one part of a city to another, or even find taxis willing to take me to further departure points.

As if sensing my growing doubt, the travel agent leaned forward slightly and smiled as he said, 'Please, there really is nothing to worry about, I'm confident that you will experience no problems whatsoever.'

'On your arrival in Hendaye it really begins to get interesting. Hendaye is the border crossing from where you will cross to Irun in Spain and it is here that the Talgo Express will be waiting for you. You will notice that the carriages on this wonderful train resemble a series of linked aluminium cigar tubes which have tinted windows to soften the glare from the sun, it really is quite spectacular. Once on board it will whisk you away in perfect comfort and luxury directly to the city of Madrid.'

Removing his spectacles, the man carefully placed them on the desk in front of him.

'Once you reach Madrid you simply cross from one platform to another to board the train which will take you directly in to Seville itself. Please believe me when I tell you that it will be a wonderful experience and one that you will never forget, in fact just talking about it is beginning to make me feel quite envious.'

With the man's final well chosen words ringing in my ears, I felt all doubts and fears evaporating like wisps of smoke drifting gently from an autumn bonfire into a cloudless blue sky before disappearing on a gentle breeze.

A piece of cake I thought, what could possibly go wrong? I'd seen Humphrey Bogart do this sort of thing dozens of times and he never seemed to have too much trouble, if he could do it, so could I… Oh, the optimism of a callow youth.

The man behind the desk smiled benignly as he posed the all important question.

'How does that option sound sir, is that something you might wish to consider?'

Now brimming with a new found confidence, I heard myself reply.

'That sounds perfect. I'll take the preliminary details and look them over when I get home, and if everything is OK I'll telephone you and we can get started right away. Will you want a deposit or do I pay when it's all arranged?

Getting to his feet the travel agent held out his hand.

'No sir, a deposit won't be necessary. Just one more thing before you go, I've deliberately left the dates open, so within reason, you can travel whenever you wish.'

Shaking the offered hand, I took the neatly written notes he had made, and feeling ten feet tall walked from the shop out into bright sunshine. The only thing left for me to do now was to go home and face my parents and tell them what I had done. But as I happily walked back towards the bus stop, I knew that whatever objections they might raise or whatever stumbling block they might place in my way, the die was cast and there was absolutely nothing on earth going to stop me from going.

I Have Something to Tell You…

Attempting a state of invisibility behind the newspaper, I tried to give an award winning performance of someone engrossed by a series of fascinating articles, but as I had been sitting in the same position for some time without turning any of the pages, it was obvious that when my mother stopped what she had been doing and stood in front of me with her hands on her hips, I knew at once that I had not been successful.

'You've been looking at that page for over half an hour and you've been very quiet ever since you came home, what have you been up to?'

I gulped. I was waiting for my father to come home from work before I mentioned my plans, hoping and praying that he would be in a good mood, otherwise I would need to wait until much later when hopefully the time would be right. From the moment I had caught the bus to come home, my mind had been in turmoil about the decision I had come to, feeling that if I didn't get it off my chest soon I would burst.

Putting down the paper I replied, 'I haven't been up to anything.'

Still wearing the same jam-stained pinafore she had been wearing earlier, she wiped her hands in her usual manner before answering.

'I know you my lad,' she replied. 'The only time you're this quiet is when you're up to something, and you've been acting very strangely since that letter arrived this morning.'

Suddenly it was decision time, did I confide in her before my father got home in the hope of gaining her approval or should I wait?

I carefully considered my options before replying. If I told her of my plans before my father got home and could convince her that my decision to go was the right one, then I would have an ally, but if I failed then I would have to argue my cause twice over, and if that happened, then I would probably be in for a much rougher ride than I had anticipated.

Looking at my mother standing there I remembered all the times she had staunchly defended me irrespective of my guilt or my innocence. On the few occasions I had found myself in trouble she had always sprung to my defence, swift to comfort but equally swift to admonish and to administer the necessary punishment. Here, without doubt, was my closest confidante and ally, surely someone I could confide in.

Taking a deep breath I plunged straight in.

'Look Mum, you saw the letter from Pam and Nick this morning and you know how they are always urging me to go and stay with them? Well I've decided to take them up on their offer and to go out to see them before I go into the air force.'

Sitting down in the chair opposite, a small smile flickered around the corners of her mouth.

'I thought it was that which was bothering you. I've known you for too long for you to think that you can hide anything from me.'

'You don't mind?' I spluttered, 'I thought you would be dead against it under the circumstances.'

'What circumstances?' she asked. 'You'll only be away for a couple of weeks won't you? You'll still be back in time to report to Cardington.'

I gulped. I hated the thought of deceiving her, but if there was ever a time for a little tactful diplomacy, this was it.

'Exactly,' I said, 'that's just what I thought; I'll have bags of time. I just think that it's an ideal opportunity to go out and see them before I get posted to the back of beyond for two years.'

'Mind you,' my mother continued, 'It won't be cheap to go all that way and back, where will you get the money from?'

'I've got some money saved and I still have some of my wages left so I should be alright. Nick has always said it's cheap to live there so I should be able to manage it OK'

My mother sniffed loudly as she continued to question my decision.

'It's all very well you saying that now, but you don't know exactly how much it is going to cost to get there do you?'

Having taken the bull by the horns I decided to carry on and throw myself on her mercy by telling her the whole story.

'Well actually I do know Mum, that's where I've been today. I went down the town to Thomas Cook's and the man there worked out how I could get there and back really cheaply.'

'What does he call really cheaply?' she scoffed. 'It's all very well him saying that but it's a long way to go and I'm sure that it's very expensive to fly anywhere.'

I suddenly felt a surge of excitement as I continued, sensing that any arguments she might possibly raise I could easily deal with.

'Well that's the beauty of this Mum; I'm going to go by train as it works out so much cheaper and I'll be able to visit other places on the way.'

'Going by train?' she snorted. 'How can you go all that way by train, you have to cross the channel for a start and I don't suppose that's cheap?'

I slowly related the whole story, reading from the notes the travel agent had given me, station by station and train by train until finally I sat back in my chair and awaited her reaction to what I had just told her.

'Well, I don't know' she exclaimed. 'You've certainly done your homework I'll give you that, but I'm not very happy about you going all that way on your own by train, anything could happen.'

'Mum,' I reasoned. 'Any minute now I have to offer myself up for Queen and Country and be sent to God knows where. With my luck, if I don't get sent to Benbecula I shall probably end up coming face to face with some lunatic with a gun who's looking to kill me, so travelling to Spain on a comfortable train surrounded by other people who might even grow to like me should be a piece of cake.'

Feeling quite pleased with the line of my arguments I waited anxiously for her next question, because knowing my mother as I did, there was bound to be one.

'What about a passport?' came her immediate response, 'You'll need a passport.'

'I've already got the form,' I replied. 'All I need to do is to get a photograph taken and send it off with the money, then when I get the passport back I just apply to the Spanish embassy for a visa. The man in Cook's said that it was all straightforward and if I sent it all off as soon as possible it would only take a week or so.'

Failing to come up with any more pertinent questions, my mother shrugged resignedly, employing that same all-encompassing ploy that mothers across the length and breadth of the country have probably used for hundreds of years.

'Well, I don't know what your father will have to say when he gets home?'

I was feeling pleased at the way things were going. Not only had my mother failed to raise any prolonged and serious objections to my plans, I now felt that I had an ally in my corner when the time came to appeal to my father. All I could do now was to hope that I could overcome his arguments just as easily.

As my mother busied herself laying the table for lunch, I sat deep in thought trying to pre-empt any questions my father might raise when I told him of my plans.

As if she had read my mind, my mother stopped what she was doing, and with hands on hips said, 'There's no point in you sitting there worrying about what you father might say, he will either agree that it's a good idea or it isn't and that will be that.'

'Actually,' she added, 'I think I can guess what he will say. He will probably try to make you change your mind by saying that he thinks it's a bit close to your call-up date, but at the end of the day I think he will say that if you're old enough to go into the forces, you're old enough to make up your own mind about it.'

The sound of a key being turned in the lock of the front door ended further conversation as a cheery call heralded my father's arrival.

'Hello, I'm home,' he called from the hallway. 'Something smells good.'

Entering the room he kissed my mother on the cheek before dropping his newspaper on to the table.

'Hello son, how are you? What have you been doing with yourself today?'

My mother turned away and headed back into the kitchen. 'Right, I must get on with lunch, it will be about fifteen minutes so if you want to wash your hands, please do it now.'

As she was leaving she turned back and gave me a thumbs-up sign, discreetly closing the door behind her as she left me to talk to my father alone.

Dropping down into his favourite armchair opposite to where I was sitting, my father let out a deep sigh before reaching out for his newspaper.

'Dad,' I began. 'We had a letter from Pam and Nick today.'

'Oh yes,' he replied, opening the paper. 'How are they both?'

'They're fine,' I answered. 'They want me to go out to Spain and stay with them for a while.'

'That will be nice,' he answered from behind the paper.

'I also had another letter from the RAF which notifies me of my reporting date. I've got to report to Cardington on July the 24th.'

'Oh well, now you finally know. You've been fretting over that for I don't know how long, at least you've still got a few more weeks of freedom left before you go.'

'Yes, that's exactly what I thought,' I replied, trying to sound casual. 'I thought I might just use that time to pop over and see them before I go.'

This time the newspaper was laid in his lap before he spoke.

'When did you say you had to report for duty?'

'July 24th.' I answered, desperately trying to appear nonchalant and offhand.

'That's only six weeks away, that's cutting it a bit fine isn't it? You haven't even got a passport and have no idea about the cost involved. Even if you found that you could afford it, by the time you made all the other arrangements it would probably be too late anyway. I think you had better forget about it for the time being, there's no way you'll be able to get all that sorted out in time.'

Picking up his newspaper, my father once again disappeared behind its pages.

'I think it will be alright Dad. I've been to see a travel agent today and he reckons that if I get my passport form sent off tomorrow together with a photograph, it will only take a few days to come back and as soon as I get it back I can send off for a visa; in the meantime he will have my tickets ready for me to collect and off I go.'

Lowering the paper once again he looked me straight in the eye.

'Look son, I know you're not looking forward to going into the forces but it's something that you've got to face up to. As much as you want to go to Spain, you don't have enough time to go swanning off all over the place before July, so just resign yourself to doing your time in the air force and making the best of it. When you get out you can give yourself a treat and then go and see Pam and Nick. You can stay for as long as you like then, that's if they're prepared to put up with you of course.'

Not prepared to give in without a fight I played what I hoped would be my trump card.

'I've spoken to Mum about it and she reckons that if I'm quick I'll probably have enough time just to go for a couple of weeks. It's nearly six weeks before I have to report and she reckons that if everything goes to plan I should have heaps of time.'

My father snorted his derision. 'Oh, and your mother knows how long it takes to get a passport and a visa does she? This sounds a bit like a conspiracy to me, what else did your mother say?'

'Nothing,' I replied. 'She just said that I should talk to you about it when you came home and that's what I'm doing.'

'Oh,' he scoffed. 'That's all right then, I'm glad my opinion still counts for something in this house.'

'Look Dad, you know what it's like; if I don't go now and I wait for a couple of years, Nick might have been posted to God knows where and I probably won't ever get to see them again. This is a golden opportunity for me to travel to Spain and catch up with them, I'd be sorry for the rest of my life if I missed it. I reckon if I get a move on I can easily be back in time to report for duty. Let's be honest Dad, National Service is always going to be there whereas Pam and Nick might not be.'

Sighing, my father picked up his paper again.

'Well, I suppose at the end of the day it's your decision. If you're old enough to go into the forces, I suppose you're old enough to make decisions like that without any help from me.'

Brilliant, I thought, good old Mum. She invariably knew what my father might say in any given situation and once again she had got it dead right.

'How are you off for money?' my father asked. 'It won't be cheap to travel all that way, and I don't want you living with them without offering to give them something for your keep. If you're a bit pushed, I could probably spare you a few quid, though for both our sakes don't say anything to your mother, I don't want her on my back saying that I'm encouraging you.'

I could have hugged him. Neither Mum or Dad ever had much money to spare, but here he was coming up trumps yet again, despite the fact he would probably have to cut down on his cigarettes for a few weeks and forego the odd pint on his way home from work, but he was still prepared to sacrifice himself for the sake of his son.

'Oh that's great Dad, thanks very much for the offer, but I think I'll be fine.'

Realising he wasn't going to get much reading done; he folded his paper and placed it on the table. 'Why don't you tell me all about it? Tell me exactly what the travel agent said and how much it's going to cost and where you'll be flying to.

Leaning forward in my chair with my elbows resting on my knees, I excitedly related the whole story from beginning to end, carefully avoiding telling him that my journey had been planned for someone who didn't have deadlines to meet or any pressing duties to perform in the near future.

When I had finished, my father nodded knowingly, a small smile on his face.

'The travel agent is right; it's the only way to travel. No rushing about everywhere in aeroplanes. The important thing about travel is to see different things and places and to meet other people along the way. I envy you son, I would certainly welcome the chance to do things like that again.'

A faraway look appeared in his eyes as he undoubtedly thought back over the years with regard to his own travels throughout India and his years in the army. As I looked into his eyes a slight feeling of guilt crept over me, I felt as if my own life was just beginning and his own expectations of future adventures were a thing of the past.

His moments of quiet reflection were banished as the door opened and my mother re-appeared carrying three steaming plates of food on a tray.

'Is everything alright?' she asked, setting the plates down on the table. 'Has he told you of his plans?'

My father nodded. 'Yes, he's told me. If he wants to go then it's up to him.'

Did I Really do This…?

Ten days had quickly slipped by since I had taken the decision to go, and although I was now the proud owner of a shiny new passport which contained an impressive looking visa duly franked and stamped by the Spanish Consulate, I had still not received word from the travel agent.

As my parents didn't have the luxury of owning a telephone, I had asked our marginally more affluent neighbour if I might use his to contact the travel agent in an attempt to speed up the proceedings. When I finally put the phone down after having been told that the tickets would be sent from their head office and I would probably hear within the next few days, I was left still feeling decidedly uneasy.

The man in the dark blue suit had assured me that he would do everything in his power to hurry the tickets along, but as the time was slipping by very quickly and the date of my conscription became ever closer, my parents were becoming increasingly concerned about the delay.

Half-heartedly picking at my breakfast, my spirits soared as they had done every day now at the sound of the rattling of the letter box, and leaping up from the table with a cry of 'I'll get it,' I flung open the door and rushed into the hallway.

Scooping up the post which lay on the mat, I quickly rifled through the various items of mail, the sight of a brown envelope bearing a local postmark and addressed to me sending my heart racing.

As I hurried back into the living room carrying the mail, I studied the outside of the brown envelope. It didn't feel very heavy and certainly didn't have the appearance of what I so anxiously awaited. Dropping the other letters down on to the table, I flopped down on to a chair as my mother came into the room.

'Well, have your tickets come?' she asked.

'It doesn't look like it,' I replied glumly. 'There's a letter for me here but it doesn't feel thick enough to be my tickets.'

Sitting down opposite, she peered at the brown envelope in my hand.

'Why don't you open it? Whatever it is, it isn't going to change by you just sitting there staring at it.'

Not feeling very optimistic, I ripped open the envelope and pulled out a single piece of neatly folded headed notepaper bearing the logo of Thomas Cook.

'Dear Mr Mardle,' it began. 'I am pleased to inform you that the tickets for your recently planned trip to Spain have arrived at this office for your appraisal. It would be appreciated therefore if you could call at your earliest convenience to finalise these arrangements.'

'At last,' I shouted, jumping up from my seat. 'The tickets have arrived at the travel agent's in town. I need to get down to the building society and draw out the money to pay for them.'

Smiling, my mother tried to stem my over enthusiasm.

'Just calm down, it's not yet nine o'clock, I'm sure they'll hold on to them for a little bit longer. I don't suppose anyone else with the same name as yours is likely to go in and claim them within the next hour or so.'

Ignoring the friendly sarcasm, I raced from the room, leaping up the stairs two at a time to my bedroom. Opening the dressing table drawer I took out my building society passbook and flung myself down on to the bed before opening it at the correct page and staring at the figures in the forlorn hope that the amount had changed for the better since the last time I had looked. Sadly nothing had changed; it still plainly showed that I remained the proud owner of the princely sum of £84-16s-10d.

Stuffing the precious book into my jacket pocket, I scooted back down the stairs to where my mother sat reading the other mail.

'I'm just going to pop down and pick up the tickets. Can you lend me sixpence for my bus fare; I haven't got any money until I've been to the bank?'

'Oh,' she scoffed. 'What's happened to this man about town who still has to ask his mother to lend him sixpence for his bus fare?'

'Come on Mum, be a dear,' I replied. 'You know what I mean; I'll give it back to you when I get home.'

Reaching for her battered brown purse which lay on the mantle shelf, she took out a half crown and dropped it into my hand.

'Here,' she said. 'Pay me back when you've made your first million.'

'Thanks Mum,' I said, kissing her on her cheek, 'you're a brick, what would I do without you?'

'Get on with you,' she said. 'You're just like your father with your old flannel, go and get your tickets and make sure everything is correct before you hand over your money. I don't want you telephoning next door while you're away to say that you've ended up in the middle of nowhere and you've run out of money.'

Rushing out of the front gate I narrowly avoided crashing into our kindly neighbour from next door, the man who had allowed me to use his telephone. I grabbed the handlebars of his bicycle as he struggled to stop both himself and his cycle from falling to the ground, one of his hands snatching at the brake while his right foot slipped from the pedal as he tried to steady himself by holding on to the garden wall.

Adjusting his cap which had slipped down to rest against the top of his spectacles he gasped, 'Steady on young man, you nearly had me over, where's the fire?'

'Sorry Mr Armitage, I've just had a letter from the travel agent and I'm off down town to pick up the tickets for my holiday.'

Smiling kindly he said, 'Ah yes, your father told me you were off to Spain to see Pam and her husband, are they both keeping well? I bet the weather there is a lot warmer than it is here, it's quite chilly again this morning.'

As he unsteadily climbed out of the saddle and stood holding his bicycle by his side, he appeared to be setting himself to have an in-depth conversation with regard to the weather both here and in Spain, the health of the rest of my family, and no doubt any other subject he might have thought relevant. Although he was a truly delightful man who liked nothing better than to stand and talk about almost anything under the sun, today was not going to be one of those days, I had things to do and I was eager to get on with it.

'I'm sorry Mr Armitage, I'd love to stop and talk but I can't, I must catch the bus into town and go to the bank, I'll pop in and see you when I get back.'

Leaving him looking perplexed at not being able to stand and talk, I sprinted up the road as fast as my legs could carry me, vowing that while I was in Spain I would buy him the best present I could find, one which would undoubtedly match his current lifestyle. God knows what that was going to be though, what did you buy a man in his late sixties who lived alone? Possibly the latest pair of Spanish state of the art bicycle clips or maybe a pair of castanets designed exclusively for the elderly?

As I stood impatiently waiting for the next number eleven bus which would take me into town, I thought of the delights which awaited me in Spain. Obviously I would become fluent in the language within the first couple of days, and that there would be dark-eyed senoritas throwing themselves at my feet everywhere I went, but even more importantly I would be spending time with the two people who, apart from my mother and father, meant more to me than anyone else on earth.

Getting off the bus in the centre of the town, I sprinted across the road, narrowly avoiding becoming another road traffic accident as a car suddenly appeared from around a corner. I waved apologetically as the driver sounded his horn, and reaching the opposite pavement I headed for the Woolwich Building Society, tapping my jacket pocket as I went to reassure myself that my precious book was still there.

Pushing open the heavy glass door, I walked up to the desk holding my passbook firmly in my hand.

A pretty young girl sitting behind the counter greeted me with a friendly, 'Good morning sir, can I help you?'

I smiled as I slipped my passbook under the glass window.

'Yes please, I'd like to make a withdrawal.'

'Of course sir, how much would you like to withdraw today,' she said, reaching forward to take my book.

Here we go again I thought, someone else obviously recognising my worldly and sophisticated manner just as the travel agent had done when he had also addressed me as 'sir'.

'Could I have eighty pounds please?'

Opening my book at the relevant page she looked up before asking, 'Do you realise that if you withdraw that amount it will only leave you a balance of four pounds, sixteen shillings and ten pence?'

Gulping, I realised that if I wasn't careful I could lose all my credibility.

'Yes, that's alright,' I replied airily. 'I have other accounts if necessary.'

The girl looked at me questioningly, clearly aware that I was probably not telling her the truth before opening the desk drawer and taking out a thick wad of money. I stared at the notes which were held in place with a band of coloured paper, the band reminding me of one part of the gaily coloured paper chains which usually formed the basis of our Christmas decorations at home during the war.

'How would you like the money, sir?'

Feeling rather grand, I loftily replied, 'It doesn't matter, fives, ones and some ten shilling notes will be fine, thank you.'

Counting out the money she placed it carefully into my opened book before closing it and slipping it back to me beneath the glass window.

Thanking her, I stuffed the book and its contents into my inside jacket pocket before making my way back out on to the street. Once outside the building, I sought the sanctuary of a nearby shop doorway, where, after cautiously looking about me, I began counting the pile of one pound, five pound and ten shilling notes. As I stared at the money in my hand, it occurred to me that I was looking at what was the equivalent of my entire wages for more than six months had I still been in gainful employment and serving what was laughingly referred to as my apprenticeship.

Assuring myself that the amount of money I had been given was correct, I put everything back into my inside pocket. Should I go and pick up the tickets first, or should I go and exchange some of my cash for some of those romantic sounding pesetas and francs? Making the decision that I couldn't wait any longer to see what this exciting foreign money looked like, I headed in the direction of the impressive looking Barclays Bank.

With my heart in my mouth, I pushed open one of the heavy doors which bore a highly polished brass nameplate stating that this was indeed Barclays Bank, the sign shining like burnished gold in the early morning sunshine as I stepped into the cool, highly polished wooden-floored interior.

I had never been in a bank before and I stood momentarily in awe at the sight of all the dark heavy oak fittings which perfectly complemented the genteel serenity that the whole building exuded. I stood for a moment and watched as people in smart business suits casually opened leather briefcases before handing bulging brown envelopes to the uniformed staff who sat attentively behind heavy glass partitions.

Oh yes, I thought. When I returned from Spain and had dutifully served my country with courageous distinction, this is to be my destiny. No more grubbing about getting filthy and going home at night needing a bath before I sat down to dinner, this is where my future obviously lay, a captain of industry, a wealthy entrepreneur used to foreign travel who would be addressed reverently by name each time I strode into a bank to deposit large sums of money into various personal accounts.

As I looked about me, I noticed a window, above which an illuminated sign proclaimed that this was where one went should help be required with 'Foreign Transactions'. Reaching into my jacket pocket, I withdrew my precious but meagre bundle of currency and walked towards the window.

'May I help you, sir?'

I swallowed hard as I looked into the calm searching eyes of the attractive lady seated behind the glass window. This was no time to act out a charade of trying to be worldly, this was a bank and the people who worked here had undoubtedly been chosen for their shrewd business acumen and their ability to sum people up in an instant. I knew that any attempt on my part to act out the role of regular tourist and man about town would be doomed to failure, I was certain that the lady behind the glass had seen it all before and would see through me in an instant.

'Yes, I hope so,' I replied. 'I'm travelling abroad for the first time and I don't really know what to do. I've got my passport with me and I know that I need some foreign currency, but apart from that I have no idea what I will need.'

Sensing my naïve embarrassment, the lady cashier smiled in a friendly and disarming manner, instantly putting me at my ease.

'Don't worry, sir, I'm sure we'll be able to help. First of all, can I ask where you're going?'

'Spain,' I replied, 'But I'll be travelling through France by train so I will need some French money as well.'

'Yes of course, but the big question is how many francs and how many pesetas do you think you will require. Do you have any idea how many of each you will need?'

'I'm not exactly sure,' I stammered. 'I don't really know how long I'll be away, but as I'm only travelling through France, I'll need a lot more Spanish money than French.'

'Lucky you,' she replied with a twinkle in her eye. 'I would love someone to take me away without me knowing when I would be coming back. Are you going out to see friends or family?'

Now feeling completely relaxed I related the whole story, carefully avoiding telling her about my impending call-up. When I had finished she sighed, 'How lovely, not many young people of your age have such an opportunity, I'm sure you will have a wonderful time.'

'Now, how much do you think you will need? I have to ask that question because you are restricted as to how much money you are allowed to take out of the country.'

Deducting the cost of my tickets I replied, 'Sixty five pounds please.'

'That doesn't seem very much for an extended stay,' she answered. 'Are you sure that will be enough to see you through? Even If we split that amount between francs and pesetas, you are still allowed to take more than that.'

I felt myself starting to blush. How could I tell this lovely lady that this was practically all the money I had in the world?

'I think that will be enough,' I answered. 'I shall be staying with relatives and I understand it's very cheap to live in Spain. If I do run a little short while I'm there I'm sure they will be able to help me out for the time being until I pay them back.'

'May I have your passport please?' she asked. 'Transactions such as this have to be entered in the back, and on your return we will buy back what you have over.'

Pushing my small bundle of money under the glass into the lady's hand, I reached inside my jacket for my shiny new passport and pushed that also towards her.

Opening the book at the page containing my black and white photograph, she quickly glanced back in my direction and smiled.

'It's a very good photograph,' she said. 'Mine is a typical passport photo which makes me look as if I'm on my last legs.'

Feeling slightly overwhelmed at this lady's open friendliness, I felt almost as if I were falling in love for the first time as I treated her to my very best smile, one that I normally reserved for members of the opposite sex for whom I had secret desires.

'I'm sure it doesn't,' I answered. 'I find it hard to believe that you could ever have a photograph taken that didn't do you justice. I think you're much too pretty for that.'

Again her tinkling laughter caused my heart to flutter slightly, and looking me straight in the eye she said, 'What a charming thing to say, you'll go a long way in life if you carry on like that. If I was twenty years younger and not married, I might just fall at your feet and ask you to take me with you.'

Although I knew she was just teasing me, I felt about ten feet tall and ready to take on the world.

After a few further light-hearted questions aimed at establishing how long I expected to be in France and if I intended to buy anything while I was there, we finally arrived at a suitable balance of both francs and pesetas, the former to get me safely through France and back without spending cash on expensive presents, while the remainder of my meagre savings were changed into pesetas to enable me to holiday in grand style in Spain.

With the sound of her good wishes for a wonderful trip ringing in my ears, I finally took my leave and walked proudly from the bank, tightly clutching a large brown envelope in which she had put my passport and my treasured foreign currency, and feeling like the man who had proverbially 'Broke the Bank at Monte Carlo', I headed down the street to the travel agents to complete the second phase of what I hoped was going to become the most wonderful and informative period in my life.

No Turning Back Now...

Standing on the platform at Luton railway station with my suitcase at my feet, I reflected on the past few days which had dragged on interminably, casting my mind back to all the preparations involved which had finally brought me to this point.

On arriving home with the tickets and money, my mother had watched as I had proudly spread everything thing out on the table, picking up several of the foreign notes and breathing in what I thought were the smells from foreign lands, she on the other hand had displayed the typically British derisive attitude of 'If it wasn't made in Britain it can't be any good'.

Carefully selecting one of the notes as if it might carry some form of highly contagious foreign disease, she looked at it with disdain, sniffing loudly before declaring, 'It doesn't even look like real money; I don't know what your father will make of it all.'

On arriving home, my father, God bless him, had thought it all wonderful, picking up some of the notes and doing exactly as I had done.

After stuffing all of the money into a large leather wallet my father had formally presented me with as a 'going away present', I had spent hours lying on my bed with the itinerary of my travel in my hands, methodically going through the tickets and memorising each station and the times of each train until it was burned into my brain.

Luton to London... London to Dover... Catch the boat train from Dover to Calais... Calais to Paris... A taxi or the Metro across Paris to the Gare du Nord... Paris to Hendaye... Cross over the French border to Irun in Spain where I would climb aboard the Talgo Express for Madrid, and finally switch platforms to catch yet another train for Seville, my ultimate destination. I had thought many times that this day would never arrive, but at last I was finally on my way.

I recalled all the hugs I had awkwardly endured from my mother, who in saying her goodbyes had shown herself to be 'über' caring as I tried to reassure her that I would be fine, sighing as she had dismissed my protests in regard to the mountainous stack of egg and cress sandwiches she had lovingly prepared for my journey. I was pretty sure that Humphrey Bogart's mother had never packed him up a pile of egg sandwiches when he went off to put the world to right, and if Humphrey Bogart didn't take sandwiches with him, I would make it my business that neither would I.

My father's brief goodbye had been an altogether different proposition. Leaving for work he had done something that he had never done before, and that was to shake my hand. Previously, when he and Mum had gone away together, even for the day, there had always been a playful clip around the ear or a pat on the back, but this time it was as if my juvenile days had finally come to the end and he was ushering me out into the big wide world and into adulthood.

Glancing at the big brown paper bag which contained the sandwiches, I felt terribly guilty as I looked around for a waste bin in which to deposit them. Mum had spent a great deal of time lovingly preparing them, but already the unmistakeable aroma of hard boiled eggs had begun to permeate the air. As I covertly dropped the bag into the bin, the station tannoy crackled into life, announcing that the next train arriving at platform three was the 8.47 to St Pancras, stopping only at Harpenden, St Albans and Radlett.

Quickly snatching up my case, I stepped nearer to the edge of the platform, peering back down the line eager to see the huge puffs of smoke and steam which would herald the arrival of the train which would carry me off on my great adventure. On its arrival, the whole station became shrouded in great clouds of swirling, pungent-smelling smoke as the train lumbered towards where I stood; particles of grit and soot from its chimney drifting down to settle on the seats, this smutty residue adding a further film of dirt to the Fry's chocolate and Wills Woodbine cigarette dispensing machines as the black steaming monster finally came to a grinding halt.

Stepping forward I saw that a number **1** had been boldly painted in white on the doors of the first few carriages. Clearly not for me I thought, these were obviously for people travelling in style. Finally after walking past several carriages all carrying this same number, I reached the first compartment which carried the figure **3**, and pulling open the heavy brass-handled door, I hauled myself up inside.

After heaving my case up on to the luggage rack above, I flopped down on to a seat, aware that there was only one other occupant in the carriage and he was totally engrossed in reading his morning newspaper. Seeing that the man was taking no interest in me at all, I checked my inside jacket pocket for the hundredth time to make sure that my money and tickets were still there. Finally, with much banging and crashing of doors, the train suddenly lurched into motion, the station platform slowly sliding past the window.

The journey to London provided me with another opportunity to surreptitiously study my itinerary, an itinerary which by now I could effectively recite backwards, the other passenger barely giving me a second glance as he continued with his paper.

Even to this day, I have never understood the English preoccupation with the compulsive study of a morning newspaper. To many it is a ritual as sacred as going to church on Sunday, and it is this fanatical study of the written word on a material, which twenty-four hours later will be the repository for a greasy pile of fish and chips which has always baffled me. My father has always been a devotee, not content with just a daily paper; he has always arrived home carrying an evening edition as well.

The stop at Harpenden came and went with no new commuters entering my compartment but it was a different story when we reached St Albans where, as soon as the train came to a standstill, the door was flung open and five more passengers each carrying a briefcase and the obligatory newspaper crowded into the carriage. With muttered apologies for jostling and pushing one another, they collapsed on to their chosen seats and, with their briefcases lying neatly on their laps, opened their newspapers with great aplomb and disappeared from sight, only to reappear as the need arose to turn the page. I felt myself smiling at the vision I had of them parading like tin soldiers, hurriedly marching down the platform to emerge on to the city streets carrying their briefcases and rolled up newspapers, and in the evening repeating the whole process as they made their way home again, only this time carrying their evening editions.

After collecting two more newspaper wielding passengers at Radlett, the train finally huffed and puffed its way slowly into St Pancras station and, after patiently waiting until all of my fellow commuters had disembarked, I hauled my case down from the rack and stepped down on to the platform. It seemed no sooner had my feet touched the ground than a porter pushing a small luggage trolley stopped by my side.

'Do you need a porter, sir?' the man asked politely.

My father had explained that I might encounter this sort of practice at railway stations, telling me although there was no charge for the service, the porter and the many others just like him relied on tips, but if I wanted to save money I would be well advised to decline such offers.

'No thank you,' I answered, 'I'm being met at the barrier.'

'Very good, sir,' he replied, quickly turning away to buttonhole a lady who, with two small children in tow, was obviously more in need of his services than I. I watched as she gratefully accepted his offer of help as she struggled to control the children, one of whom cried fitfully and tugged repeatedly at her skirts.

As the porter loaded her very large suitcase on to his baggage trolley, I heard her sigh as she picked up the child in an attempt to console it, wiping away its tears as it continued to weep uncontrollably.

'I told you not to unwrap your chocolate yet,' she said. 'I knew that it would end up under the train. You'll just have to wait until we get to the end of the platform and hope that there are other chocolate machines there.'

Sweeping past me, the porter headed off at full speed for the barrier, pushing the trolley in front of him while the lady desperately tried to keep up, dragging one of the children by the hand while the other continued to scream and wail in its demand for more chocolate. Following much more slowly in their wake, I handed my ticket to the collector at the barrier before walking through on to the busy station concourse and out on to the street, where a line of black London cabs waited at a rank to pick up their fares.

As I approached the first in the long line of taxis, a big burly cabby wearing a flat cap and smoking a hand-rolled cigarette got out from behind the steering wheel and stepped back to open a rear door.

'Where to guv?' he asked as he took my case and threw it nonchalantly into the back.

'Waterloo station please,' I replied as I slid down on to the well-polished leather of the rear seat. I had never ridden in a taxi before and, feeling like royalty, relaxed back on to the comfortable and well-worn upholstery and looked out of the window.

More of my father's sound words of advice before leaving for work that morning were, 'When you get to St Pancras, don't ask a taxi driver how much the fare will be because that will let him know that you're a stranger and he'll probably take you all round the houses before you get there to get more money out of you'.

Wondering if my dad had found this out to his cost, I mentally ticked off the first of my completed journeys and reached inside my jacket pocket for my tickets to study once more my timetable and the rest of my departure times.

Suddenly looking up from what I was doing, I noticed the driver watching me in his rear-view mirror.

'Where are you off to then?' the driver asked as he casually leaned his elbow out of the window while expertly weaving his way through a convoy of cyclists who suddenly appeared from nowhere.

'I'm going to Spain to visit some relatives,' I answered proudly, scooping up the tickets and returning them to my pocket.

'Lucky you,' the taxi driver said. 'Is this your first time or have you been out there before?'

Before I had time to reply he carried on with the conversation.

'I keep saying to my old woman that one of these days we'll go abroad somewhere but I don't suppose we ever will. She's no traveller you see, she even feels sick in the back of the cab so I reckon that rules that out unless of course I win the old football pools and we can travel in style. That's a bit of a pipe dream, though mind you having said that, I came up on the old three draws a couple of Saturdays ago, I only won a few quid but it was enough to take us to Southend and back and we had a smashing time. We both had a belly full of cockles, winkles and whelks and a few brown ales to wash it all down, really handsome it was.'

I laughed at the man's broad cockney accent and his references to 'his old woman', thinking that if my dad ever referred to Mum as 'his old woman', he would probably end up with a clip around the ear for his trouble.

'How long are you going for then, a couple of weeks? Mind you, it's that far away it's not worth going for just a week is it? What part of Spain are you going to?'

Before I could reply, he carried on as if he hadn't asked a question at all.

'I fancy that Ibiza myself, they reckon it's lovely, but with my old woman being the way she is, I'll be lucky if I get a weekend on the Isle of Dogs. I've gotta say though, you know what sort of food you're in for on the Isle of Dogs. I don't rate none of that foreign rubbish meself, give me a good old plateful of jellied eels and a few whelks and I'm as happy as a pig in muck. Cor blimey guv, can you imagine going all that way and spending all of your holiday in the carsey.'

I fell back in my seat and laughed out loud at his colourful use of the English language. I had never heard that expression before but I knew what he meant. I laughed as he continued to reminisce about his only experience on foreign shores which turned out to be serving in the Army Catering Corps towards the end of the last war, spending nearly two years diligently serving up greasy food beneath the confines of a huge marquee that served as a mess tent. He went on to describe how his one aim in life at that time was to sample the delights of the multitude of mademoiselles which he had heard frequented the bars and the brothels of Paris. His dreams had failed to come to fruition when he was told by his commanding officer that his house had been demolished in an air raid, whereupon he had immediately been shipped home without even seeing Paris, something it appeared he seemed to regret even more than having his house flattened by a doodlebug.

As the taxi sped across the city, the jovial driver continued to regale me with hilarious tales of his exploits while in the service of king and country. Typically, his stories of times spent in uniform were punctuated with the most colourful and graphic language, most concerned with getting his own back on people he had fallen foul of while dispensing their food at meal times, the more inventive of his outrageous and unhygienic methods of revenge causing me to convulse with laughter.

Finally the cab drew to a halt at the kerb beneath a huge sign which proclaimed it to be Waterloo Station, and with a leap that did someone of his stature credit, the driver jumped from behind the steering wheel to open the rear door, dragging my case out from next to where I had sat before placing his hand on my shoulder.

'Look son, a word in your ear,' he whispered confidentially. 'I know it's none of my business, but if I was you I wouldn't keep all that gear you're carrying in the same pocket. There's a lot of dodgy geezers out there who wouldn't think twice about turning you over for that little lot, especially your passport and your cash. You're a nice kid so I hope you don't mind me marking your card for you. Do yourself a favour, use different pockets for different things so it's not all lumped together, and take a little of your cash and keep that separate for little things like drinks and stuff, that way you're not showing the world and his wife what you've got.' He touched the side of his nose in a conspiratorial manner, 'Know what I mean son?'

Feeling sheepish but grateful for his worldly advice, I carefully took out my passport and tucked it away in another inside pocket, at the same time separating my tickets from my cash before offering the taxi driver his fare.

'Thanks very much for that, how much do I owe you please?' I asked.

'Two and a tanner to you son and we'll call it quits,' he said holding out his hand.

Dropping a shiny half crown into his big hairy hand I spluttered my thanks.

Patting me on the back with such force it nearly knocked me over, the man grinned and said, 'Now, you go and have a great time and don't forget what your old Uncle George has told you, just you be careful and keep your eyes skinned, right?'

Jumping back behind the wheel, the taxi driver slammed the door, waving cheerfully out of the window as he sped away.

As I followed in the wake of other people walking towards the entrance to the station, I became conscious of my small imitation leather suitcase, gazing in envy at some of the more expensive luggage on view. I watched as several well-dressed couples strolled casually arm in arm while following in the footsteps of scurrying porters who pushed heavily laden pushcarts containing huge leather-bound trunks.

I looked wistfully at the carefully stacked luggage on the porters' trolleys, noticing that some of the cases and trunks carried stickers announcing that the owners had visited exotic sounding destinations like Biarritz, Venice and Barcelona. Feeling a little envious at the sight of such stylish luggage, I began to feel conscious that my own small case exuded newness and post-war inelegance, but despite that, I was also travelling on the boat train, so in spite of the ostentation they displayed, our most immediate mode of transportation was exactly the same.

Scanning the numbers of the platforms in front of me I noticed a large sign which read, '**Boat Train Passengers This Way**' and, with my heart beating faster at the prospect of boarding this famous cross channel boat train to Dover, I hurried towards the gate at which a uniformed ticket collector stood quietly whistling between his teeth, ready to confront the people coming towards him as he slapped his ticket punch purposefully into the palm of his other hand.

Putting down my suitcase, I reached into my inside pocket where I had so recently put all of the tickets, and taking out the folder, peeled off the top one before handing it to the collector. The man smiled, and with an almost theatrical flourish, deftly twirled the heavy looking tool, and with a sharp squeeze on the handles, punched a neat little round hole in the designated square on the card.

'That's the one you want, sir,' said the ticket collector, pointing to a train that stood quietly puffing out steam at a nearby platform. 'She'll be leaving in about twenty minutes. There's a buffet car towards the front of the train if you want a decent cup of tea and something to eat.'

I hurried through the barrier and headed towards the waiting train, stuffing the folder that contained my tickets back into my jacket pocket as I walked. Looking into the carriages through the open doors, I felt happy that not too many people appeared to be travelling to Dover at that time of the day and, finally coming to the first compartment which carried a large figure three painted on its door, I jumped up on to the step and clambered inside, slamming the door closed behind me.

For several minutes I just sat there, looking around at the interior of the compartment, running my hand along the upholstery of the seat and breathing in the distinctive smell that trains all over the world seem to have, a unique smell that comes to mind even today, despite so much having changed with the advent of diesel trains and the modern upholstery materials which are now used.

Finally, I heaved my case up on to the luggage rack above my head and gazed at the pictures adorning the carriage, posters advertising the delights to be had in places like Cannes and Nice, colourful images of girls in bathing costumes throwing gaily coloured beach balls to each other as they laughed and frolicked beneath brilliant blue skies. This is definitely the life for me I thought; pretty soon I too would be enjoying clear blue skies and wallowing in that same holiday atmosphere that is to be found on foreign shores.

Breathing a huge sigh of pure contentment, I settled back to watch the world go by, watching fellow passengers hurrying along the platform looking for a carriage in which to deposit themselves and their luggage. As I watched I began to regret disposing of the sandwiches my mother had packed for me, feeling the pangs of hunger beginning to gnaw at my stomach, wishing now that I had been a little less hasty in making that decision. Getting to my feet I pulled hard on the wide leather strap which lowered the window and leaned out, hoping that by keeping the door shut and filling the window with my body, no-one would be tempted to try to enter the compartment.

After several close calls with one or two people glancing in my direction and hesitating but continuing to hurry by, I checked my watch and saw that if the train was to leave on time there remained only three minutes in which other potential occupants might be tempted to invade my space. Finally, there was a huge cacophony of sound as the engine belched out an enormous wreath of snowy white steam which soared majestically upwards in rolling, swirling plumes to become trapped by the heavy steel girders of the station roof, and as the train whistle screamed out its warning that it was about to depart, the station guard walked quickly down the length of the train noisily slamming all the doors which still remained open. As the last door slammed shut, the guard put his whistle to his lips and gave a piercing blast, no doubt to notify the engine driver that he had safely accomplished his task and we could now be off.

Without further warning there was a series of short deafening bursts of escaping steam from somewhere up ahead and with a jolt that slammed my head against the side of the window frame, the train lurched into motion. With my head ringing, I massaged my right ear and watched as the train slowly gathered momentum as we began our journey to Dover.

A Voyage of Discovery...

The beginning of my journey from Waterloo to Dover came as something of a shock, and under any other circumstances I would have been thoroughly depressed by the sights which stared back at me through the train window.

As the train rattled its noisy way out of the station, I could barely believe my eyes as I looked out at row upon row of drab, and sometimes dilapidated, terraced houses. Of the houses which still retained some semblance of being habitable, grimy smoke-stained chimneys looked down on small unkempt gardens enclosed by crumbling brick walls, and the dirty cracked windows which sported grubby net curtains did little to disguise the horrors that this part of London must have experienced during the war.

How did people exist in such an environment? If these decaying and shattered houses were occupied, were the huge piles of rat infested rubble playgrounds where children still gathered? With the railway practically running through their gardens, how did people manage to get their washing clean and how did they sleep at night?

Occasionally a tiny oasis rose up in this desolate landscape where the occupants had valiantly attempted the cultivation of a small garden, and with it, wilting and bedraggled flowers which bore testament to the undoubted pollution caused by the continuous passage of trains. Happily, as the terraces of houses began to disappear, they were replaced by green fields as the train began its journey across the Kent countryside, and looking at my watch for the hundredth time during the last half an hour, I saw that we would be arriving in Dover in the next forty-five or so minutes.

Continuing to stare out of the carriage window, I tried to visualise what the next twenty-four hours had in store. Would things go according to plan or would there be something, or indeed someone, waiting in the wings to disrupt and throw into disarray our meticulously drawn up plans, a lurking fickle finger of fate hovering and ready to throw a very large spanner into the works? Shrugging off an alarming vision of me sitting on my suitcase at the side of the road in some hot and dusty Spanish village, I decided that there was probably no better time than now to go and get a cup of tea and a sandwich of some description, and getting to my feet I mentally kicked myself for having disposed of the sandwiches my mother had lovingly prepared for me.

Entering the buffet car, I looked around for an empty seat, noticing that not many people had decided to avail themselves of the mouthwatering delicacies that LMS currently had on offer, and trying to appear nonchalant and worldly, I scanned the display of plates covered by circular glass domes before making my selection.

After selecting two cheese sandwiches, an ice covered bun of indeterminate age and texture and a cup of deep brown coloured tea poured from a huge aluminium teapot, I carried my goodies to an unoccupied table, desperately trying not to spill any of the thick brown liquid as the train lurched and clattered across a series of points.

Finally reaching the table without slopping too much of the tea into the saucer, I put down my plates and my cup and slid into a corner seat by a window. No sooner had I taken my first bite from one of the sandwiches than the train's tannoy crackled into life announcing that the train was running on time and we would be arriving in Dover in twenty-five minutes.

Picking at the rather dry and tasteless sandwiches, I came to the conclusion that this was probably why the buffet car was practically deserted. Obviously those more discerning customers with the expensive items of luggage I had seen earlier, had done this journey many times before and they were obviously acutely aware of the standard of British Rail catering, which was undoubtedly one of the contributory reasons why they were in a position to purchase expensive luggage and travel to exotic destinations, and I wasn't.

People in Britain had endured a very long period of 'make do and mend' and had suffered long years of deprivation during the course of the Second World War. Rationing had not long ended and it would be a long time before the country returned to any semblance of normality with regard to having a great deal of choice of food to eat, and this being the case I should have anticipated that the quality, and indeed the variety of food available on trains would not be very startling. Despite the poor quality of the sandwiches, the sugary iced bun washed down with the cup of strong sweet tea made me feel much better, and with my spirits now restored to a new high I made my way back to my compartment in readiness for disembarkation.

Poised in readiness for a quick departure, I impatiently awaited a further announcement that would herald our arrival into the port of Dover, and as I reached into my pocket for the next ticket I would need, the train began to slow. Several minutes later the insistent clickety-clack of the train wheels on the track began to grow less impatient and the urgent squealing of the brakes signalled its approach into the station. Once again I began to feel a flutter of excitement; shortly, I would be in a foreign country and my travels would begin in earnest. Just me, a limited amount of foreign currency and my wonderful blue and gold passport in which it clearly stated that this document would 'allow the bearer to pass freely without let or hindrance, and would offer the bearer such assistance and protection as may be necessary'. Surely there could be no better insurance for the start of a great adventure than that.

Grasping the wide leather window strap, I jerked it upwards and lowered the window before sticking my head out to try and see something of the station ahead. Almost immediately a piece of sooty smut landed squarely in my eye, and quickly ducking back inside I rubbed my eye for a few seconds before pulling out my handkerchief and peering into the mirror which was conveniently placed between the holiday posters on the carriage wall. Despite probing and digging with a corner of the handkerchief in an attempt to remove the piece of grit, I finally resorted to pulling the upper eyelid down over the lower one until finally it began to feel as if this had done the trick. Despite the fact that it was likely to happen again, I poked my head out of the window and squinted down the track, eager to find out what lay ahead.

Ahead of me I could see what appeared to be large warehouses and some sort of heavy gantry which ran alongside the railway line on which we were now travelling, and beyond that more warehouses forming the main part of the dockyard, and beyond that still, the sea. Excitedly, I took in every detail of the approaching station and what I could see of the harbour, watching the seagulls as they screeched and wheeled high above the cliffs which were now clearly visible from where I stood.

Stretched out into the distance, there appeared to be a long, wide jetty where the railway tracks clearly ran beneath the various gantries and wrought iron girders, intricate spider's web structures that supported the roof high above the station platform where uniformed porters awaited the arrival of the train.

Slowly, the train inched its way forwards into the station and with a final enormous puff of steam and nerve-jangling squeal from the brakes, the engine finally came to a grinding halt. Ducking my head back inside the compartment, I grabbed my case from the seat beside me, and turning the big highly polished brass door handle, flung open the carriage door and leaped down on to the platform.

In front of me I could see several porters climbing into the first class compartments to retrieve the luggage of the more well-heeled passengers, while further back down the train the more humble passengers such as myself struggled to deposit both themselves and their suitcases down on to the platform.

As I walked towards where the ticket collector stood watching the horde of passengers heading his way, I blinked at the sight of the biggest ship that I had ever seen tied up at the quayside. To me this ship looked just about as impressive as the pictures of the *Queen Mary* that I had seen in magazines, and even if it wasn't of the same stature and prominence of the

Queen Mary, to me it was everything that I could have wished for.

Handing my ticket to the uniformed man at the barrier, he pointed towards the side of the vessel where I could see a wooden gangplank with a handrail being tended by several men wearing navy blue, roll neck sweaters and sailors' caps which bore the logo of the shipping line.

'You'll be boarding down there on the right, sir, where those chaps are standing by the wooden gangway. Be careful when you get down there though, you don't want to go tripping over any of those ropes and hurting yourself.'

Eager to get on board, I picked up my case and hurried down to where the men were standing beside the gangplank. As I approached I looked up at the immense bulk of the ship as it towered above me, stepping over ropes which were thicker than a man's wrist which rose and fell as the ship strained against its moorings.

Reaching the foot of the gangplank, one of the men asked if I had a cabin reservation. I shook my head.

'No,' I replied, 'I want to go up on to the top deck.'

'That's fine, sir. Just turn to your right at the top of the gangplank and go up the first of the three sets of stairs on your left and just keep on following the stairs right up until you reach the top deck. Just be careful that you don't bang your head as you go up the companionway, it's quite low between the decks. If you require food,' he added, 'there's a snack bar on the first deck towards the bow and the main restaurant is situated amidship on the second deck, you'll see the signs.'

Breathing in smells that were entirely new to me which told me that this was going to be an experience that I would never forget, I hurried towards the painted steel stairs which led to the deck above. As I hurriedly placed my foot on to the third step, the recent warning given to me by the sailor below was already a vague and distant memory as I whacked my head with a sickening thud into the superstructure above. Dazed, and seeing far more stars than those on the flag of the United States, I crashed back down on to the companionway below, my case falling from my hand as I sat down with an almighty bump.

Struggling to focus and come to terms with what had happened I was aware of a pair of black shoes and dark blue trousers coming swimmingly into my line of vision. Following the line of the immaculate crease in the trousers before me, I let my befuddled gaze continue upwards until it reached a double-breasted, navy blue coloured uniform jacket, complete with gold rings on each sleeve on which shiny brass buttons perfectly complemented the white shirt. Highlighting the smartness of the uniform, an immaculately tied tie declared this whole outfit as belonging to a more senior member of the crew.

'Are you alright sir? You gave yourself a nasty whack.'

I gingerly put my hand up to my head and felt something both warm and sticky on my fingers. Glancing down at my hand I shivered at seeing the amount of blood now covering my fingers, the sight of which suddenly made me, again, feel extremely dizzy and rather sick.

Reaching down to grasp my arm, the man in the uniform said, 'Here let me help you, I think we need to have a look at that cut.'

I took the offered hand and struggled to get to my feet, my head spinning as I tried to make light of it.

'I'm OK thanks,' I replied, trying to dismiss the matter as something that usually happens to me on a regular basis. 'It just shook me up a bit that's all. I'll be alright in a minute.'

Bending to retrieve my case I felt my legs beginning to buckle beneath me and it was only the man's restraining hand that stopped me from crashing back down on to the deck.

'Come on sir, let's not be silly, I'm the chief steward and I think we had better get you looked at. We have a doctor on board and I think it best if he gives you the once over, I think that cut might need a couple of stitches.'

At the sound of the word 'stitches', all attempts at pseudo bravado quickly left me, and with one arm supporting my sagging body and the other hand scooping up my case, the steward began leading me along the companionway in totally the opposite direction I had originally intended to go.

With my handkerchief clamped firmly over the cut on my head, the steward managed to half drag and half carry me towards a door that carried the word **PURSER**, and dropping my case down on to the deck he turned the brass handle and shoved open the door with his foot, helping me across the step and into the cabin.

After helping me into a big leather swivel armchair that stood in front of the desk, he retrieved my case from where he had left it and brought it into the small cabin, pushing it back against the wall with his foot.

'Right,' the steward said, perching himself on a corner of the desk, 'Let's take a look at that cut, I think it's still bleeding pretty badly.'

Carefully peeling off the blood-soaked handkerchief, he gently parted my hair and whistled between his teeth as he looked at the cut.

'That will definitely need several stitches,' he said. 'I'll give the doctor a shout and he can get down here to take a look at it, he'll know what to do to put you right.'

Not relishing the idea of having someone sticking a needle into my head which I felt had already suffered enough punishment for one day; I tried to argue my way out of it.

'Honestly, thanks for all your help but I'm just a bit shaken up that's all. If you've got a plaster or something I can stick on it and I could rest here for a bit I'll be fine.'

The steward took out a clean handkerchief from his own pocket and clamped it back over the wound.

'I'm sorry,' he said, 'there's no way I can let you go looking like this, I'll get the doctor.'

Resigning myself to what now seemed inevitable I sat back in the chair and tried to pluck up some courage to face the impending ordeal, watching as the steward picked up the telephone and spoke into the mouthpiece, describing to the person at the other end what had occurred. When he had finished he replaced the receiver and, turning back to me said,

'The doctor's coming to take a look at you, don't worry, he'll soon have you sorted out.'

Instructing me to hold the handkerchief tightly on to the wound, the steward opened a wooden cabinet and, taking out a glass, poured a measure of golden liquid from a bottle which he handed to me.

'Here, drink this,' he said. 'It will make you feel better.'

'What is it?' I asked.

'Brandy,' he replied. 'It will stop you feeling sick and it will help to put some strength back into your legs.'

As I sipped the fiery-tasting liquid which was the first brandy I had ever had, the cabin door suddenly opened and in walked a tall dark man carrying a leather bag. The white jacket he was wearing sported shiny brass buttons and, on his shoulders, gleaming gold-coloured epaulettes suggested that not only was I looking at the doctor, but an officer as well.

Dropping his bag on the floor beside me, the man bent to look at my head, discarding the handkerchief and parting my hair as the other man had done.

'Umm, that doesn't look too pretty; I think I'm going to have to put a couple of stitches in that. How did you do it?'

I related the story as he bent to open his bag, taking out a small bottle of brown liquid which he placed on the desk before pulling on a pair of thin rubber surgical gloves.

Turning to the steward he said, 'Pop along and fetch me a bowl of warm water and a towel please, I'll sew him up here rather than take him up to the infirmary.'

Not much liking the thought of me being 'sewn up', I tossed back the remainder of the brandy in one gulp, the fiery liquid catching the back of my throat and making me cough.

'Steady on old chap. I should take it easy on that stuff if I was you, you've done enough falling about for one day, we don't want any more accidents do we?'

Before leaving the cabin to fetch the water, the steward turned to explain.

'I'm sorry, sir, but that's my doing. I gave him that for strictly medical reasons; he looked as if he needed a stiff drink.'

As I leaned back in the chair I tried to ignore the snipping sound as the doctor began cutting back my hair, moments later the steward re-appeared carrying a bowl and a towel, placing it on the desk by my side. Thanking him, the doctor picked up the sponge which floated in the water and began cleaning the cut, the warm water in the bowl, turning red and stinging my scalp, before trickling down my neck.

Closing my eyes, I steeled myself for further pain as the doctor injected my scalp. Keeping my eyes firmly closed, I waited until the anaesthetic took effect, feeling only my fingernails digging into my palms as the doctor went to work.

Five minutes later he straightened up and, with a sigh, said, 'There you are young man, all done, nearly as good as new.'

Scarcely able to believe my ears, I heard myself saying, 'Have you finished already? I didn't feel a thing.'

'We aim to please,' the doctor laughed, 'it's all part of the service. You shouldn't have any more trouble with it, but don't forget that when you get to wherever it is you're going you will need to have the stitches taken out in about ten days' time. Just pop along to a doctor's surgery or a clinic and they will be able to do that for you.'

After throwing the bloody handkerchief and the used rubber gloves into the blood-stained water in the bowl, he bent to pick up his bag, pausing to look at his handiwork before opening the cabin door.

'The next time you feel the need to run up a flight of stairs, particularly on a ship,' he grinned, 'just take a little peek at what might be above your head, you may not be quite so lucky next time.'

As the door closed, my gut feeling was that if this was me being lucky I could do with a lot less of it as my head began to throb and sting, reminding me of what had just occurred. I got unsteadily out of the chair and thanked the steward for his kindness and all the trouble he had taken, picking up my case, determined in future to heed the doctor's words.

'Thanks for everything,' I mumbled sheepishly. 'I'll see if I can manage to reach the top deck without getting into any more trouble.'

The steward smiled and held out his hand. 'Like the doctor said, just be careful in future.'

Slowly and very deliberately I climbed the remainder of the steel stairs up on to the top deck until finally I stood and breathed in clean fresh air. As I looked about me I could see the town of Dover stretching out behind me and directly over the rail in front of me, the vast expanse of the English Channel.

Flopping down on to a long wooden bench, I leaned back and watched the seagulls as they wheeled and screeched in the clear blue sky above me, the warmth of the morning sun washing away the recent trauma as I looked forward in anticipation of what might lay ahead.

After several minutes of watching the seagulls whirling and diving above me as they performed intricate manoeuvres to catch scraps of food being thrown out by passengers on the decks below, I pushed my case beneath the seat and strolled towards the ship's rail, watching the sailors below as they went about their allotted tasks. Forklift trucks arrived and left, while drivers, aided by some of the seamen, unloaded the heavy boxes and crates which in turn were manhandled up the wooden gangplank to be despatched into the bowels of the ship far below.

As I continued watching all the activity, I became aware that the procession of vans and trucks had ceased while the men working below appeared to be awaiting further orders as they talked into small two-way radios, peering aloft at the superstructure above me.

Coming to the conclusion that this suspension in activities might herald our imminent departure, I crossed to the seaward side of the vessel and looked down to see bubbling white water streaming from the side of the ship below the waterline. All of a sudden an ear splitting blast exploded from somewhere high above me as someone whose apparent task it was to deafen all and sundry, announced the ship's imminent departure by activating the vessel's booming siren.

Crossing back to the opposite side of the ship, I looked down over the rail and watched as the seamen unhooked the great heavy ropes from the bollards on the quayside, the same ropes that had previously secured the ship to the dock.

With an enormous rush of water from somewhere deep below the waterline, the ship slowly began to move away from the quay and, with a further huge blast from the ship's siren above, it proudly announced to the world that it was now unfettered and free of its land-based restrictions and had hoisted up its skirts ready to set sail to new and exciting shores, at least, that's what I imagined it said.

As the ship steamed serenely and gracefully from the harbour and headed out into the busy shipping lanes of the Dover Straits, I watched the panoramic shoreline come into view until finally catching sight of the breathtaking sight of the world famous white cliffs of Dover which glowed creamy white in the hazy sunshine.

How many soldiers, sailors and airmen had lined the rails of the hundreds of troop ships returning from the continent at the end of the Second World War, cheering as they looked at the same view that I was also now seeing, relieved and grateful at once again seeing the country they had so valiantly fought for, in particular those brave and defiant men returning from the evacuation of Dunkirk.

Alone with my thoughts, I tried to imagine how those heroic men must have felt as they reached the homes of their loved ones, anticipating once again meeting the wives and children they must have thought they would possibly never ever see again.

Watching the magnificent chalk cliffs gradually getting smaller in the distance, I remembered the words of that much-loved war time Vera Lynn song, suddenly feeling incredibly emotional as I quietly hummed those nostalgic and poignant verses...

'There'll be bluebirds over the white cliffs of Dover,
Tomorrow, just you wait and see.
There'll be love and laughter and peace ever after,
Tomorrow, just you wait and see.

The shepherd will tend his sheep; the valley will bloom again,
And Jimmy will go to sleep,
In his own little room again...'

Despite the anticipation and excitement of what lay ahead, a feeling of sadness swept over me as I tried to imagine what it must have been like for the thousands of our brave young men, who, like me, headed out towards France, but in their case, sadly wondering if they would ever return to witness this wonderful sight again.

Shivering slightly in the cool breeze which was now sweeping unchallenged across the deck, I tried to rid myself of the sombre images that remained so clearly etched in my mind and decided to retrace my steps to a warmer part of the ship, but this time in a much more careful manner.

Picking up my case, I slowly made my way back down the metal companionway to the lower decks, conscious of the throbbing in my head which reminded me of my earlier encounter with the metal structures all around me. Reaching the deck on which the bar and restaurant were situated, I felt grateful for the comfort and the warmth which greeted me as I walked in through its doors.

Pushing my case out of sight beneath the table at which I had chosen to sit, I went to the glass-covered counter and tried to decide what I should have to eat. Finally, I thought that I would take on the role of the itinerant continental by ordering the French onion soup, crusty French bread followed by some sort of chicken dish whose name I couldn't begin to pronounce, all washed down with a bottle of French lager beer, something else I had never tried before. Paying for my chosen fare, I retired to my seat to enjoy the food and look out of the window from where I could see the horizon appear and disappear in a graceful and majestic manner.

Some two hours and two more bottles of the French beer later, the steady watching of the rising and falling of the horizon finally claimed yet another naïve victim as I relinquished my short-lived hold on my lunch as I confined my first taste of continental cuisine to the deep.

Withdrawing my aching head from over the rail for the third time in as many minutes, I began to wonder if this foreign travel was really all that it was cracked up to be. I felt reasonably confident that Humphrey Bogart never had all this trouble when he set forth to save the world, yet here I was having been on board for less than two hours and already I had accumulated several stitches in my head and had been seasick. Catastrophes like this didn't happen when I had been to Ramsgate in the past and I was quickly coming to the conclusion that maybe I should restrict all future activities to much closer to home.

Despite the warm sunshine prickling the skin on the back of my neck, I felt thoroughly wretched and longed to feel the firmness of solid earth under my feet again as I sat on the hard bench with my head in my hands. As I fought to avoid another stomach wrenching journey to the ship's rail, I vowed there and then never to sample the dubious delights of either sea travel, foreign food and foreign beer, but to stick instead to things about which I was far more familiar.

Coming to with a start, I realised that I had dropped off, the change in the pitch of the ship's engines waking me as the vessel began to slow. Staggering unsteadily to my feet, I looked out over the rail in front of me and saw in the distance my first view of what lay ahead. To my right, a long sandy beach stretched as far as the eye could see and, directly in front of me, I could see the concrete pincer-like structure of the harbour wall as it reached out to welcome visiting ships into its protective embrace.

In an instant I began to feel much better as I eagerly took in the scene ahead of me.

Slightly to the left of the harbour entrance I could see what looked like a huge fortified building and the spire of a large church which appeared to look down upon the whole town, while the roofs of the smaller buildings shimmered in the warm sunshine.

As the ship slowly nosed its way between the two huge breakwaters which marked the entrance to the harbour, I could see on the left-hand side of the vessel the entrance to what appeared to be a series of inner harbours and wharves that contained a number of smaller cargo vessels being serviced and emptied by large cranes whose arms swung majestically across the quay. And from those arms, chains as thick as a man's wrist supported pallets and platforms as they were lowered expertly on to the decks and down into the bowels of the various vessels to re-emerge moments later laden with other various forms of cargo.

On the right of the ship, a long, cobbled and concreted footpath ran at the base of the high harbour wall offering shelter from the prevailing wind. This pathway, stretching back towards a series of sheds and warehouses where porters and seamen clad in various styles of uniforms hurried about their business, obviously in readiness for the arrival of the cross channel ferry.

As I hurried towards the companionway that led down to where the gangplank would soon be lowered, it dawned on me that in a few minutes I would be taking my first steps on foreign soil. Up until now I had certainly been less than streetwise, and if I was to survive this trip and enjoy myself in the process I would need to be far more circumspect and aware of what was going on around me, something which certainly hadn't been the case so far.

The Land of Snails, Garlic and Strong Cigarettes...

To say that my first glimpse of the French at home was a surprise is an understatement. Everywhere I looked, men appeared to be engaged in serious arguments which to my untutored mind seemed likely to lead to bloodshed at any moment. As they shouted and gesticulated in a most alarming manner, I couldn't believe that here was a past adversary that had led England to the very brink.

Porters waved their hands in the air and shouted hysterically as they were given instructions by passengers disembarking from the ship. They tossed cases and trunks on to trolleys as if there was an ongoing enmity between themselves and the owners of the luggage, determined that their baggage should suffer as a result. Coupled with each noisy tirade, there appeared to be an inordinate amount of hawking and spitting.

As I watched, it soon became clear that this was in fact perfectly normal French behaviour, this was simply how the French behaved, totally the opposite of what passed as acceptable behaviour in Britain. These men were on home territory and were exercising their tradition of 'Liberty, Equality, Fraternity' and if you didn't like it, any objection was likely to be greeted with a shrug and they would saunter off to find another victim who might be less inclined to object.

As I watched, engrossed at everything that was going on around me, a man wearing a black beret and sporting at least three days' growth of thick stubble on his chin approached and stood directly in front of me. Dangling from his lips was the foulest smelling cigarette that I have ever encountered, and without removing the offending object from his mouth, greeted me in his native tongue.

'*Bonjour Monsieur*,' he growled, 'Porter?'

With great emphasis on the first letter of the word 'Porter', I took the whole unadulterated pungent smell of day old garlic full in the face. This was the first time I had ever encountered this exotic culinary outcast, and the effect of this innocuous looking bulb sent me reeling. Trying to appear that this was not a new experience to be nasally assaulted in such a way, I shook my head, and with a dismissive shrug, he loudly cleared his throat and spat on the ground at my feet, strolling away in search of a more responsive customer to his less than obvious charms.

The harsh and bitter smell of strong French tobacco, garlic and strong coffee saturated the still air in the enclosed space of the covered dock area but I happily breathed it in as I immersed myself in everything that went on about me. Porters, dock hands and others who seemed to have nothing to do except wave their hands in the air and shout at each other, appeared to me as a contradictory breath of fresh air.

With the train for Paris not due to leave for just over an hour, I looked around for the possible source of the mouth-watering smell of coffee. Spotting a small café near to one of the huge sheds, towards which a steady stream of men seemed to be headed, and picking up my case I followed in their wake.

Opening the door was like switching on a radio at maximum decibels as the cacophony of sound had the same effect as being hit with a hammer. The place was literally bulging at the seams and, everywhere I looked, people were engaged in those same voluble heated arguments I had witnessed outside. Being inside was not a deterrent to arm waving or beating tables to emphasise a point, seemingly everything became clearer if you shouted louder or beat the table harder than your colleague.

Spotting a single empty seat at the end of the bar, I squeezed my way through the throng of chattering people and flopped down on a rickety stool which teetered and threatened to collapse under my weight at any second. Dropping my case on the floor I dragged it back with my heel so it remained partially hidden beneath my seat.

'*Monsieur?*'

I looked up to see a man standing behind the counter wiping his hands on a grubby wet cloth which, moments before, he had undoubtedly used to wipe cups and glasses. My big moment had arrived, it was time to show Johnny Foreigner that we English knew exactly what it was all about and that we could hold our own at any level.

'*Bonjour monsieur. Café au lait sil vous plait.*'

Without replying, the man casually leaned forward to give the counter at which I sat a half-hearted wipe with the cloth, the same cloth on which he had wiped his hands only moments before and with this act of dubious hygiene completed, he wandered off to process my order.

Disappointed that my attempt at the language had received no acclaim and not even merited a '*Merci*', I watched the man reach up to a shelf in front of him and take down a cup and a saucer. I shook my head in disbelief as the cup and saucer received the same treatment as the counter, the dirty wet cloth being used again as the man wiped around the interior of the cup into which he would now pour my coffee.

Coming to the conclusion that going native and using the same establishment as the locals was probably not the best idea I had ever had in my life, I tried to console myself with the thought that if I only took a small sip of the coffee, I might get away with just a mild dose of hepatitis C, or a fleeting attack of cholera. Being acutely aware of all the arm waving and shouting nearby, the last thing I wanted was to become the centre of attention over a cup of coffee, anyway I reasoned, with luck the hot water used in the making of the coffee would probably kill off most of the bacteria.

With much gurgling, slurping and belching of steam, the antiquated machine at the back of the counter obligingly coughed out a frothing stream of tarry black liquid into the cup before the man completed his culinary masterpiece by adding the tiniest amount of milk to his creation. Walking back to where I sat, still with the wet cloth draped across his arm, he banged the coffee down in front of me, the now deep khaki-coloured liquid spilling into the saucer as he demanded his fee.

I reached into my trouser pocket and pulled out a handful of small change, coins I had received as change after paying for my ill-fated food and drink while on the boat. Placing them on the counter in front of me for the man to help himself, he gave a loud sniff and, after wiping his hands on the disgusting looking cloth, looked at me as if about to say something but instead gathered up a few of the small coins and strolled off to serve someone else at the other end of the counter.

Tentatively, I picked up the small cup and took a tiny sip, aware that the man was looking at me as if anticipating some comment. Surprisingly, the coffee exceeded my expectations; this was the first real coffee I had ever had. Normally the stuff we had on rare occasions at home came out of a bottle and it tasted nothing like this, the only problem that I had now was that I had no sugar. Did I attempt a bit more schoolboy French, or did I just grit my teeth and drink it? What would Humphrey Bogart have done I thought? Sod Humphrey Bogart, I decided, I'll do it my way.

Placing my cup back in its saucer, I glanced across to where the man was still watching me.

'*Pardon Monsieur,*' I called. '*Avez vous sucre sil vous plait?*'

Giving me a toothy, tobacco-stained glare that said, 'I knew you'd want the bloody sugar', he had obviously been waiting for me to say something as he deftly scooped up a chipped and stained bowl from beneath the nose of a startled looking customer wearing a black beret, leather waistcoat and a red and white striped T-shirt who was just about to spoon some of its contents into his own coffee. Carrying the sugar, he picked up another teaspoon from the counter and walked towards me.

Grinning, he put them both down in front of me with a flourish and said. '*Sucre, Monsieur. Bon appetite.*'

Now it was my turn to smile as I acknowledged his sardonic good humour with what I hoped sounded like a sarcastic '*Tres bien Monsieur, merci.*'

Feeling surprisingly at ease having enjoyed this little Anglo/Gallic duel, I happily sipped my coffee until the cup was completely drained, and putting the cup back in its saucer I slipped off the stool and recovered my case before turning to the café proprietor to bid him goodbye.

'*Merci Monsieur, au revoir,*' I called, and with his own cheerful reply ringing in my ears, I strode out the door and back on to the station concourse.

I looked all around as I walked down the platform away from the ship, noticing the repairs to what were once great holes in the roof and remains of buildings which were still standing, seeing two massive twisted girders where both German and Allied bombers had taken their toll. Everywhere I looked, I could see evidence of the amount of building work which had already been carried out including the new shiny railway tracks which glistened and shone as they rested on the bright new wooden sleepers, each one lacking that tarry, oily appearance that came only with the passage of time.

I remembered things I had read and had been told of the heroic desperate stand at Calais, where English troops had obeyed Sir Winston Churchill's order and had fought until virtually the last man and the last bullet in a desperate attempt to stop Hitler's advance. I also knew that less than twenty miles down the road lay the much bombed town and beaches of Dunkirk, where the gallant rescue of thousands of Allied troops by men and women in small boats had turned an inglorious defeat into a magnificent victory as they ferried survivors of that horrendous bloodbath back to England and safety.

Feeling moved, almost to the point of tears, by the images which raced through my mind, I gazed back beyond where the ship in which I had so recently arrived lay. Looking back still further into the distance, I could just make out the outline of the white chalk cliffs of Dover and I imagined what horrors those poor souls endured as they desperately fought for their lives. What must it have been like trying to find some scrap of shelter from the merciless pounding of German artillery while continuing to repulse wave after wave of infantry and enemy tanks, yet still able to look back over their shoulders and see their homeland tantalisingly less than twenty-five miles away, knowing that in many cases they would never set foot there again.

Visitors arriving today at the ferry terminal need to look only a few yards to their right to see a simple sandstone cross dedicated to those gallant souls who gave their lives so that we might be free; a sombre and poignant reminder of the vicious conflict which claimed so many lives, many of those who died probably falling on the very spot on which I now stood.

With a rather heavy heart I walked towards the barrier against which four *gendarmes* wearing smart blue uniforms and the traditional round *kepis* leaned nonchalantly against the metal structures. As they talked, they took no notice of the steady stream of people who produced documents and passports to be scrutinised by two others who busily stamped passports, checked tickets and answered questions with regard to the direction to be taken to get to their next departure point. Standing patiently, waiting in line to pass through the barrier, my attention was drawn to the shiny black leather holsters on each of the *gendarme's* hips from which protruded the butts of the first real guns that I had ever seen.

Fascinated, I couldn't tear my gaze away from these deadly military accessories. Obviously, I had seen images of weapons before on the screens in cinemas but I had never seen weapons such as these in real life, these images making me aware of how far removed I now was from my previous relatively comfortable and safe existence, where any minor wrong doing would at worst be rewarded with a clip around the ear from a member of the local constabulary, but here doing the wrong thing, one could possibly end up by being shot.

Finally, tearing my gaze away from the uniformed men and their weapons, I handed over my shiny new passport and tickets, proudly staring at the stamp which now adorned its first vacant page. Feeling that the world was my oyster, I walked proudly along the platform towards the train waiting to take me to places that I had previously only read and dreamed about.

Why Can You Never Find a Gendarme When You Want One?

It didn't take long for me to find an empty carriage, but as it began to fill up I became disappointed to find that the nationality of my travelling companions proved to be English to a man. I had been hoping that, when we reached Calais, my fellow travellers for the next leg of the journey to Paris would be perhaps French or maybe Spanish, and that being the case I would have the opportunity of discreetly studying 'Johnny Foreigner' first hand in the hope of gaining some sort of insight into what made them tick. In the station café I had observed what could loosely be described as the French working man at play, but this had been very brief and the only person I had any real contact with was Monsieur Le Patron.

Dad had often spoken in less than complimentary terms with regard to the French, and although I considered him to be a very honest and fair man, I did find some of his more defamatory remarks somewhat confusing. On several occasions I had attempted to establish the reasons for his dislike of the French as a nation but he had simply shrugged and told me that someday sooner or later I would probably find out the answer for myself, and it was for that reason I had hoped my fellow travellers would be of the local variety enabling me to quietly observe them first hand.

As the flat countryside flashed past the window, I became fascinated by the amount of poplars that lined each side of the straight country roads. Standing tall and erect they disappeared into the distance, echoing the perspective painted by the great French impressionist painters, pictures of which I had seen in books and magazines and I began to imagine what it must have been like for French infantry men as they marched towards the carnage that became the Battle of Waterloo.

With the scenery outside remaining unchanged for mile after mile, the rhythm of the wheels rattling on the track became a soothing lullaby as I slowly succumbed to its hypnotic beat, my eyelids becoming increasingly heavy until finally I surrendered to the tiredness which swept over me as I snuggled down in my seat for a quick forty winks.

The insistent voice of the conductor and his gentle shaking of my shoulder brought me back to wakefulness with a start.

'*Pardon Monsieur*, your ticket please? We will be arriving in Paris in fifteen minutes.'

Shocked and surprised by the intrusion into my dreamless sleep, it took me several seconds to realise where I was and what was happening. Pulling myself upright from where I had slumped in my seat, I fumbled in my jacket pocket for my tickets, blinking up at the conductor who stood impatiently waiting for me to produce the right piece of card, the expression on his face telling me he was eager to find other people who had also lost the battle to stay awake, they too having tired of the flat uninteresting countryside outside.

Handing my ticket to the conductor, I noticed the man sitting opposite watching me, a half smile playing about his lips as I desperately tried to come around and appear reasonably intelligent and alert.

'How long have I been asleep?' I asked self-consciously.

'An hour or so,' he replied. 'You dropped off just as we were going through Arras. You haven't missed anything,' he smiled. 'Personally I think all this flat French countryside and skinny tall trees is a bit overrated, it's a bit like Norfolk on a good day but with different horticulture. You needn't have worried; I would have given you a nudge if the ticket collector hadn't beaten me to it.'

Standing up and stretching, I muttered my thanks, trying to get myself together as I stuffed the remainder of the tickets back into my pocket, trying to ignore the pins and needles which pulsed through my right arm against which my head had rested.

'With all those tickets you have, I guess you're not just heading for Paris?'

'No,' I grinned, 'I'll be catching a few more trains after Paris. I'm travelling down through Spain to Seville, I have relatives there that I haven't seen for some time so I'm going to see what Spain is all about and how the other half live.'

The man whistled softly, 'Boy, that's some trip. I envy you doing it like that; it's got to be far more interesting than just getting on a plane at one end and getting off at the other. Do you have deadlines to meet, or is this something you've been planning for some time and you're taking time out to do it?'

'Something like that,' I answered. 'It's a golden opportunity for me to do it at this time and if I don't do it now, I don't know when I might get the opportunity again.'

After chatting for a few more minutes and thanking him for his good wishes, I felt any doubts and misgivings I might have had fade away as I settled back in anticipation of my first glimpse of the suburbs and outskirts of Paris.

I still found it hard to believe that I was now heading for this great city, famed the world over for all its wonderful sights together with its art galleries and museums, and I searched for my itinerary to get some idea of how long I would have before I needed to catch my connection for Hendaye. I knew that planning my time carefully was important but this was an opportunity I was not going to miss. Carefully studying my typed itinerary, I saw that I had just over three hours to kill, time enough I thought to perhaps see the Eiffel Tower or take in the Louvre or the Musée d'Orsay, but I realised that I would have to consider my options very carefully.

Art had always interested me, even as a small boy, and I had invariably spent the majority of my week's pocket money on books about paintings and the great artists of the world, particularly books that carried coloured illustrations by the wonderful French impressionists and post-impressionists which were always on the top of my 'must see' list.

Reasoning that I could always find time to visit the more touristy places on my way home, I happily decided that my first priority would have to be a visit to the Musée d'Orsay, and then, if time allowed, a flying visit to the Louvre.

With a feeling of excitement at simply having made that decision, I began to worry that it might not be possible to fit it all in. Deciding that not knowing how things worked in respect of finding my way around on the Metro, it could be money well spent if I travelled by taxi, after establishing of course that the price charged was affordable. In doing this, hopefully I would be taken directly to where I wanted to go.

Barely able to contain my enthusiasm, I checked that all my tickets and money were where they were supposed to be, and in anticipation of the train pulling into the station, pulled my case down from the rack above and placed it at my feet, ready to jump off at the very earliest moment eager to save as much time as I possibly could.

Before the train had come to a standstill, I flung open the door and leaped from the compartment, and with the sound of my fellow passenger's voice wishing me a safe journey I rushed for the ticket barrier and my exit on to a brave new world, hurrying towards the exit as fast as my legs could carry me. Three hours to spare I thought, no time to stand and stare but to get to a taxi rank as quickly as possible before other passengers from the train also descended on the hopefully waiting taxis.

Emerging from the station into the bright sunlight I spotted a line of taxis on the opposite side of the road, the drivers standing in a group at the side of their vehicles seemingly not interested in seeking out potential customers, preferring instead to fill the air with pungent smoke from strong smelling cigarettes as they shrugged, gesticulated and waved their arms violently in the air to emphasise some point or other. As I walked towards the edge of the pavement to cross the road, two men stepped from behind a pillar, catching up with me as I reached the kerb. Flanking me on either side, one reached down in an attempt to take my case.

'*Pardon monsieur,*' he said, 'are you wanting a taxi?'

Instinctively I pulled my case out of his reach, stepping to one side to avoid the man's groping hand, coming into contact with the other man who stood slightly behind my shoulder. I now found myself closely pinned in between the two.

'Permit me,' the man said as he again reached down to snatch my case. 'We have a taxi just across the road. Where is it you wish to go?'

Once again I snatched the case away, knowing instinctively that these men weren't bona fide taxi drivers but probably bag snatchers preying on tourists leaving the station. Quickly looking around to see if there were any *gendarmes* nearby I was dismayed to see that not only were there none of the local constabulary in the vicinity, it also appeared that no-one else seemed to have noticed what was going on either.

Shrugging off the man's fierce grip on my arm, I attempted to get away in the hope of dashing across the road to where the taxi drivers stood talking, but the man on my right stepped directly in front of me, pushing me back towards his companion who now stood directly behind me, blocking any possible retreat in that direction. With my heart pounding I tried desperately to stamp on the feet of the man behind, hanging on to my case determined that there was no way that they were going to have my belongings without some sort of a fight.

The man in front of me thrust his unshaven face right up against mine, his breath heavy with the smell of stale garlic and tobacco as he sandwiched me even more tightly between him and the man standing behind me, this further contact making me suddenly aware of something hard digging into the small of my back.

'Drop the case on the ground and give me your money and passport and you will not be harmed,' he hissed.

Despite feeling petrified I was adamant that whatever happened there was no way that this French thug was going to rob me of my hard-earned money, the thought of having to telephone home to say that I had only got as far as Paris before being robbed stirring me into sudden violent action. This was not the time to think what Humphrey Bogart might do under similar circumstances, it was obvious that I needed to act quickly because this wasn't the cinema and no-one was going to come round in the next few minutes and serve me with chocolate or an ice cream.

With the thought of being stranded in Paris with no money, no tickets, no passport and no luggage, the feeling of being afraid quickly evaporated into a bitter hatred.

I had been given my first boxing gloves at the age of ten and it had been instilled into me that gentlemen always boxed according to the rules, but this was different, no rules existed for scenarios such as this. What happened in the next few seconds must surely have had the Marquis of Queensbury spinning rapidly in his grave.

The crack of my forehead meeting the bridge of the nose of the man in front of me together with his gasp of pain was enough to stir me on as I smashed my knee hard up into his groin. Slamming my case into the side of his body, he gasped for air as he fell to the ground, his fall giving me the opportunity to jump to one side to momentarily avoid whatever it was that being rammed into the small of my back. Scrambling over the man's body I made a desperate dash for the opposite pavement, frightened that at any moment I would be grabbed from behind by the injured man's compatriot.

Halfway across the road I glanced behind me looking for signs of pursuit but both men were as eager to get away from the scene as I was, the one I had knocked down being half carried and half dragged away by his companion. Reaching the relative safety of the opposite pavement, I dropped my case on the ground and stood panting for breath, looking around in the hope that there might be a *gendarme* somewhere nearby, but to my dismay not only were there no *gendarmes*, but it seemed no-one else in the vicinity had witnessed what had occurred either.

As I quickly considered what to do, it seemed unlikely that even if I found a member of the local constabulary and tried to explain what had happened, he probably wouldn't be able to speak English anyway and by the time I had managed to make it clear to him what had occurred, the men would be long gone. It also crossed my mind that even if I did find an English speaking *gendarme* and he made a note of all the facts, he would in all probability haul me off to the local nick for my story to be investigated, and that being the case, not only would I not have time to do the things I wanted to do, I would probably end up by missing my train as well.

Trying to think it through, I felt myself being jostled by people scrambling for a taxi, and thinking that if I didn't quickly come to a decision, I would still be there when everyone else had gone. With no witnesses to substantiate what had happened, I felt it likely that the outpourings of a young Englishman who bore no marks of any struggle may be construed as a callous attempt to deride the good name of honest French citizens simply going about their lawful business. Weighing up all the pros and cons, I realised that I had been lucky, I had also had the satisfaction of dealing out some rough justice to a couple of potential thieves who may or may not think twice about trying a similar stunt in the future, and with that thought in mind I opted for trying to forget the whole ugly incident and put it down to experience.

Manners and the forming of orderly queues appeared to be something that the French had not quite got the hang of as I was pushed, trodden on and generally roughed up by people who clearly had lots to learn about common courtesy as they battled each other for the sanctuary of the quickly diminishing line of taxis. Realising that in continuing to stand back and adopt the principle of 'women and small children first' was going to get me precisely nowhere, it spurred me into action. Acting upon the alternative adage of 'when in Rome do as the Romans do', I immediately disregarded all the lessons which had previously been instilled in me with regard to good manners, and with elbows and shoulders fending off others who were intent on securing the services of the taxi I had earmarked for myself, I used my suitcase with further deadly effect to cut a swathe through the mass of heaving, sweating humanity. Finally reaching my goal, I tumbled gratefully into the back of a battered and rusting taxi to once again inhale the now familiar aroma of stale garlic and cigarettes, plus on this occasion, an overwhelming smell of body odour.

The taxi driver, full of the Gallic charm of which I was now becoming familiar, simply leaned his head back over the front seat and puffed a cloud of pungent smelling tobacco smoke in my direction before adding some unintelligible phrase in his native tongue which I took to mean, 'Where do you want to go?'

Good question. I did a mental check on how many francs I had already spent before answering, knowing that I needed to be careful before embarking on any extravagant sightseeing tour of the city. I remembered too what my father had said in respect of the cost to a local person, thinking that it was quite likely that it could go up quite considerably for foreign visitors such as me. As the driver awaited my answer, I decided to ask for the Musée d'Orsay in the hope that I would not appear to be a stranger to Paris and that I had done the same journey many times before and therefore would be taken to my chosen destination rather than be taken for a ride.

'*La Musée d'Orsay s'il vous plait*'.

With no indication that he had heard me, the driver leaned forwards to press a button on the scratched and scarred dashboard, at which the engine coughed and clattered into life. After pushing and pulling a strange looking lever which protruded from the centre of the dashboard panel in front of him, the ancient car lurched forwards and spluttered away from the kerb amid clouds of black smoke, completely obliterating the view from the rear window of people still jostling for a cab.

Amid much crashing of the gearbox and loud mutterings from the driver who I assumed was apportioning blame for the mechanical state of his vehicle to people like the Duke of Marlborough because of his annihilation of the French at Blenheim, Napoleon who fared little better, and latterly to General Charles de Gaulle, I soon began to relax, the memory of my encounter with the two thugs slowly fading into the background as I sat back and began to fall under the spell of the French capital.

Swinging out of the station concourse into the wide avenue of the Rue la Fayette, I watched enthralled as the scenery began to change from small shops and houses to more vibrant and bustling boulevards where shops, houses and spectacular looking apartments began to take on a more elegant feel.

Shouting and gesticulating through the open window at two cyclists who casually and romantically held hands as they rode side by side along the busy thoroughfare, the morose looking driver expertly hauled the ancient vehicle around a large roundabout, crossing an equally busy Boulevard Haussman into the Rue Halevy, where directly in front of me, I could see the world famous opera house which seemed to rise up through the pavement like a huge living Gothic monument. With mounting excitement I drank in the atmospheric names of the streets like an alcoholic salivating in anticipation of his next drink, names that I had only read about coming to life as more and more of the city came into view.

Glancing back through the rear window at hearing more Gallic expletives; I saw that he had narrowly avoided a scooter rider and his passenger, the driver of the scooter seemingly far more preoccupied with his pretty pillion passenger than other road users. As I continued to watch the couple on the motor scooter, I blinked in disbelief at the sight of the young girl dressed in a flowing long skirt and simple white cotton blouse with a red and white spotted scarf holding her hair in place, casually riding side saddle behind the driver, their animated conversation liberally punctuated by much laughter and waving of hands. The driver of the scooter, dressed equally simply in corduroy trousers and striped T-shirt was even more animated than his attractive passenger as he waved and gesticulated, even reaching behind him to place his hand lovingly on the young girl's thigh. Seeing the happy laughing faces of these two young people who weren't much older than me, it became clear to me why Paris over the years had become known as 'The City of Love'.

In an instant, I decided that this was to be the life for me; the idea of me becoming a successful businessman travelling the world in utter luxury disappeared in a flash. I knew then what I wanted from life, happiness and just enough money to get by, all that coupled with the opportunity of making love to as many pretty girls as possible. I had been in Paris for less than an hour and I was seriously contemplating becoming French. I even pondered on how I would look wearing open toed sandals, a striped T-shirt and a black Basque-style beret. Dashing I thought, simply dashing.

With the taxi driver still muttering under his breath, he heaved and struggled to drag the cab around a large roundabout, the name of one of the avenues leading away from where we were now headed catching my eye. I looked again to make sure that I had read it correctly; it was the famous Rue de la Paix, a name so familiar to me that I felt sure I had been here before, maybe I had, but in a previous life.

Now completely at ease and oblivious to the smoke that billowed around me from the cigarette that dangled from the taxi driver's lips, I even leaned forwards to peer over the driver's shoulder to see what lay ahead. Now that I had decided to become French, small things like choking to death on someone else's cigarette didn't seem to matter any more; there were other things which now took precedence.

I stopped myself from being thrown forwards as the driver suddenly decided to obey a traffic signal, screeching and squealing to a halt at the junction of a huge boulevard that proudly told the world that this was the Rue de Rivoli. As the light turned to green, he hauled on the steering wheel to point the front of the car in the general direction of where he wanted to go, at the same time pulling and twisting the strange looking gear lever which protruded from the centre of the dashboard, flicking a switch that spat out an equally battered arm type indicator to indicate to whoever might be watching that this might or might not be the direction he intended to go.

Succeeding with this heavy handed 'multi-tasking', we turned into a magnificent wide avenue, immediately turning right again after a few yards, this time without offering any indication of the direction he intended to take before emerging into a fairy tale part of Paris which surely must have been photographed a million times.

'*Regardez-vous,*' the taxi driver muttered proudly over his shoulder, pointing through the windscreen. '*Le Place de la Concorde et des Avenue des Champs Élysées.*'

It was like déjà vu as I stared ahead at the magnificent vista that suddenly opened up before us. I had seen hundreds of pictures and photographs of the scene ahead, but no photograph or painting could have prepared me for the view that now unfolded before me.

The stunningly beautiful Jardin des Tuileries basked in the bright sunshine, its magnificent ornamental pools and fountains glittering and sparkling beneath the glory of the chestnut trees which surrounded them, giving the whole area a feeling of peace and tranquillity despite the traffic which seemed totally alien in such a beautiful setting.

Gazing about me in absolute awe, it barely seemed possible that only a few years earlier Adolph Hitler and his hated German army had also driven down this very boulevard as France was brought to its knees by its much hated adversary, ordinary victorious German soldiers looking at the same scene that I too was now admiring.

Totally absorbed by my surroundings, the driver also gave the impression that he was seeing this magnificent sight for the first time as he excitedly called out the names of monuments and various beautiful buildings of significance.

As we passed the wonderful Grand Palais on the left-hand side of the boulevard, I could see ahead of us the huge monumental central feature of the Champs Élysées, from which radiated the twelve avenues of the Place de l'Étoile.

As the car spluttered and coughed its way into this beautiful and chaotic amphitheatre which braced itself for the onslaught of taxis, motor scooters and cyclists all travelling in different directions at hugely varying speeds, I waited for the accident which must surely happen. To my intense relief we somehow manoeuvred our way forwards together with the multitude of other vehicles without mishap.

Despite being brought up in the birth place of the Vauxhall motor car, the number of cars travelling on the streets of Luton was microscopically small by comparison and one had to travel to London to see a comparative volume of traffic to that which I was now seeing. Even in London I was confident that the number of cars seen on the streets of our own capital was still significantly smaller than it was here.

Driving past the stunningly beautiful Arc de Triomphe I gasped at its design and architectural elegance as we were dwarfed by its massive arch, the bones in my neck cracking as I swivelled my head around to gaze upon it again through the rear window, not wishing to tear my gaze away from probably one of the most photographed pieces of architecture in the world.

Slumping back on the battered and worn leather upholstery of the taxi, I thought what it would be like to live in this wonderful city, imagining myself driving along beside the River Seine, the wind blowing through my hair as I rode my bright red Italian scooter with a beautiful girl passenger sitting side saddle behind me whispering sweet nothings in my ear as we headed for some romantic little bistro. Yes, there was no doubt about it, I was definitely going to change my nationality and become French. In fact I would probably even join the Foreign Legion when I finally tired of all the female attention that would undoubtedly be lavished upon me, courageously volunteering to go and fight in some desert war like Beau Geste and his fellow legionnaires had done. Mentally I began compiling my letter home... Dear Mum and Dad, I have decided to become French and join the legion etc. etc.

As I dreamed of what it would be like living in some garret apartment overlooking the rooftops of Paris, I was thrown to one side as the taxi driver made a sudden turn and headed back in the direction from which we had just come. Feeling slightly uneasy after my brush with the two attempted muggers at the station, I wondered what was to come next. Was this a detour designed to separate the tourist from his money by taking the longest route, or had the driver genuinely taken a wrong turn? The driver half-turned in his seat and in broken English pointed out of the window.

'Observe monsieur. Le Seine et la Musée d'Orsay.'

Surprised at his attempt to be courteous, the driver then asked in broken English if I had enjoyed his little tour. Undecided as whether to be grateful or to feel angry at the liberty he had taken, I nodded, trying to imagine what this beautiful yet unscheduled sightseeing tour might have cost me, also wondering what would happen if it transpired that I had insufficient French francs to pay him.

Worriedly, I glanced in the direction the driver had indicated, my earlier thoughts disappearing as we crossed the famous Pont Solferino to pull up at the kerb beside this world-famous building. Staring at the elegant stone façade of this former nineteen hundred World Fair railway station, it seemed incongruous that it now housed some of the most important and beautiful paintings in the world. I picked up my suitcase and braced myself in readiness for what was to come before opening the door.

Stepping out on to the pavement I moved around to where the driver still sat idly watching me as I reached into my pocket for some money. Now, for it I thought, this is where it could become extremely embarrassing and decidedly difficult.

Leaving the few French currency notes I still had in my inside pocket, I pulled out a handful of small denomination coins hoping that by doing this the driver might understand that I wasn't a rich English tourist and as such he might just take pity on me by charging me the going rate.

'*Merci monsieur, combien s'il vous plait?*' I muttered, hopefully holding out my hand which contained all of my loose change.

Answering me with some unintelligible figure in French, the driver showed no emotion as he peered into my outstretched hand, leaning out of his cab to sift through the small pile of French coins. Scooping up some of the shiny little centimes which lay among the duller but larger denominations, he selected what he wanted before picking up a small battered leather bag from the seat beside him, tossing the small handful of coins inside.

Briefly touching the front of his greasy black beret as acknowledgement of the payment, he smiled before wishing me '*Bon Chance*' and without another word the battered car coughed and clattered its way back down the road in the direction of that from which we had initially come.

Heaving a huge sigh of relief at not having to face the ignominy of not having enough money to pay the fare, I shook my head in disbelief as I watched the swirling screen of smelly dense smoke obliterating the sight of the taxi as it rattled away to seek out another fare before picking up my case and hastily making my way into the gallery.

For Some, a French Dream, for Some, a Nightmare...

Remembering every little detail of the paintings I had seen in the Musée d'Orsay, I still couldn't believe that I had stood in awe in front of great works of art by artists like Renoir, Monet and Degas. Apart from the incident with the two miscreants at the station, it was turning out to be a wonderful day and if anything else I saw came close to the magnificence of what I had just seen, it would have to be really special.

After gathering up every free catalogue and flyer available in the gallery, I pored over them attempting to translate the wording beneath each small picture and illustration. Sitting comfortably on the train I glanced out of the carriage window and saw that the weather had turned noticeably dull and overcast, but inside my head all I could see were the vibrant colours which had been used to such great effect by those great artists and despite the disappointing weather outside, the world had now become a much more colourful and beautiful place.

Reflecting on the events which had occurred since leaving home, I began to wonder if I might be turning into a more enlightened and mature person. I had already dismissed the incident at the station as something that happened in a less than ideal world, preferring to remember instead the taxi driver whose civic pride had gone a long way in redressing the balance with his impromptu and informative tour.

Reluctantly, I had dragged myself away from the gallery to summon a passing taxi for my return to the station, enjoying once again the beautiful boulevards and buildings, the sight of which, together with the memory of the magnificent paintings I had seen, making my first trip to Paris one which I would never forget.

On my arrival at the station, I was directed to a train which waited to take me on the next stage of my journey, one which would carry me closer to my ultimate destination and one step nearer to seeing my cousin and her husband. As I thought about the stories I would have to tell, it crossed my mind that I was experiencing what it must be like to live alone with no-one to share your thoughts and memories. I realised too that one of the things about travelling was that by not having anyone to tell of the things you had seen and done, the impact of those things would be sadly diminished, as part of the joy of any travel lay in the telling of such stories.

Prior to getting on the train, I walked the length of the platform with growing apprehension, as every carriage I had looked into contained simple wooden slatted seats which would have been far more suitable surrounding a bandstand than on a train. My anxiety grew even more the further I went, as I certainly didn't fancy sitting on something that resembled a park bench for the length of time I would be travelling.

Finally, to my relief I found some compartments at the rear of the train which were equipped with substantially more comfortable seating than those that I had seen previously, and I assumed from this that the former were probably of a lower class. Although none of the carriages carried numbers on the doors to suggest that this was the case, the one in which I now sat seemed far more suitable for travelling longer distances. While firm, the seats were at least upholstered, happily a more comfortable option than the slatted variety I had seen earlier. Gratefully, I clambered into an empty compartment which was linked to others by a corridor, stuffing my case up on to the luggage rack above before getting myself settled for the journey ahead.

Before getting on to the train I had found a kiosk which sold soft drinks and assorted rolls, and seizing the opportunity I bought a couple of rolls and some orange juice together with a small map with which I intended to try to trace my progress through France. With the rolls and juice on the seat beside me, I opened the map and began to trace the thin line which denoted the railway down through France until it reached the Spanish border.

To make sure that I had got it right and had not got on the wrong train, I got out my tickets and compared all the place names that were listed on my typed itinerary. The first name on the list was Orléans, followed by Tours, Poitiers, Angouleme and Bordeaux until finally heading out on the last leg to Bayonne where we would cross the border at Hendaye before travelling the short distance to Irun where I would need to change trains once again.

Referring to the scale at the bottom of the map, I worked out that the total distance from Paris to the Spanish border was about seven hundred kilometres, sighing as I realised that I was in for a long haul with only a few brief stops at the towns I had on my list. Grimacing, I contemplated the long trip ahead knowing that I would be spending a long time on trains without the luxury of a sleeping compartment, but I knew that, whatever happened, it was important to snatch whatever sleep I could.

As I looked around the carriage thinking how I might make myself more comfortable, I saw the skies beginning to darken outside and glancing at my watch I figured that it would be at least an hour before we reached the train's first stop at Orléans where perhaps I could get off and stretch my legs and hopefully find a café or a kiosk where I might be able to get some other form of refreshment.

Thinking about what lay ahead, my attention was drawn to a noise outside in the corridor; sliding open the door I looked to see what was happening. Outside, uniformed men made their way along the corridor carrying heavy kit bags, and intrigued at what was going on, I watched as more and more men walked past where I stood; some of them looking at me but none attempting to enter the compartment.

Eaten up with curiosity, I stared up and down the corridor.

On either side of the doorway, several of the men flopped down on to the floor, their backs resting against the sides of the compartments while others perched uncomfortably on top of their light khaki coloured kit bags, the majority of them appearing to be not much older than me, and all of them carrying rifles.

The peculiarities and nuances of my fellow man have always intrigued me, and my mother had often chastised me when she had seen me curiously watching people, saying 'It's rude to stare, you know what curiosity did don't you?' On this occasion her homespun philosophy was particularly appropriate as I continued to watch what was going on, my curiosity soaring to well over one hundred on the nosiness scale.

Reluctantly coming to the conclusion that she was right, I began to close the carriage door, as I did so I heard a voice asking in near perfect English if I had a light. Looking around, I half expected to see a fellow British traveller, but instead I was surprised to see a young man about my own age also clad in army uniform standing by the doorway of the next compartment casually holding a cigarette in his hand, smiling as he squeezed past his companions to head towards me.

'I'm sorry,' he said, 'but you are English aren't you?'

Shoving my hand into my jacket pocket for my matches I nodded as I replied.

'Is it that obvious?' I asked feeling slightly embarrassed.

It was the young man's turn to look embarrassed as he lowered his gaze.

'Please accept my apologies,' he said. 'As you do not look French, I just assumed that you might be English.'

'That's OK,' I replied, striking the match on the side of the box and holding the flame out towards him. 'I suppose I must look a bit like a tourist.'

The young man who was deeply tanned in contrast to his pale, sandy coloured uniform laughed as he reached into his tunic, producing a crumpled half-empty cigarette packet.

'Once again I apologise,' he said. 'Perhaps you would care for one of these? They're Gauloises, you may find them a bit strong after your English cigarettes, but I think you might like them.'

Accepting his offer, I thanked him, looking at the softly rolled cigarette before putting it between my lips, lighting it from the still flickering match. I wasn't ready for the impact from the strong tobacco as the smoke hit my lungs and I burst into a fit of uncontrollable coughing, tears streaming down my cheeks as I spluttered and attempted to regain some sort of dignity. The brand of cigarettes I normally smoked were much milder and also benefited from some form of cork tip, the strength of this raw unfiltered tobacco taking me completely by surprise.

After several more coughs, wheezes and general spluttering, I managed to stop before gasping my apologies.

'Wow, please excuse me, it just caught me off guard, I wasn't expecting something quite that strong.'

To an accompaniment of laughter from his colleagues who were watching what was going on, the young man smiled as he said, 'I did mention that they were probably stronger than the cigarettes that you normally smoke, but I didn't think they would affect you like that. Perhaps it is because that here in France we begin smoking much earlier than you do in England and are much more used to it.'

I thought back to my usual Craven A's with the cork tip which were extremely mild by comparison, vowing that I wouldn't be caught out like that again. Recognising that this was probably the strong smelling tobacco I had smelled earlier in the café, I made up my mind that I would try stronger brands in future, knowing that both Pam and Nick's choice of cigarettes had always been the stronger toasted American brands like Camel, Lucky Strike and Pall Mall.

Gently inhaling slightly less smoke than my initial lung jarring introduction to French cigarettes, I began to enjoy this newfound taste as I continued to chat to the young soldier. Inviting him into my compartment to share my orange juice and rolls, I was surprised as the young man looked anxiously over his shoulder and back down the corridor as he sadly shook his head.

'I'm sorry, nothing would give me greater pleasure but I'm afraid it is not possible. If my sergeant even saw me talking to you like this he would discipline me.'

His admission that he was not allowed to talk to me made me think of my own imminent foray into a life of discipline and I wondered if I too would find myself in this sort of situation where I might fall foul of military rules and regulations.

As we continued to talk, the young man's eyes continued to dart left and right, perpetually looking back over his shoulder, ready at a moment's notice to ignore me and continue in the role of an obedient French soldier. It was obvious that he, together with his young comrades, was clearly in transit to God knows where.

The brittle tenseness which emanated from him and his colleagues began to fill me with unease as if I too should also fear the approach of this dreaded sergeant, someone whose very presence on the train seemed to generate an unquantifiable fear.

From somewhere nearby, the haunting strains of a harmonica drifted along the corridor, its haunting reedy lament causing my new friend to look desperately sad, his whole demeanour becoming nervous and unhappy where previously he and his companions had appeared to be in relatively high spirits.

Eager to try and recapture our light-hearted conversation of earlier, I asked his name.

'Eric,' he replied. 'My name is Eric Besancon.'

'Do you live in Paris?' I continued, hoping that by getting him to talk about his home and family, his jauntiness might return.

He nodded. 'Just on the outskirts of Paris, in the Val-de Marne department. We have a small patisserie there, my father is a baker and my mother and sister help in the shop.'

As the young man ground out his cigarette on the floor, I became increasingly uneasy at the gathering quiet that hung heavy in the air, a silence broken only by terse whispered conversations coming from the men squatting uncomfortably on their kit bags, while the continuing sombre strains of the harmonica added their own solemnity to the moment.

Gradually I began to realise that this air of despondency which now permeated throughout the whole length of the carriage was not brought on by the sad lingering refrains of the harmonica or even by the omnipotent presence of this anonymous and much feared sergeant, I began to sense that there was much more to it than that.

Staring into the deep brown eyes of the young soldier, the name of Beau Geste suddenly popped into my head as I recalled the stirring adventures of him and other French soldiers who had fought so valiantly against Arab hordes, and with my imagination running riot I began to wonder if these young boys were also being taken to fight in some God forsaken war zone that I had never heard of.

'Please don't answer this if you feel that you shouldn't, but where exactly is it that you are going? I have a feeling that you're not exactly overjoyed about it?'

Eric hesitated before answering, looking nervously up and down the corridor, bending his head towards me as he whispered his reply.

'I should not be telling you this, but as I am quite sure that you must have read much about it in your English newspapers, I don't think that it can matter that much.'

Again he looked up and down the corridor before answering, speaking quickly in French to one of his colleagues who nodded and pushed his way past the others to stand at the end of the carriage by the connecting door.

'We are being sent to fight in the war in Algeria. Do you in England know anything about this war?'

I reluctantly shook my head. 'No, not really; I know that there is a great deal of trouble there and that the French people have become involved, but I only know what has been published in our newspapers.'

The young soldier sadly shook his head.

'I have always suspected that it is a case of the rest of the world not knowing exactly what is happening here in France.

'Basically what is happening is that our president, Charles de Gaulle, insists that Algeria is a part of France, but in reality it is far removed from belonging to France.'

He glanced nervously in the direction of his friend at the end of the corridor before continuing.

'Algeria is a Muslim country and I believe that it is the right of the people living there to rule Algeria as they see fit without any interference from our politicians here. I personally believe that there is only one way that this war can end.

'It is obvious to me and many of my friends, and with other young people of our age group that this is just simply a political and religious struggle.

'I think a word that I have read in your English newspapers is the word attrition and this is an example of a war of attrition. President de Gaulle is intent on ruling Algeria at any cost as colonialists, as we currently do in French Indo China, but in this instance it is not possible. There is already much unrest and bloodshed which is directed at both our soldiers and our civilians working there and I think that before very long we will be involved in an all out war.'

I marvelled at the young man's understanding of his country's politics and felt ashamed at knowing so little of what went on even in my own country.

Looking up and down the corridor he leaned even closer before continuing.

'If the struggle in Algeria goes the wrong way for us, as it almost certainly will, we think that the President will realise this when it is all too late and he will simply walk away. When this happens, the Marxists, who are there already waiting in the wings, will take up arms and carry on the fight with the Islamic fundamentalists making all the sacrifices my gallant countrymen have already made even more futile. It is very sad, and it is this situation which saddens us all.'

Eric shrugged his shoulders, raising his hands in a simple act of supplication.

'My friends and I want no part of this war but what can we do? I'm sure that it is the same in your country when your own politicians do something that you do not agree with, but this is a war no-one wants, this is why we are all sad and frustrated.

'Already there have been thousands of my fellow countrymen captured, tortured and slaughtered, and in retaliation we have done the same to them in the name of so-called liberty. Personally, I do not think that we should become involved in the politics of a foreign country which does not belong to us, and if you were to ask any of my friends on this train what they think, I'm sure they will tell you the same.'

He took another cigarette from his pack also offering me one, accepting my brief shake of the head as a refusal before continuing, bending his head to light his own from the match I held out for him.

'We are not afraid to fight as we proved to everyone when we bravely fought along with your own soldiers against the Bosche during the last war.'

I said nothing as I remembered my father's criticism of the French and what he described as having to fight both the Germans and also the government of Vichy.

'We are desperately struggling to rebuild our country after the last war and now we are being plunged into another, it is sheer lunacy, it is a war we cannot possibly win. These are a people who do not fight in a conventional way, they fight secretly, not out in the open, they fight from doorways and they plant booby traps. They have no artillery, no tanks and they have no air force and we continue to bomb what our generals call strategic targets, but on the ground in the towns and villages, we just send out patrols to try to keep some sort of order in the streets but they just ambush our patrols and butcher our soldiers.

'They are the experts at this type of street fighting. When we do manage to capture a few prisoners and try to make them tell us where their leaders are hiding, these fanatical mullahs, or whatever it is they are called, crawl back into hiding to re-appear somewhere else, it is like fighting shadows.

'I have lost three of my best friends this year, people I grew up with who lived in the same department as myself. Two of them were shot while on patrol and the other one was snatched as they searched a mosque. When he was discovered, he was tied to a telegraph pole and had been tortured and his body mutilated, these are the people we are asked to call fellow citizens. They hate us so how can we be expected to live side by side when they want us out of their country and just to govern themselves.'

Suddenly, from somewhere further down the train, a soft sharp whistle was repeated again and again as it travelled quickly through the ranks of the assembled men, the sound being taken up as a warning of the approach of a superior officer. Quickly, Eric stamped out his cigarette and moved away, returning to his comrades where he squatted uncomfortably on his kit bag.

'Sorry,' he said over his shoulder. 'I mustn't be seen talking to you, please stay in your compartment and we will talk again later.'

As I sat back in my seat I looked towards the window in the hope of seeing who had caused this young man to be so concerned. I didn't have long to wait as a man dressed in the same coloured uniform as those worn by the soldiers outside came into view, but that's where any similarity ended.

Walking slowly along the line of men, he looked at them with disdain and almost hatred. Wearing a sand coloured uniform, the colour of that of the young soldiers, he wore on his head a round *kepi*, and above the peak an insignia which resembled a flaming gold torch resting on a dark blue background.

His jacket was beautifully tailored with a shiny black leather belt around its waist on which a pistol hung encased in an equally shiny black leather holster, and on his breast several lines of medal ribbons contrasted dramatically to the colour of his coat. On the precisely pressed sleeves were three braided stripes of a different colour to that of his jacket but it was his face that caused me to sit back in my seat.

Beneath the cap, closely-cropped iron-grey hair framed a face which in the past had undoubtedly seen its fair share of action both in bars and on the battlefield, a face which only a mother could love and then possibly only while under the influence of drugs or alcohol. His was a countenance that could strike the fear of God into mere mortals with just a glance, a face which was capable of turning ordinary soldiers' legs to jelly, both in times of conflict and on parade grounds.

On the man's right-hand cheek, a deep scar ran from beside his nose to his ear, this horrific scar underlined by a grey waxed moustache, the colour of which matched exactly that of his hair, a moustache bristling with undisguised antagonism.

As I studied the figure outside, he suddenly became aware of me watching him, glaring back at me through the glass. Unable to tear my gaze away, I found myself looking into the coldest blue-grey eyes that I had ever seen; eyes that stared unblinkingly back into mine, turning my blood to ice and sending a shiver running through my body. I now realised why my new found friend and his colleagues had appeared so nervous and full of apprehension, here was a man who was undoubtedly a strict disciplinarian, a brutal man whose presence demanded instant obedience and anyone unfortunately falling foul of him would certainly live to regret it.

Turning his attention back to his charges in the corridor, he growled a command in French to one of the men who positively cringed with fear as he adjusted his uniform to his superior's reluctant satisfaction. What stories did this cruel looking individual have to tell as I again remembered the story of Beau Geste; was he now, or had he ever been a soldier in that romantic sounding branch of the army, the French Foreign Legion?

I thought back to my earlier dreams of living in France and in time joining the Legion, suddenly coming to the conclusion that this last part of my dream was probably not the best idea I had ever had in my life.

As this frightening looking figure moved from my line of vision I waited for a few moments before gingerly sliding back the carriage door. Obviously what went on in the corridor outside was none of my business and clearly this malevolent looking character certainly had no jurisdiction over me, but the last thing I wanted was to be seen to be even remotely interested in their comings and goings.

On hearing the carriage door slide back, Eric glanced quickly in my direction and with a tight-lipped frown on his face, shook his head as a signal to me that it would be unwise to continue our conversation. Quietly closing the door again, I reluctantly decided that the wisest thing for all concerned would be to wait until the young man contacted me again, and slumping back into my seat, I took one of my rolls from its greaseproof paper and began to eat.

Finishing the first roll, I took a long swig from the bottle of orange and stared out of the window. It was now quite dark outside and I could see very little of the countryside as the train continued its rattling progress on into the night. Outside in the corridor, the young soldiers still perched on top of their kit bags, some of them eating while others just sat and talked. I longed to hear more from my new found friend but there was no indication that he was going to make any further contact.

Tiredness began to overtake me as I felt my eyelids beginning to droop, and resting my head back on to the seat cushion behind me I closed my eyes, travel weariness suddenly overcoming me as I drifted off into an uneasy sleep.

The noise of the carriage door being slid back brought me back to a state of reluctant wakefulness and turning my head I was disappointed to see the ticket collector standing in the doorway instead of the young soldier.

'*Billet monsieur, s'il vous plait.*'

I reached into my inside jacket pocket for my tickets, glancing past where the man stood waiting to where some of the young soldiers still lay sprawled awkwardly on their crumpled and sagging kit bags, some of them nodding in an attempt to snatch whatever sleep they could.

With a cursory glance at my ticket, the collector thanked me, touching the peak of his cap before punching a neat round hole in the piece of card before stepping back out into the corridor, carefully stepping around both the soldiers and their kit. Knocking over a rifle which rested against the wall, it clattered to the floor causing its owner to wake with a start as he reached out to pick up his weapon.

Getting to my feet, I followed the ticket collector out into the corridor, looking towards where I had last seen my new found friend, but although his rifle and kit bag were still in the same spot there was no sign of the owner.

Several heads turned in my direction as I stood debating what to do next. Would it be wise to try my schoolboy French in an attempt to try to discover the whereabouts of the young soldier or should I just forget about it and say nothing? As I struggled to make up my mind what to do, one of the soldiers called to me in broken English.

'*Pardon mon ami.* If you are seeking Eric Besancon, he has been taken away by the sergeant and has been ordered to bring food for us. I think that he was reported after he was seen speaking to you and he has been given this duty as a punishment, I think that you may not see him again.'

Thanking him for the information I stepped back into the compartment and closed the door, flopping down on to my seat and feeling guilty that by talking to him I may have got him into serious trouble with the fearsome looking sergeant. I desperately hoped that this punishment of serving food to his colleagues would be sufficient to wipe his slate clean and he would not suffer further at a later date.

I reflected that it had been less than twenty-four hours since leaving home and already I was beginning to realise how comfortable and uncomplicated my life had been. My happy upbringing had sheltered me from extremes of hardship and danger, something brought about by the cushioning security of having two loving parents who guided and advised; this guidance brought about by their own experiences in life.

The regular melodic sound of the train wheels rattling against the tracks again began to have a soporific effect as I felt my eyes starting to close despite my attempts to stay awake, and accepting the inevitable I folded my arms across my chest and put my feet up on the seat and was soon fast asleep.

Harsh sounds of screeching and tortured metal brought me back to a state of semi-awareness as the train driver applied the brakes, slowly reducing its speed to a crawl.

Jumping up, I wiped the steamed up window with my hand and looked out to see a few flickering street lamps together with brighter, smaller lights shining from the un-curtained windows of several small houses some distance away. More nerve jangling sounds of metal against metal together with the accompanying juddering and lurching of the carriages bumping together brought the train to a shuddering halt, a notice on the platform outside telling me that we had arrived in Orléans.

Ignoring the billowing smoke from the engine and the odd raindrops which splashed against my face, I lowered the window and looked out. This was certainly nothing like the throbbing bustle of the Gare du Nord. In fact, the station appeared at first glance to be deserted, but as I watched, several people emerged from the shadows clutching bags and dragging small suitcases behind them as they looked for unoccupied carriages.

At first glance I thought that I had been lucky and would continue to have the compartment to myself but it was not to be as a lady and a young girl of about my own age appeared, each clutching a suitcase and walking in my direction.

Accepting the inevitable, I opened the carriage door and reached down to take a small case from the young girl's hand, dragging it in and stepping to one side to allow her room to enter. The more elderly lady who I guessed might be the girl's mother, handed up her own suitcase with a strength that took me completely by surprise. As I gripped its handle, the combined weight of both the case and its contents caught me unawares and caused me to pitch forwards and fall against the side of the carriage, the impetus of my fall threatening to drag me out of the train and down on to the platform to where she now stood. Behind me, I could hear the young girl giggling as I struggled to retain some sort of dignity and extricate myself from this embarrassing situation.

Half carrying and half dragging the heavy case into the compartment, I felt my face burning and turning red, not simply with the effort of getting the case on board the train but also as a result of my undisguised embarrassment. As I continued to drag the case backwards there was a shriek from behind as I stepped on the girl's foot, my shame was now complete.

'I'm so sorry, please excuse me,' I stammered, turning to face the girl who was hopping up and down on one leg, 'I did not know you were there.'

With a pained smile and a few muttered words, the girl flopped down on the seat opposite to where I had been sitting, watching while her mother clambered up into the compartment.

Hitching the heavy case up on to the seat prior to giving it the final 'heave ho' up on to the luggage rack above I paused, this time there would be no embarrassment, this time the case was going up on to the rack above even if I suffered a hernia in the process. Just as I was about to take a deep breath before giving it my best shot, the lady smiled sweetly and brushed away my hand before swinging it up on to the rack in one easy flowing action.

Feeling totally inadequate, I felt disappointed at not being given the opportunity of demonstrating my masculinity in front of the girl. Watching the older lady taking off her coat and placing it on the rack above beside her case, I flopped back down on my seat, looking up to see her smiling pleasantly in my direction as she tried in broken English to thank me for my efforts.

After several minutes of embarrassing silence, I was relieved when the train began to pull away from the platform; clouds of steam billowing past the window as it slowly gathered momentum. As I turned away from the window to glance at my new travelling companions, I wondered if I should try to initiate some sort of dialogue between us, particularly if we were to be travelling any sort of distance together. As if in answer to my dilemma, the older lady who sat opposite again thanked me in broken English for my efforts with the case, introducing herself and her daughter Avril, informing me that they were travelling to Bordeaux where they would be visiting relatives they hadn't seen since before the outbreak of the war.

With the train rattling on into the night I began to hear of the traumas and suffering of the people of France during the German occupation. The young girl who spoke excellent English, interrupted every time her mother became stuck for a word or a sentence while I looked from one to the other trying to imagine what life must have been like living under that sort of tyranny.

Enthralled, yet horrified, by the stories of misery and near starvation, I listened to horrendous descriptions of German soldiers banging on the doors of houses with rifle butts at all hours of the day and night. I tried to picture the scene, imagining what it must have been like to see loved ones dragged out into the street and loaded on to the backs of lorries often never to be seen again.

As I listened, I became aware of Avril showing what I imagined to be a more than a passing interest in me, looking at me in a quizzical manner as she tried on several occasions to question me about where I lived and of my own recollections of the war, but with her mother in full flow she found it impossible to interject.

After about half an hour of continuing tales of unbelievable near famine conditions and of make and mend due to the lack of practically everything imaginable, my mind began to wander as I kept repeating the young girl's name over and over in my head.

'Avril.' Was ever a name so lovely?

'Avril.' Could this be an omen of things to come, Avril in Paris and all that? Here was I recently departing the French capital, albeit not quite in springtime but near enough for my impressionable mind to consider that fate had suddenly come calling.

In the background, the steady Gallic drone of her mother's voice continued, but all I could think of were myself and the lovely Avril skipping hand in hand through meadows filled with bluebells and buttercups, while, overhead, a skylark announced to the world that Avril and I were in love. Steady I thought, I hadn't yet been given the opportunity of speaking at length to her, and already we were practically betrothed.

The insistent dull background babble continued unabated as her mother continued with her saga as I mentally switched off to consider how I could obtain the lovely Avril's address and possibly even a telephone number. Suddenly I was brought back to the present as Avril leaned forwards to touch my knee, repeating a question that her mother had obviously asked while I was still dreaming of the paradise that would be ours to share.

'My mother asked where do you live in England and if you saw any of the war?'

Grateful of the opportunity to direct some of my attention towards Avril, I talked of home and of the Vauxhall motor car plant on the outskirts of the town, explaining that the factory had been redeveloped and altered to manufacture the Churchill tank, mentioning also that there were two aircraft factories located just outside the town. I also spoke of other factories located in the town itself that produced vast quantities of ball bearings and shell casings which were destined to help the war effort, pointing out that because of these vital targets, we too had been victims of attacks from German bombers and V1 rockets.

I waxed lyrically about, although only being five, my father had held me in his arms in our garden at night, pointing towards London where the glow of fires in the burning city could be clearly seen from a distance of over thirty miles away. I spoke too of the heroism of the crews manning the anti-aircraft batteries that had been strategically placed around the town who were responsible for the shooting down of numerous German bombers as they tried to target these manufacturing plants. I explained how these anti-aircraft crews would attempt to shoot down the bombers before they managed to drop their bombs, also how they had shot down many more as they tried to limp back across the channel after having been savaged by our Spitfire and Hurricane pilots.

As our conversation became more personal and less about the war, I thought it time to discover more about the lovely Avril, turning the conversation to a point where I felt that it was time to obtain an address and perhaps a telephone number.

'Do you live in Orléans?' I asked, hopefully trying not to appear too obvious by carefully directing my question to Avril's mother.

Before her mother had a chance to respond, my spirits soared as Avril jumped in to answer my question, telling me that they lived on the outskirts of Orléans, a town in which she had been born and lived all of her life; she, in turn, asking where I lived and what was the purpose of me being on this train so late at night.

Feeling that it was all going exceedingly well, I told her about my reasons for travel as her mother began to feature less and less in our conversation until finally, sighing heavily, she closed her eyes and resting her hands in her lap, settled back in her seat. Seizing the opportunity, I quickly slipped on to the seat next to where Avril was sitting, apologising profusely as my hand 'accidentally' brushed against hers.

Subtly trying to phrase my questions delicately in an attempt not to appear too obvious or too pushy, I tried to find out more intimate details in respect of her age and marital status without actually appearing to do so.

'Do you also work in Orléans or do you attend a college or university?'

Now completely at ease with the situation, she began to confide in me with regard to life at home, telling me that she was single and on her return from Bordeaux she would begin work in the local mayor's office and, if she worked hard, she could become responsible for a department which dealt with the issuing of the necessary permits and licences which allowed alterations and renovations to be carried out on some of the historic and imposing manor houses and chateaus throughout the region.

Confident that I had now reached a stage where I felt that my chances of being rebuffed were fairly slim, I played what I hoped would be my trump card.

'That's amazing,' I said, blatantly lying through my teeth. 'I've always been fascinated by stately homes and the history behind them, it looks as if we have something in common. When you get home perhaps we could keep in touch and maybe you would write and let me know how you are getting on?'

Holding my breath I reached into my pocket for something to write on.

'Look, let me write down my name and address, and if you would like to you could give me yours, it would be nice if we could write to each other once in a while. If you have a telephone, let me have the number and perhaps you will allow me to call you.'

Without hesitation she took my pen and the piece of paper and began writing down her name, address and telephone number. Feeling as if all my birthdays had come at once, I did the same, except of course as we didn't have a telephone and hoping that Mr Armitage next door wouldn't mind, I jotted his number down as well.

Staring at the neat handwriting on the piece of paper she handed back to me, I wondered if I should really push my luck and question her about any potential men in her life, but a little voice inside my head told me that 'softly, softly catchee monkey', and I should keep those sort of questions until a much later date.

With the train rattling on through the darkness we happily continued to speak of our respective lives and ambitions, the conversation finally turning to my imminent secondment into the RAF and my reasons for being on a train heading for Seville. As I talked of my hopes and plans for the future, I could see that my mentioning the RAF had unwittingly scored me a few hundred 'brownie points', as it transpired that, unhappily, her father had been shot by the Germans as a reprisal for him assisting the French resistance in aiding the escape of several English air crew who had been forced to parachute from their stricken aircraft into occupied France.

The stations at Tours, Poitiers and Angouleme came and went with nobody joining us in our compartment, the absence of other people giving me uninterrupted time with the beautiful Avril until finally the train began to slow down as it headed into the station at Bordeaux.

'I think this is where we must say *au revoir*,' she said, glancing at her mother who still sat with her eyes closed and her head resting against the carriage window.

'Please write or telephone to let me know how you are and what you are doing. Perhaps when you join your RAF you might be sent to somewhere which would enable us to meet, it would be very nice to see you again.'

Bending forwards, Avril placed her hand over mine, leaning forwards to kiss me lightly on both cheeks, the delicate smell of her perfume arousing a feeling in me that I found hard to control as I responded by kissing her gently on the lips. Instead of turning her head away she stared into my eyes, the expression on her face telling me that she was sorry that we would not be spending further time together.

'When will you be back in Orléans?' I asked, still holding her hand, but before she had time to answer her mother suddenly sat up with a start and began to wipe the carriage window.

'*Alors Avril, nous sommes arrives.*'

With a screeching of brakes, the train jerked and clattered to a standstill, catching the older woman unawares as she reached up to the luggage rack above, sending her pitching backwards to sit unceremoniously on to the seat opposite. Leaping to her feet, she tried again, this time managing to drag the case down from the rack above.

Determined not to repeat my earlier embarrassment with the heavy case, I chose instead to deal with Avril's much lighter one, easily lifting it down from the luggage rack and placing it on the seat, leaving her mother to open the carriage door and clamber down on to the platform before dragging her suitcase behind her. Avril followed dutifully in her wake as I dropped down on to the platform behind her with her much smaller battered case in my hand before she turned back to where I stood.

'We will be back in Orléans in ten days time, if you feel that you would like to, you could telephone me then.'

Ten days time, could I possibly wait until then? My answer was drowned by a shrill blast from the guard's whistle, this being followed by another more urgent double blast telling me that if I wanted to travel any further on this particular train I needed to get back on board and shut the carriage door.

As I gazed at Avril standing forlornly on the dimly lit platform, I climbed back inside and lowered the window, knowing precisely how Trevor Howard must have felt as he waved goodbye to Celia Johnson in the film *Brief Encounter*, and with the train slowly heading off into the night, I waved and turned away from the window.

Staring out into the night I tried to shrug off the image of her face, wondering how I might be able to telephone while staying in Spain. I knew that if either Pam or Nick even suspected that I was telephoning a girl I had just met on a train, life would degenerate to become hell on earth with their almost certain incessant teasing.

The more I thought about it, I knew that I was not going to be in any sort of position to meet up with her again in the immediate future. I made up my mind that I would telephone, but any future meeting would have to be put on hold.

Feeling that Humphrey Bogart probably had this sort of encounter all the time and it was all part of becoming the international traveller I now was, I delved into my pockets for my tickets. Knowing that the next stop on my journey would be Bayonne where, shortly afterwards, I would be crossing the border into Spain, I looked again at my itinerary and tried to estimate the time of our arrival.

The stop at Bayonne brought no new passengers on to the train but it did bring increased activity from the corridor outside as the young French soldiers began to stand up and tend to their kit, their obvious despondency made even worse by several older NCOs marching up and down their ranks barking out orders and instructions to the hapless young men.

Realising that they were preparing to disembark, I wondered if they would continue their journey by catching another train which would take them down through Spain, or were they headed for a military airfield from where they would fly directly into Algeria, it was clear however that wherever it was that they were going, they were certainly not going by choice. I also realised, from watching the frantic activity going on in the corridor outside, that there would be very little chance of me seeing my young soldier friend again before they left.

As I watched, two men dressed in official looking uniforms struggled to push their way through the mass of young soldiers, fighting to make their way down the corridor until finally they reached my compartment.

'Your tickets and passport please monsieur. We will be crossing the border shortly.'

Handing my passport and ticket to one of the men, I watched as he flicked through the pages of my passport, studying the photograph inside and then me. Satisfied, he produced a rubber stamp, and with a flourish, brought it down on to one of the opened pages before handing it back. Eager to see how my bright, shiny new passport had been officially vandalised, I waited until he had left the compartment before looking inside to see what had been done.

On turning to the page which carried the impressive looking Spanish visa with its other official consular stamps, I saw that it now also boasted a small black lozenge-shaped stamp which read 'SURETE NATIONALE HENDAYE' together with the current date. As I looked at it, I thought back to when I had disembarked in Calais, I had been asked for my passport but rather disappointingly it contained no stamp.

With the two officials now having moved further along the train, I stepped out into the corridor hoping that I would see my young friend but he was nowhere to be seen, even his kit had been moved away from where it had remained unattended for so long.

Feeling sorry for the rest of the young soldiers who stood dejectedly smoothing down their uniforms and checking their rifles and kit bags, I thanked my lucky stars that I would not be going with them. Thinking back to what Eric had told me with regard to the unpopular war in Algeria, I returned to my seat imagining what horrors they might see and how many of these reluctant heroes would be returning home in one piece, their bodies whole but their minds in turmoil.

Wiping the steamed up window with my sleeve I saw that it had stopped raining and ahead I could see the bright lights of the Spanish border station of Irun welcoming the train as it nosed its way up to the platform. Casting my mind back to when I had excitedly stood on the platform of Luton railway station with my egg and cress sandwiches, it now seemed light years away, and despite all that had happened so far, I sent up a little prayer of thanks for me having actually arrived relatively unscathed in Spain.

A sudden sharp barking of orders from the corridor outside sent the soldiers scurrying to pick up their belongings as they prepared to leave. As I looked at their tired and worried faces, they were herded like cattle towards the doors which had been flung open as a prelude to their disembarkation, their kit bags being thrown unceremoniously down on to the platform below.

Even today, I still remember the faces, tired and anxious as they slowly followed each other like sheep towards the exits, boys younger than I, probably about to die for things they didn't understand or even care about, sent to fight in a country which would possibly only be seen by future generations as having an interesting sounding name in some battered school atlas, but not remembered for what went on there.

As the corridor slowly cleared of soldiers, I was once again confronted by two more uniformed figures who again asked for my tickets and passport. This time the men were darker skinned and attired in totally different uniforms, and although I had never encountered Spanish guards or soldiers before, there was no doubt that these dour looking individuals were there to forcibly deny unauthorised access into Spain.

While one of the men leaned against the side of the open door with his hand resting easily on the butt of his holstered pistol, the other took my ticket and passport, staring hard at my face as he compared it to the photograph inside. Almost grudgingly it seemed, he produced a rubber stamp much like the one used by the French officials moments before and brought it down on the opened page, and with a brusque and surly 'Gracias', he thrust it back into my hand.

Welcome to Spain, I thought sarcastically, staring at the new stamp which now adorned the same page as the last, but this time because of the attitude of the two officials, this latest stamp seemed to be much more sinister. It was again lozenge-shaped but inside, it stated 'POLICIA – IRUN' together with the current date followed by the word 'ENTRADA'.

Who Said Eating a Banana was Easy...

The Talgo Express to one whose only previous travel experience had been restricted to third class, oozed refinement, offering, as it did, single reclining seats separated by individual tables on which stood small vases of real flowers. At the window, elegant tasselled curtains hung; curtains which could actually be drawn. Not on this train the heavy fly-specked canvas blinds which normally adorned the windows of the mundane rolling stock on which I had previously travelled in England.

I sat back and revelled in the luxury of the seating, pressing a button on the armrest of my seat which gently and silently lowered me back into a more reclined position, the subdued lighting above my head gently bathing the table in front of me in a soft halo of light. If this style and opulence was typical of what I could look forward to throughout my journey to Madrid I was pleased that I hadn't bothered with a sleeping compartment, happy in the knowledge that if I decided to sleep for a couple of hours I could do so in far greater comfort than I had previously imagined.

My initial glimpse of the train had lived up to all my expectations as it crouched at the side of the platform, poised and ready to launch itself into the blackness of the Spanish night. Each carriage was a streamlined shiny aluminium cylinder, the doors of which stood open to welcome its passengers, and at the side of each door a uniformed attendant stood poised ready to whisk each person's luggage into the sanctuary of this masterpiece of modern engineering. Not only were they ready to escort the owners of such luggage to their seats, I was sure that they were also well versed in the subtle art of smilingly accepting gratuities for such a service.

Before boarding, I stood and stared at this gleaming apparition, thinking of the description given by the travel agent in Luton when he had compared it to a series of linked aluminium cigar tubes. To a degree, his analysis had been reasonably accurate but I certainly hadn't expected anything like this.

Throughout the length of the train, oval tinted windows gave the impression of aerodynamic simplicity which offered an insight into the future world of travel, a glimpse of things to come, a design which would undoubtedly become the norm in our own country in the twenty-first century. (Oh yeah?)

Discreetly studying other passengers in my compartment, it was obvious that these were people who were comfortable with this type of lifestyle, no doubt perfectly relaxed and at home in what I considered to be outstanding and elegant surroundings.

Sitting two seats in front of me on the opposite side of the central walkway, a dark-skinned rotund gentleman dressed in a soft, grey, beautifully cut, lightweight suit had taken a cigar from an embossed leather cigar case and was in the process of nipping off the end with a gold and horn cigar cutter. This was the first cigar cutter I had ever seen and I watched in fascination as he inserted the end of the cigar into the hole at the end, and with a deft pressing of his thumb, the rounded end of the cigar was expertly removed. No sooner had he dropped the cutter back into his pocket and placed the prepared cigar into his mouth, than a uniformed attendant appeared as if by magic to apply a lighted match. With barely a nod of acknowledgement, the man sank back into his seat, and with a huge sigh of contentment sent a rolling cloud of blue smoke towards the ceiling.

I had never sampled the delights of a cigar but had always loved the smell, and the aroma that drifted back to where I sat reminded me of Christmas when my father would invariably receive a packet of five small Wills's Whiffs cigars as a present. My mother being a non-smoker and hating the smell of cigarette smoke, always insisted that he went outside if he wanted to smoke, and if it happened to be raining he could be found sitting comfortably in a deckchair in his shed at the top of the garden, or similarly if the downpour was so severe that he couldn't reach his shed without becoming soaked, he would normally retire to the 'comfort' of the outside toilet. Christmas though was altogether different, when the 'smoking in the house' ban was relaxed, and after presenting him with these little cigars, she would proudly watch as he sat back in his armchair after lunch, contentedly puffing away at his once a year treat where we would all sit in anticipation of the Queen's speech at three o'clock.

Closing my eyes and happily breathing in this festive aroma, my thoughts drifted fondly back to my mother and her unstinting generosity in all things. Even despite her worries and fears with regard to me travelling to Spain in this way, she had unhesitatingly opened her purse and given me that half crown for my bus fare into town to collect my tickets.

I remembered her smiling face as she joked about me making my first million, feeling guilty at having discarded the sandwiches she had lovingly prepared, reflecting that it was hardly an ideal way to show my love and appreciation.

A sound from further down the compartment interrupted my thoughts and I peered around the side of the seat in front to watch another male passenger settling himself into his seat. It suddenly crossed my mind that this might be a 'men only' smoking compartment, but with that, a beautifully dressed dark haired woman aged about thirty suddenly appeared to join him. Unable to take my eyes off this incredible vision of loveliness, I watched as she spoke to her companion before she too sat down. Before sitting down she glanced in my direction and smiled as she caught me staring at her, and despite feeling embarrassed at being caught in the act of watching her, I managed to conjure up my best smile in return.

Her hair, the colour of a raven's wing, complimented perfectly her wonderfully smooth tanned skin. Being a happily married man, Nick had obviously never mentioned anything in regard to the beauty of the fairer sex in Spain, but I was confident that there couldn't be too many women anywhere in the world that could be compared to her. I smiled to myself as I thought back to my previous encounter with Avril, less than an hour ago I was almost prepared to throw myself from the train for the love of a young French girl, now I could barely remember what she looked like. Wonderful stuff this travel I thought, it certainly broadens the mind and widens one's horizons.

Sinking back into my seat, I thought about what might lay ahead. The reunion with Pam and Nick was something I was really looking forward to, but because of the possible ramifications of what awaited me on my return to England in respect of my call-up, I was determined that this was going to be one trip that I would never forget.

A discreet cough at my elbow brought me back to the present and I turned my head in the direction of the sound. Standing in the central aisle smiling down at me stood one of the uniformed attendants I had noticed earlier. Speaking in hushed tones and saying something that sounded a bit like 'excuse me', he continued in Spanish.

'I'm sorry,' I stammered, 'I don't speak Spanish.'

The man repeated what he had said, this time pointing down the compartment in the direction from which the beautiful young woman had appeared.

A sudden panic gripped me as I guessed he was telling me that I shouldn't be here, and that peasants like me should be confined to a less sumptuous part of the train. I should have realised I thought, that luxury like this was not for the likes of me, and now I would have to face the embarrassment of being thrown bodily from the train.

Deciding to play the innocent in the forlorn hope that I might get away with it I shrugged my shoulders, lifting my hands in the time honoured fashion of someone who had not understood what had been said.

'This man is telling you that there is a buffet car in the next compartment.'

I turned my head to see who it was that had come to my rescue, and saw that it was the new great love of my life looking even more stunning as she stood smiling in the aisle. She raised her hand and pointed towards the end of the compartment.

'If you would like something to eat or drink it can be served to you there.'

'It can be served to me there!' God, is that really what she had said. 'It can be served to me there?'

This is what true love must be like. Not only was I not going to be thrown off the train, this vision of loveliness had actually made the first move indicating that she too was in love with me. Telling me that there was a buffet car next door was simply a ploy where she would be waiting to throw herself into my arms.

At the thought of perhaps having something to eat and having the merest morsel of something Spanish to drink, it was clear to me that it would be rude not to visit the compartment 'where it can be served to me'. After all, the new love in my life had gone to great lengths to make sure that I did not starve or become dehydrated, so it was clear that not only did she love me, she had my dietary interests at heart as well.

Attempting to give my best 'man about town' smile and not leer lasciviously, I brushed past this escapee from heaven to be immediately transported to a place where the sound of angel's voices filled the air. Bluebirds hovered amongst trees heavy with blossom, from which the exotic fragrance of her perfume drifted provocatively past my nostrils in the same way as it appeared in the advertisement featuring the Bisto Kids and the gravy. Behaving like the innocent victim of a hypnotist, I floated on air as I opened the door to the buffet car and stepped inside.

On each side of the carpeted compartment, deep comfortable leather armchairs were grouped in twos and threes around circular tables containing shallow glass or cup holders, each of the tables strategically placed beside the big tinted windows. At the far end stood a leather padded bar behind which glass shelves supported a huge array of glasses and bottles containing various coloured liquids, each one sparkling enticingly beneath concealed lighting which shone from above. For a brief moment I stood and gazed open-mouthed at the selection of drinks displayed before me. Thus far in my comparatively young and innocent life, the only drinks I had come into contact with were either Watneys Red Barrel or bottles of J.W. Green's brown ale.

Remembering the French beer I had unfortunately committed to the deep while on board the cross channel ferry, I thought that although the beer here might be different, it might not be the wisest thing at this time of the night to repeat the performance of earlier; instead I would have something different with less impact.

As I slipped on to one of the leather covered bar stools and scanned the various bottles lined up before me, I tried desperately to think what I should have. Having never seen such an array before and not recognising any of the labels, I began to panic slightly as the steward stopped polishing an already sparkling glass and came towards me. What was it Nick had told me in one of his letters? 'You can get a Cuba Libra in Spain for what it would cost you for a cup of tea in England'. Yes, that was it, a Cuba Libra, that sounded pretty harmless, that's what I would try.

Speaking in very good English the barman smiled and said, '*Si señor*, what is it I can get for you?'

'I'll have a Cuba Libra please,' I said, sounding far more confident than I felt, aware that I had no idea what a Cubra Libra might be, but surmising that if for some reason I didn't like it, I could always order something else.

'Would you like ice with that *señor*?' the steward asked as he took down a tall straight glass from one of the shelves.

What, being asked if I would like ice in a drink in the middle of the night, sat on a bar stool on a train somewhere in Spain, I couldn't believe it, particularly as I had never had ice in anything in my life, surely this was a taste of life in the fast lane?

'Yes please,' I answered, hoping that I was giving the impression that this was something I did all the time.

Watching what the man did, I looked on in anticipation of what was to come as he took down a bottle of clear watery looking liquid from the shelves, the label declaring it to be something called Ron Bacardi. Removing the lid from an ornate ice bucket on the bar, he scooped out several cubes before tossing them into the glass.

Removing the screw top from the bottle, he poured a generous amount of the clear liquid over the ice before placing the glass in front of me. As I naively reached forwards to pick up the glass, the barman deftly flicked off the cap from a bottle of Coca-Cola and splashed half of the contents into my glass, placing the half empty bottle by its side.

Aware that I had just let my ignorance of what constituted a Cuba Libra show, I reached into my trouser pocket for some money as the barman busied himself below the bar in front of me. Completely ignoring me, he continued with what he was doing before finally straightening up and placing a small dish consisting of small pieces of meat and a few olives covered in with what looked like some sort of thick tomato sauce by the side of my drink, finally adding a small fork.

'*El cerdo señor,*' he said as he walked away.

Staring at the plate in front of me with one hand still poised in my trouser pocket, I began to wonder whether coming into the bar was such a good idea, what the hell was I supposed to do with this, I didn't think that I had ordered it or maybe I had. Maybe this strange little platter was all part of a Cuba Libra? I suddenly remembered reading somewhere that if you ordered Tequila in a bar in Mexico you were given half a lime and some salt, maybe this was something similar.

Not knowing if I should just drink what was in the glass and leave the rest, I began to think about the amount of Spanish money I actually had. On one hand, this being such a luxurious train, could this little snack thing just be a little freebie that you were given when you ordered a drink or was it going to cost me dear? I knew that some pubs in England placed bowls of peanuts or cheese on the bar for people to help themselves, but this was without doubt a great deal more upmarket than that.

Oh the hell with it I thought, just eat the bloody thing and worry about it afterwards, but first things first, try the drink, anything that contains Coca-Cola couldn't be that bad could it?

I picked up the half filled glass and raised it to my lips not knowing what to expect as I took my first tentative sip. The sweet taste of the Cola hit my expectant palate, quickly followed by the bitter taste of the Bacardi, the two tastes coming together to create a drink I knew instinctively might become habit forming. Reasoning that this unknown drink might have less embarrassing side effects if watered down, I tipped in the remainder of the Coca-Cola. With a further look at the small plate of food sitting on the bar in front of me I cautiously picked up the fork.

In saying that, the very first small mouthful of that food began a love affair with Spanish cuisine that was to stay with me all my life is not an understatement. The pungent taste of the garlic combined with the mixture of herbs, onions and creamy tomato sauce which covered the succulent meat, (something I later discovered to be pork), sent my tastebuds into orbit. (Eat your heart out British Rail).

Surely this was what life is meant to be all about, foreign travel, foreign food and the other man's point of view, maybe I was growing up. I'd never thought like this before and I had only been away from home for less than twenty-four hours.

As I finished both the delicious food and my drink I wondered what would happen if I ordered another. Would my next drink be accompanied by a totally different example of the wonderful food, or did what I had just had come as standard every time you ordered a Cuba Libra? No wonder Nick had said it was cheap to live in Spain, it seemed that all you had to do was to go out and have a couple of drinks and the food part of the budget was automatically taken care of.

Deciding that solely for the benefit of mankind generally it was necessary in terms of research to establish if that was indeed the case, I decided that I would order another and sit at one of the comfortable seats by the window, but that in itself would present me with another little conundrum. As the man behind the bar had not asked for any money, would he grab me by the collar and demand payment for the first drink, or would he present me with a bill as I left? It wasn't easy this continental way of life, what would Humphrey Bogart do? Yes of course, Mr B. would simply get up and gesticulate that he was going to sit in the window and that he needed another drink; and what was good enough for Mr. B was good enough for me.

As I slid off my stool the barman looked up, and pointing first at my empty glass and then at a seat in the widow, I breathed a small sigh as the man nodded in acknowledgement. Feeling extremely pleased at having sorted out what, to my mind, could have been an embarrassing moment; I slid into one of the comfortable leather seats and stared out at the empty platform, almost immediately there was a shrill blast from somewhere up ahead and the slamming of carriage doors as the train prepared to leave the station. With my head resting against the back of the seat I watched as the train slowly pulled away from the station platform. I glanced at my watch, bang on time, if things carried on like this I would be in Seville in less than six hours.

The arrival of the steward with my drink plus more food interrupted my thoughts, only this time it was slightly more bizarre. In addition to the delicious meat dish I had previously been given, I was surprised to see another small plate on which sat a banana complete with its skin. I was not disappointed to see that the steward had obviously sized me up and had my dietary interests at heart and had included fruit into my menu, but it was the accompanying knife and fork that prompted a small frown to wrinkle my brow.

Thanking him, I poured the remainder of the new bottle of Coca-Cola into my glass. Clearly the answer to my question of did one receive food with each new drink had been answered, but I still had absolutely no idea what this was going to cost me, and more importantly, how the hell did you tackle a banana with a knife and fork?

With drink in hand I stared at this wretched piece of yellow fruit and tried to decide what I should do. Was one supposed to peel it with one's fingers before putting it back down on the plate and use the knife and fork with which to eat it, or alternatively were you meant to just use the knife and fork to peel the bloody thing?

With a half smile on his face that seemed to indicate that this may have been a potential problem he had encountered many times before, the steward leaned discreetly across the table, picking up the banana with one hand and the small fruit knife with the other.

'*Perdoneme señor,*' he said as he expertly slit the top off the banana revealing the fruit inside, and with a swift incision down each side of the outer skin, he popped the banana from the opened skin before dropping it deftly on to the plate. Not once had he touched the fruit itself with his fingers and he finished this doubtless well-rehearsed act by placing the knife and fork together with a napkin at the side of the plate.

While watching the skilful way in which he had dealt with the banana, I was subjected to the second-hand aroma of garlic on the waiter's breath, an experience to which I was becoming gradually accustomed.

As I replaced my knife and fork after having eaten both the delicious meat dish and the banana desert, I leaned back in my seat suddenly feeling decidedly tired, and thinking that if I was to be bright-eyed and bushy-tailed for the remainder of my journey, it was time to head back to my seat and get some rest. Decision made, I picked up my drink and drained the glass with a couple of quick swallows, easing myself out from behind the table before heading up to the bar to settle my bill.

'*Señor?*' The steward smiled at my approach as I pulled out some peseta notes from my pocket.

'How much do I owe you *señor?*' I asked nervously, hoping and praying that I would be able to pay without putting too much of a dent in my budget, offering up a handful of notes of various denominations for the man to help himself.

Taking just one of the notes from my hand he walked to a small till at the other end of the bar, counting out what seemed an inordinate amount of money as my change. Returning to where I stood, he placed a small saucer containing my change in front of me on the bar which had in it a smaller denomination note and numerous coins.

Glancing down in disbelief, I quickly calculated that the cost of everything I had eaten and drunk had cost me less than seven shillings (35p). Thinking that he had made a mistake and given me too much, I looked at my change and then at the man's face. With a smile and a slight shrug he looked at me as I scooped up the change, smiling even more broadly as I left several of the coins in the saucer as a tip. I had no idea how much I had left him but I knew that it couldn't be very much, but it was as if I had been overly generous as his face literally lit up.

'*Gracias señor. Via con Dios.*'

The first thing I noticed as I pushed open the door to my compartment was the beautiful Spanish lady curled up in her seat, her jet black hair cascading down on to a blanket which was pulled up beneath her chin, the blanket rhythmically rising and falling as she breathed, her face made even more beautiful by the innocence of sleep. Her male companion glanced up as the door closed behind me, the look on his face telling me that future conversation or contact of any kind was not going to happen. Showing him that I was not fazed by his intimidating glare I smiled tauntingly as I passed, my show of bravado fuelled by the drinks I had just consumed.

Slipping into my seat, I breathed a huge sigh of contentment as I snuggled up against the sweet smelling leather and thought about the journey. I had now completed more than three quarters of my journey and, on reaching Madrid, my next and final stop would be Seville where hopefully Pam and Nick would be waiting. As I thought about finally meeting up with them again, I felt my eyes beginning to close as a contented dreamless sleep finally caught up with me.

A gentle shaking of my shoulder by a uniformed steward awakened me with a start as he spoke quietly in my ear.

'I am sorry to disturb you señor, but we will be arriving in Madrid in twenty minutes.'

Yawning and rubbing my eyes, I struggled to get back to reality, stretching and rolling my head from side to side in an attempt to rid myself of the stiffness in my neck.

Through half opened eyes I watched the steward continue down the length of the compartment, watching him stopping briefly beside the seats occupied by my current love interest and her companion. I looked on as the man slowly woke, the steward turning his attentions to a seat further forwards in which the sleeping figure of the large man with the cigar cutter I had noticed earlier lay in a crumpled heap.

Lying back in my seat, I became aware of the sour taste in my mouth from the food I had consumed earlier, wishing now that I had had both the discipline and the good sense to clean my teeth before dropping off to sleep.

As the other passengers began to ready themselves for their imminent departure from the train, I stood up and pulled down my case from the rack above, opening it to look for my toilet bag, determined to freshen up and clean my teeth while I still had the opportunity. Finally digging out the bag from the bottom of the case, I made my way down the compartment towards a door I had noticed earlier on which a polished copper sign indicated that this was the door for the 'Señors' rest room.

Locking the door behind me it was obvious that none of the refinements had been overlooked in this more down to earth and less glamorous part of the train. The toilet itself had the appearance of having been meticulously cleaned only moments before and, on a shelf above a small hand basin, several bottles of perfumed soap and other men's toiletries stood in a neat line behind a small brass rail obviously designed to stop them crashing to the ground should the train come to a sudden stop. The crowning glory of this display of understated opulence was another shelf on which were stacked a neat pile of pristine white hand towels.

Shaking my head in disbelief I thought back to the scruffy trains on which I had previously travelled in England, trains which displayed notices ordering passengers to refrain from using the toilet while the train was standing in the station. Sadly, It also occurred to me that had we have been in England, this quiet oasis would have been sullied and depleted of its luxuries within moments of it leaving the station.

After sampling the soaps and other toiletries on offer and as a result smelling much sweeter than I had done since leaving home, I cleaned my teeth and stepped back outside, practically colliding with the ticket inspector who asked for my ticket. Dropping my toilet bag down on to an empty seat I produced the relevant ticket from my jacket pocket and watched as the man scrutinised the piece of card before punching a small neat hole in one half of the ticket, leaving the other half intact for my homeward journey.

It must have been fairly obvious to any of the other passengers in my compartment that although I was indeed sharing this luxurious means of travel on this wonderful train with them, and theoretically I could order the same food from the same menu, this was where the similarity ended as there was not the remotest similarity in our respective mode of dress or with the luggage we owned.

I watched intrigued as my other travelling companions finalised their preparations for their departure as exquisite leather hand luggage were opened and smaller matching bags containing items for personal grooming were removed in readiness for visits to respective rest rooms. What did people like these do to earn a living I wondered? One thing I was certain of however was that none of them probably worked as hard as either my mother or my father, and as I looked at their obvious displays of opulence, life suddenly seemed a trifle unfair.

Barely conscious of the slowing down of the train I continued my surreptitious observations. The corpulent owner of the elaborate cigar cutter stood up from his seat and picked up his jacket which he had draped across the seat opposite and delved into an inside pocket, pulling out a bulging leather wallet which was stuffed to bursting point with what looked like large denomination peseta notes. The wallet appeared to contain so much money that it was kept closed by an incongruous looking thick rubber band which looked totally out of keeping with the man's wealthy demeanour. Flicking back the rubber band on to his wrist, he furtively checked the contents, quickly glancing about him to see if anyone was watching.

What would the esteemed Mr Bogart have made of all this? Was the man opposite an arms dealer who had just concluded his latest transaction, selling guns to be used against the young French soldiers I had so recently seen, or was he perhaps a secret white slave trader on his way to Casablanca to stock up his harem?

I was brought back to reality as the door at the end of the compartment opened and the incredibly beautiful Spanish woman who I had so recently fallen madly in love with glided back to her seat.

This was clearly a woman who knew precisely the effect she had on members of the opposite sex and she used that power without having to think about it as she again reduced me to a quivering wreck with the most wonderful flashing smile. Here was I, together with other passengers on the train looking as if we had slept all night in some hay loft, while this goddess from another planet appeared to have just stepped out of the pages of a glossy Hollywood fashion magazine.

Whatever the man she was with possessed, be it rank, title, wealth or an unbelievably wonderful personality (which I seriously doubted) he would certainly need to make sure that he lost none of it if he was to keep this goddess by his side, for this was, without doubt, an extremely high maintenance and desirable woman. Clearly her consort was very aware of the admiration displayed by other men, the glare he had given me earlier leaving me in no doubt on that score, and I was also sure that I was not the only person to have become the object of his displeasure as a result of her natural friendliness.

Finally, without a trace of a jolt or a shudder the train drew slowly to a halt and I jumped to my feet for my first view of this microscopic segment of the Spanish capital. From where I stood, it was just the usual trappings that all stations seemed to have on offer that were visible. I don't know what else I was expecting, but once again it was just another railway station, albeit much larger than the majority of the others I had seen, but nevertheless, still just a station.

'Hi Buddy, What Have You Done to Your Head?'

The excitement of jumping on and off trains in foreign towns and cities was beginning to wane and the only thought in my mind now was to get to Seville as quickly as possible, and sadly, as I bade a fond farewell to the luxury of the Talgo Express, I knew that apart from my return journey on this wonderful train, it would once again be back to a far more basic mode of transport.

With nearly three quarters of an hour to kill, I felt the need to stretch my legs, and with case in hand I walked briskly towards the big arrivals and departures board which informed me of which platform I now needed, this also telling me the relevant time of my train to Seville. Memorising the number of the platform and the time of the train, I looked around in the hope of finding a news-stand of some description that might have magazines or newspapers printed in English.

Finding nothing printed in English, (I would even have been happy with a copy of *Tropical Fish for Beginners* had one been available), I suddenly caught sight of a garish and colourful magazine devoted to bullfighting. The front cover featured an exquisitely dressed matador plunging a sword into the neck of a huge prancing black bull, whose front feet were actually clear of the ground as it attempted to sink its huge horns into the man's body. I knew that bullfighting and the ritual killing of bulls watched by hundreds of spectators in an arena was considered to be the number one attraction in Spain; and whether it was considered to be a sport or an art I didn't much care, it was something with words and pictures that I could look at.

As I thumbed through the pages I became more and more fascinated by those images. Men with utter disdain etched on their faces gallantly tested their courage to the limit as they stood in the path of huge animals. Armed only with what appeared to be a small piece of blood-red cloth, the animals thundered by with their massive horns passing only inches away from the bodies of death defying individuals whose purpose in life seemed to be to show the spectators how brave they were.

The sound of the kiosk owner's voice startled me as I became increasingly fascinated by the images and gory photographs in the magazine. Assuming that the elderly lady behind the counter was informing me of the price, I held out a small handful of coins inviting the woman to help herself.

With a brusque '*Gracias señor*', she took two of the small brassy coins from my hand before dropping them into an open wooden tray by her side. Little did I realise that, by this simple act of buying this magazine, this chance purchase was to start a passion in me which would never be extinguished, one which would take me by the hand and lead me into a world where that great writer Ernest Hemingway had also stepped, whereto Kenneth Tynan had also witnessed both the death and the glory.

Clutching the magazine in my free hand, I made my way towards a man selling small cups of thick black coffee which noisily oozed from a machine, this weird contraption sounding as if it was about to explode at any moment, while the counter on which it stood vibrated violently to each belch and squeal the machine emitted.

Glancing at my watch I saw that it was just after six thirty, leaving me with plenty of time before I needed to board the train. Deciding to live dangerously and risk the wrath of the machine, I dropped my case down on to a nearby bench and turned to the coffee seller.

'Coffee *señor*, please?' I said, again digging into my pocket for my dwindling stash of small coins.

'*Si señor, con leche?*'

Not understanding what the man had said, I grimaced, telling him in English that I didn't understand.

The man shrugged in an offhand way and pointed at a jug that was doing its best to sashay along the rickety counter in time with the shuddering vibrations from the noisy machine. I peered into the jug and saw that it contained some thick yellowy white liquid which resembled cream rather than milk. I shook my head not wanting to risk trying something that appeared to have been loitering there for the past few days.

Taking one of the small cups in one hand and firmly grasping a lever which protruded from the front of the machine with the other, he held the cup beneath a blackened and battered metal spout which at one time appeared to have been chromium plated, jerking the lever viciously downwards, at the same time muttering something which sounded decidedly uncomplimentary under his breath.

Immediately the machine coughed and spluttered into life and began spouting steam and thin jets of boiling water in several directions at once.

I leaped back in dismay as the coffee machine leaped about an inch into the air before crashing back down on to its unsteady perch before it again began its chorus of wheezing and belching. Suddenly without warning there was a sound like that of a very large horse breaking wind, and from its spout a trickle of black viscous coffee oozed its way into the waiting cup.

Noticing my alarm at the antics of the bucking machine, the man shrugged apologetically before giving the offending appliance an almighty smack with his free hand; something I'm sure that wasn't advocated in any of the chapters in the accompanying manual entitled 'How To Look After Your Machine', assuming of course that it had come with such a booklet in the first place. The chastening whack appeared to have the desired effect as the roaring and belching settled down to a more placid and serene gurgling, obviously this manoeuvre having been one of the more technical tactics used many times to subdue his ancient apparatus.

In a noticeably happier frame of mind now that he had given the machine a well practised thrashing, he again placed the cup beneath the nozzle and pulled down on the lever… nothing, nada, not even a strained or wheezing cough. A puzzled frown creased the man's brow as he tried again, still nothing.

By this time I was beginning to feel that I had made a mistake in trusting both the man and his ancient contraption and was on the point of leaving, when, with a series of muttered oaths among which I'm sure I heard the words '*Diablo*', '*Bastardo*' and '*Madre de Dios*', the man gave the machine another huge smack... After several seconds of eerie and uncanny silence there was a maniacal scream of protest coming from somewhere within its bowels, this hideous scream being followed by a scalding burst of steam which hissed out from the machine to engulf the poor chap's hand.

With an agonised scream which harmonised almost perfectly with the noise made by the coffee machine, he dropped the cup which smashed into sticky fragments on the floor as he proceeded to leap around his tiny coffee emporium, at the same time waving his injured hand in the air in much the same way that a morris dancer might have done after having his fingers bludgeoned by one of his colleague's cudgels. It was like watching a scene from an old Keystone Cops movie as I desperately tried to stop myself from laughing out loud at the poor man's dilemma, and feeling rather guilty at being the cause of the man's discomfort, I picked up my case and slunk away unnoticed towards the waiting train.

After showing my ticket to a bored looking individual with a pock marked face leaning against one of the barriers, whose incessant yawning and scratching of his unshaven jaw made me feel even more tired and travel weary than I already was, I walked along the platform looking for an empty compartment.

At that time of the morning not many people appeared to be travelling to Seville, so with half of the train to choose from, I found an empty compartment and climbed aboard, throwing my case on to the luggage rack above. Lacking the elegance of the Talgo Express, the train was comfortable enough and I noticed that it had a corridor, and where there was a corridor it stood to reason that it also had a toilet.

Catching sight of my reflection in a mirror on the wall of the carriage when I tossed my case up on to the rack, I realised that although I had gone through what I thought was a thorough cleaning up process less than an hour ago, I wasn't prepared for how dishevelled I looked. I was in desperate need of a shave, and where the ship's doctor had tended the wound on my head, my hair was sticking up on end and the wad of bandage and sticking plaster had worked loose and was now covering nothing. Although I had washed, where the blood had run down my neck it had soaked both the collar of my shirt and also my jacket; as a result I looked like someone who had spent the night on the streets and had been mugged in the process.

Studying my head from all angles it was clear that I couldn't continue looking the way I did, so plucking up all the courage I could muster, I took hold of one corner of the sticking plaster and bandage and pulled. To my immense relief, what was left of the pad came away with nothing worse than the addition of a few hairs adhering to the plaster that had been tugged out by the roots from around the wound. Gingerly touching the uncovered cut, I glanced at my fingertips and saw that the wound remained dry and that it no longer bled.

Taking down my case, I flipped open the catches and took out my toilet bag, throwing the case back up on to the rack before heading out into the corridor to look for the toilet where hopefully I could shave and tidy myself up. Ten minutes later I had managed a painful shave in cold water and got my hair into a more respectable state, and finally looking in the mirror I felt reasonably happy with what I had done. Back in my compartment I took out a clean shirt and packed both the bloody shirt and my jacket in the bottom of my case together with my toilet bag before flopping down on to the seat to flick through the pages of my newly acquired magazine.

Despite the earliness of the hour and having already lowered the window as far as it would go, I could already feel the stuffy dry heat permeating into the compartment from outside and it wasn't long before I tired of the magazine, tossing it to one side to stand with my head and shoulders out of the window, staring listlessly up and down the platform. Finally, from a carriage window near to the rear of the train, the head and shoulders of a uniformed guard appeared and with much waving of his arms and vigorous blasts from his standard, Spanish railways, regulation issue, for the use of guards whistle, his over the top dramatic and theatrical hand signals to the driver resulted in the train slowly lurching into motion.

Once out of the station, I began to catch fleeting glimpses of the city where impressive ancient church towers and elegant stylish homes basked in the early morning sun, the white walled houses nestling beneath rounded pink and orange roof tiles. Everywhere I looked, beautiful black wrought iron balconies were made even more stunning by drifts of scarlet and purple bougainvillea cascading down snow white walls, bleached even more dazzlingly white by the sun.

As the splendour of the urban spectacle began to recede, more solitary houses began to take their place as the broader panorama of the countryside began to unfold. Rambling isolated farmhouses and smaller, more humble looking dwellings began to replace the sophisticated town houses, each one looking more romantic and intriguing than the last as I became swept up with a landscape, the like of which I could never have imagined.

With my imagination racing into overdrive I stared out at the dusty arid landscape, visions of Don Quixote and Sancho Panza riding out to tilt at windmills appearing vividly in my mind's eye. El Cid must have also witnessed sights not dissimilar to these as he fought to drive the Moors from Spain, until at last the fall of Granada in 1492 finally ended the Muslim rule which had lasted from the eighth century.

Even from the modernity of the train, I could still sense an overwhelming feeling of the history and the drama that had taken place across this parched landscape, a place where once the dried earth had been moistened by the blood of the fallen.

Derelict farmhouses slipped by as I imagined both Moors and Christians sheltering in turn from the blistering heat in the shadows offered by ancient and crumbling walls, home now to only lizards and scorpions, unchallenged residents in a land that had changed very little since the days of those epic battles, a dry and barren land on which very little grew except oranges and plump juicy olives, a land baking in the heat of the fierce Spanish sun.

Mile after mile flashed past the window as I sat transfixed by the surreal landscape outside, this baking dusty landscape like nothing I had ever seen before or could have possibly imagined. Occasionally a small oasis of green and sparkling white came into view where both men and women bent double as they tended the vines from which grew luscious grapes to produce the many varieties of fine wines for which Spain is famous, in particular the rich full bodied Rioja which seems to epitomise the very lifeblood of Spain itself.

As the train rattled on, larger fields came into view surrounded by low stone walls, and within the confines of these laboriously built, meandering stone enclosures, trees, heavily laden with oranges, thrived; the colour of the glistening fruit contrasting sharply to the lime green of their leaves, the whole wonderful landscape taking on the appearance of a huge panoramic oil painting, the clear blue cloudless sky framing this immense canvas which typified life in this vast open dry plain.

There appeared to be no rivers or lakes from which water might be drawn to irrigate these precious crops and I wondered how things managed to survive. I had noticed several dried up river beds and arroyos but nothing which suggested a constant source of water.

I thought back to Don Quixote and his windmills. Although I hadn't seen anything that vaguely resembled the windmills still being used in Norfolk, I had noticed some spindly looking structures with big fragile looking blades which hung precariously from wooden shafts which protruded from the towers themselves. Maybe these were the legendary windmills that Don Quixote and his fat friend had been tilting at, or maybe these simple structures were used for pumping up water from wells located deep within the stony and barren ground.

As I pondered the nuances of crop irrigation and meagre water supplies, the train clattered across a wide bridge beneath which ran a fast flowing river, a sign at the side of the bridge declaring that this was the Rio something or other, the rest of the sign having been made unreadable by some would-be John Wayne who had used the sign for target practice.

As I continued to watch the unfolding panorama outside, it became clear that the landscape was slowly beginning to change. In place of the dry arid fields, more and more trees began to appear, thrusting their way upwards between tumbling rocky outcrops which themselves were covered with green mosses and lichens.

Slowly the train's pace began to slow as we began to climb. Through the windows on both sides of the carriage I could see tall languorous pines, their tops moving gently as they swayed in the light breeze which whispered through the towering hills and mountains high above, their foliage glistening darkly in the early morning sun.

The sudden transformation from the dry arid plains of before to the green and verdant forest through which we were now travelling was made even more remarkable by the sight of a pair of broad winged eagles floating majestically high above the tree tops, swooping and gliding as they soared ever upwards in the thermals of warm air rising from the hot earth below.

Quickly lowering the window I watched enthralled at this aerial ballet being performed high above me as they wheeled and circled in some form of courtship routine, their shrill cries clearly audible even above the noise of the train, their huge wings scarcely beating as the warm currents of air carried them across the sky. In the blink of an eye they were gone, taking with them a sublime feeling of peace and tranquillity which had enveloped me as I had marvelled at their effortless unhurried flight, their regal and dramatic departure leaving me with a sense of sadness at the possibility of perhaps never again being lucky enough to see such a sight.

As it began its descent from the mountains, the train's speed began to increase and I reflected on how lucky I had been in not having to share my compartment with other travellers, but I knew that before I reached my ultimate destination there were three more major stops, Cuidad Real, Puertollano and then the magical sounding Córdoba. Surely I thought, it has to be too much to hope that my luck will hold and I can continue my journey free of the hindrance of others.

As the train began to slow down as we approached another river bridge, I saw that by its side a further battered and shot-riddled sign declared that this too was also a Rio. I began to wonder what people had against signs such as these. Did the people who did this sort of thing have grievances against the local water board and imagined them to be the face of Spanish authority, or were they modern day Don Quixotes who, instead of tilting at windmills with a lance, used a shotgun instead?

Minutes later, the train slowed to a walking pace, shuddering to a stop near a large station sign fixed to the wall of what looked like a workman's rest room. From every direction, a stream of coughing and spitting men in overalls and aprons came and went, probably coughing and spitting as a result of inhaling the thick smoke which billowed out from the inside of this shabby looking shack at each opening of the door, the sign on the wall declaring that I was witnessing the delights of Cuidad Real.

Outside the window I could see the usual plethora of sheds and warehouses and numerous other neglected looking structures indicating that this was the commercial end of the station, and even at this early hour, men wearing predominantly black berets and overalls could be seen pushing and pulling handcarts, laboriously transferring crates and boxes to another waiting train, this one being without passenger carriages and consisting only of open trucks and closed freight cars.

Pulling down the window, I idly watched the comings and goings of the people outside, my attention being drawn to a wizened little character who appeared to be hobbling on only one leg. Despite his obvious handicap he was struggling manfully with a small flat-topped handcart on which appeared to be an appliance for the production of tea or coffee, an outdated machine which appeared to be remarkably similar to the lethal contraption I had seen earlier in Madrid.

Stepping down from the carriage in order to stretch my legs, I watched the shabbily dressed little man half dragging and half pushing his small cart towards where I stood, using the handles of the cart as crutches as he dragged himself along. Unable to draw my eyes away from his faltering and painful gait, I sensed that I was the intended target of all of his efforts as he drew near to where I was standing.

'*Café señor?*' the old man croaked. '*La torta*?'

The word for coffee needed very little translation, but whatever a *torta* might be I had no idea, but the sight of this broken little man struggling to earn a few measly pesetas despite his severe handicap sent waves of pity sweeping over me. Whatever it was that this desperate little man might be selling, I knew that I had to buy some, even if it meant having to hide it and throw it away when he wasn't looking.

Praying that I wasn't about to purchase anything that resembled something that had recently been run over on the road and tasting very much the same, I held out a few coins for the man to help himself. Gratefully he selected a few of the coins, and with a smile that exposed rotten and blackened teeth he proceeded to coax his machine into producing something that looked and smelled remarkably like coffee.

Fearful that I might be about to witness a repeat performance of that in Madrid, I stepped back out of the line of fire but was surprised by the smooth and quiet running of his antiquated appliance. Instead of belching steam and roaring its defiance, it produced a small cup of wonderfully smelling thick black coffee. Putting the cup down on the cart in front of me, he bent down and produced a small paper napkin on to which he carefully placed a piece of sticky looking pastry, something that resembled a cross between a yellowy coloured, triangular sugar-coated cake and a custard cream slice.

Balancing my coffee and my gooey delicacy of unknown taste and flavour, I was about to climb back on to the train to sample this unknown culinary delight when the old man touched my arm, pointing to a nearby bench, indicating that he wished me to leave the empty cup there for collection when he returned to this part of the train. I nodded as the man smiled and thanked me.

'*Gracias señor, muchas gracias,*' he said before continuing his painful journey along the rest of the train.

To say that his was the best tasting cup of coffee I have ever had would not be an exaggeration, and even without the benefit of some form of sweetener or cream it was absolutely delicious.

As I stared at the small cake-like object lying on the napkin, I decided to be brave, and after a couple of tentative sniffs I plucked up courage and took a small bite. It was like a small taste explosion in my mouth as the sweet, sugary pastry literally dissolved on my tongue; I felt that I had died and gone to heaven. Whoever was responsible for the man's catering achievements was a genius, but in view of the man's tatty and ragged appearance I felt that it wouldn't be wise to dwell on what the process entailed or what the state of his kitchen might be like, but instead I decided to opt for seconds. Gulping down the remainder of the coffee and popping the rest of the cake into my mouth, I leaped down from the train to pursue the little man as he dragged his broken body along the platform.

Hearing my approach, the man stopped and turned, looking puzzled as I handed back the empty cup before signalling for a repeat performance of both coffee and cake, this simple gesture being rewarded by another glimpse of the man's horrendous teeth as he grinned from ear to ear. Repeating the process with the coffee machine, he again carefully placed one of the pastries on to a fresh napkin before thanking me several times, his smiling gestures seeming to indicate that we had just cemented a relationship that would undoubtedly last for as long as we both should live.

After a more leisurely and appreciative repast, I climbed down from the carriage to leave my cup on the bench nearby as he had requested, looking back along the platform to where he still endeavoured to sell his wares to other passengers. As I watched I was filled with pity at his plight as nobody appeared to want to try the delicacies he had on offer, this probably due in no small part to his ragged and pitiful appearance. Before getting back on board, I tipped the few remaining brass and copper coins I had left in my pocket into the empty cup, hoping that he wouldn't think that I was being patronising and that he would accept this gesture as a small token of my gratitude for the quality of both his coffee and his food.

Satisfied and ready to face the rest of the journey, I sat back in my seat pleased that once again I had been spared the company of others, knowing that should I want to, I could put my feet up and have a little nap. I thought back to the old coffee seller and wondered how he had come to lose his leg. Was it a result of the civil war or was there a much simpler explanation? He was the first person I had ever encountered who was disabled in such a way and, as hard as I tried, I found it difficult to erase the picture of the tragic little figure from my mind.

I knew of people who had lost practically everything as a result of the war, families living in the East End of London where life had been difficult enough before due to unemployment and ill health, but I had never thought that I would witness such poverty and distress as that which I had just seen. I knew a little about the Spanish Civil War and had seen pictures of the destruction that had been caused. I also knew that General Franco still ruled as he had previously done while we had been at war with his German allies, but I had never expected to witness first-hand such a tragic sight. Half-heartedly, I flicked through the pages of my magazine as the train rumbled on through the countryside, not really aware of what I was looking at as I wondered if what I had seen was typical of what I might expect to see when we reached Seville.

Aware that the train was beginning to slow down, I dropped the magazine on the seat beside me and looked out through the window, seeing various buildings and houses coming into view as we slowly drew into Puertollano station. Not bothering to get to my feet to see if other passengers might be waiting on the platform, I took out my map and itinerary to check how much further we had to go, checking my watch to see if we were still running on time.

On hearing the carriage door being opened, I looked up and watched as three other people clambered aboard. One was an incredibly handsome young man with jet black wavy hair and brooding dark eyes, someone who I estimated to be in his early twenties. Immaculately dressed in a pale grey, lightweight suit made even more stylish by a dazzling white shirt and pencil-thin black tie, he was a picture of health and vitality, his polished soft black leather loafer type shoes giving the appearance of someone whose image was carefully cultivated and of singular importance in promoting an image of himself in whatever it was he did in life.

By contrast, the two other passengers were an elderly couple who, on sitting down, immediately became preoccupied with the contents of two bulging paper bags which they placed on the seat between them, the bags obviously containing food for their journey, but it was the young man who held my fascinated attention.

In a clumsy attempt at discretion, I adopted one of the ploys I had seen my old buddy Humphrey Bogart use on numerous occasions, turning my head as if looking out of the window, but instead studying him in the reflection from the glass. As I watched, it became obvious that all three were equally curious about me as they too cast inquisitive glances in my own direction, in particular the young man whose eyes constantly flicked between the magazine I had left on the seat and back again to me.

Suddenly the young man addressed me in Spanish and pointed to the magazine. I looked away from the window to acknowledge his smile, shrugging my shoulders to indicate that I hadn't understood what he had said. Picking up the magazine, he came and sat next to me, pointing to the picture on its cover.

'*El Corrida*,' he said. '*El Maestranza de Sevilla.*'

Speaking with a soft Andalucian lisp which was later to become so familiar to me, his breath was heavy with the smell of garlic as he leaned towards me.

'This is the *Maestranza,*' he repeated in English. 'It is the most beautiful Plaza de Toros where I am soon to fight.'

I sat back in disbelief, wondering if I had heard him correctly.

'You're a matador?' I gasped, hardly able to believe what he had just said.

He shrugged. 'I am still a *Matador de Novillos*,' he said, 'but I am to take the *alternativa* in the plaza in Sevilla, then I will become a Matador de Toros.'

Noticing my puzzled frown, he began to explain.

'You are not familiar with the *Corrida*?' he asked. 'I saw the magazine and thought that you must be an aficionado?'

I shrugged before replying.

'No. I bought the magazine in Madrid just for something to read.'

'I am sorry,' he said. 'When I noticed the magazine I thought you knew of our fiesta *brava.*'

Intrigued by the young man and his deadly art, I shook my head.

'Please don't apologise,' I said. 'I know that people fight bulls in an arena here but I don't know anything other than that.'

He offered me a slightly patronising smile that seemed to say, 'Well you are a foreigner, why would you know anything about things that go on here in Spain?'

His next comment caused a substantial rise in my blood pressure and I left him in no doubt as to the extent of my feelings.

'You must be German?' he said.

'No, I certainly am not German,' I snapped back at him, 'I'm English.'

'I'm very sorry,' he replied. 'Please excuse me but I have never met any English people before.'

It crossed my mind that he had probably never met a German before either, but I grudgingly accepted his apology and grasped his extended hand as he continued.

'As I said, I am already a *novillero torero* and have killed many bulls, but if I wish to become a great matador and fight in all of the big plazas all over the world, I must take the *alternativa.*'

A puzzled frown wrinkled his handsome face as he struggled to find a word to illustrate more fully the meaning of the word *alternativa*.

I ventured a word that I thought might be appropriate.

'Do you mean that you have to graduate to get to a higher level?'

Excitedly he seized on my suggestion.

'*Si*, graduate, that is what I must do. I must work very hard to graduate to become a Matador de Toros and once I have done this, I too may become one of the truly great matadors like Belmonte, Arruza, Ortega and Parrita, or perhaps even become as good as Manolete, the greatest of them all.'

He reeled off the names with the reverence of someone reading from a Bible.

'After I have taken the *alternativa* in the *Maestranza* in Seville, I will then be given the honour of fighting in the monumental, the wonderful Plaza de Toros in Madrid where my *alternativa* will be confirmed, and only when I have done this will I be able to call myself a Matador de Toros.'

Clearly excited and passionate about his dangerous career path, his dark eyes flashed as he talked about his upbringing.

'I come from Toledo and have seen many wonderful fiestas there, and if you had been a follower of the *corrida de toros*, you will have known of that great day when Parrita, Manolete and Carlos Arruza performed in the plaza near where I was born.'

He sighed as if remembering the occasion.

'When did this happen?' I asked. 'Did you see it?'

He shook his head.

'No, I was only a small boy, but I have been told many times that it was the greatest corrida ever seen and that there will never be another like it. People still talk of it as if it were yesterday.'

I watched the faraway look in his eyes as he clearly visualised himself in the role of the greatest matador of them all, fighting and killing bulls to rapturous applause, happily receiving favours from some of the most beautiful women in the world.

'When you take this *alternativa*, what exactly happens?' I asked. 'Are you given a certificate or something that tells people what you have done?'

He looked puzzled and struggled with the pronunciation of the word

'A cerfiticate? What is a cerfiticate?'

'A certificate,' I said, correcting his attempt at the word. 'It's a piece of paper or a diploma that proves that you have accomplished certain things.'

The young man threw back his head and roared with laughter, causing the couple opposite to pause momentarily in their search through the bulging paper bags for something to eat and to stare over in our direction.

'No,' he laughed, 'it is a ceremony that goes back to the early days of bullfighting when Francisco Romero and his brothers and sons became the first *chulos*, or *matadors*, to fight on foot. This is a ceremony that first began in Ronda before seventeen hundred and it is the root of all of the ancient traditions of the corrida.'

'Firstly, there will be posters which will tell people that I am to take the alternativa in the Plaza de Toros in Sevilla, and on that day I will drive to the Plaza with my *cuadrilla*. My cousin, who is my dresser, will help me into my *traje de luces* and when that is done I will go to the chapel. When I have prayed and given thanks, we will then be ready to enter the ring in the magnificent parade. The trumpet will sound and the keys to the *toril* where the bulls are kept will be thrown down, after which I will receive my muleta and sword from the senior matador of the day, this act tells the people that I have been given the honour of fighting and killing the first bull.'

The young bullfighter chuckled. 'I think this is much better than just receiving a cerfiticate don't you?'

'To be given the first bull by the senior matador is the greatest honour possible and when I have killed this bull in an honourable manner, I will have become a Matador de Toros and will be allowed to wear the pigtail or the *coleta* as it is called. There are six bulls which will be fought in the afternoon and each matador will kill two bulls each. We will pray that the bulls will be brave and fight well.'

As the young man described the afternoon as being wonderful, it crossed my mind that it might not be too wonderful for the bulls, but it was the excited anticipation on the young man's face that told me that it would be more polite to say nothing.

The talk of bulls and bullfighting continued punctuated only by his animatedly turning the pages of my magazine to show me extraordinary pictures of men clothed in beautiful costumes performing heroic passes with blood red capes. Some of the more dramatic pictures showed what happened when things went drastically wrong, with men feeling the might and the aggression of the bull as they found themselves being knocked down and trampled before being impaled on the deadly horns.

As he turned the pages he explained what was happening in each photograph in turn, telling me the name of each pass being executed, sometimes standing to demonstrate how these passes were accomplished, his energetic gyrations and foot stamping causing the two other occupants of the compartment to momentarily forget their forays into the bags of goodies to concentrate on what the young man was saying. Clearly they had no understanding of the English language but the older man in the carriage was obviously an aficionado, as a quietly muttered '*olé*' followed some of the more complicated manoeuvres being demonstrated before him.

The slowing of the train pulling into the station in Córdoba caused my young companion to stop his demonstrations to peer out of the window.

'Córdoba,' he said wistfully. 'Do you remember that I mentioned the great Manolete? Well it was here in Córdoba that he was born and sadly where he also lost his life in a small town called Linares not very far from here. In most people's opinion he was the greatest matador of them all and when he was so tragically killed, the whole of Spain mourned his death for a whole week. The bells in the churches all over Spain were rung and people dressed in black, he was truly a great, great man.

'What happened?' I asked. 'Was he killed in the ring?'

The young man nodded sadly, obviously reliving the tragedy which had occurred.

'Yes, he had been engaged to fight with Luis Miguel Dominguín and Gitanillo de Triana where all the bulls to be fought would be the deadly Miura bulls. Manolete did not fear these bulls but he did not like them. The sorting of the bulls is done in the morning of the fight and it is a matter of luck which bull the matadors draw, also in which order they will be fought. That morning Manolete had the bad luck to draw a cowardly and vicious animal called Islero.'

He shrugged.

'Obviously at this time no-one could know that this brute would not fight honestly as all matadors want or that it hooked badly to the right, and for a bull to do that with Manolete's style of fighting meant that he could not have drawn a worse animal.

'Islero was Manolete's second bull and the fifth of the afternoon but he was horrified when he saw his *banderillero*, a man named Gabriel González place his second pair. González was lucky to escape with his life when he had to leap the barrier to save himself after the beast hooked when the *garapullos* went in. When Manolete saw this he knew that this was a very bad bull and it was not going to be an easy afternoon. His first bull had also been cowardly but this one looked even worse.'

'Why wasn't the fight stopped if these bulls were so bad?' I asked. 'Surely they had another bull which could have been sent in as a substitute?'

'This does not happen,' he retorted. 'When a bull enters the ring it must be fought and killed. If you draw a bad animal that is just your bad luck, you have to fight it.'

Taking up the story again he continued with a shrug of his shoulders.

'After talking with his *banderillero* he stepped from behind the barrier and headed for the centre of the ring where

Islero waited. Manolete called and goaded the beast and somehow managed to get the animal to charge, and despite this ugly brute not wishing to fight, he showed the crowd why he was the greatest matador in the whole world by giving the bull three brilliant right-hand passes, standing so still and so close to the horns that the crowd thought he must surely be killed.

'When Manolete used the sword it was always perfection. He would line up the bull with its two front feet together, turning slightly sideways with the muleta held in the left hand and the sword poised just below his chin. He would look along the blade to where he would plunge the sword and throw himself forwards over the horns to bury the sword up to its hilt; this is called a *volapie,* the most dangerous way to kill. This is called the "moment of truth", but when Manolete did this it was called "*la suerte suprema*", in English I think you would call it "the supreme destiny".'

'Is this when he was killed?' I asked.

The young man nodded. 'He was not killed immediately, but he died later.

'When Manolete used the sword it was beautiful, always as if in slow motion. As the sword entered, Islero hooked, just as González said it would. The horn buried itself deep in Manolete's right thigh, picking him up and spinning him around. At first it did not look serious, just a bad tossing, but the *cornada* was enormous with the horn severing this big artery in the leg here,' he pointed to the inside of his thigh.

'Manolete's *cuadrilla* rushed out and carried him out of the ring to the infirmary, but the blood was pumping from the *cornada* like water gushing from a tap and they could not stop it. He was given two blood transfusions in the infirmary before they decided to take him to the hospital of San José in Linares where the doctors and the surgeons worked on his wound. He was given much more blood but it was no use and he grew weaker. All of the doctors and the surgeons who were there and had worked on him knew that it was the end but they continued to try everything they could but it was all in vain and the great man finally gave in and died.'

'That's so sad,' I said, watching my companion's face as he imagined the whole hopeless scenario.

He looked out of the window not seeing anything, a glazed look clouding his eyes.

'He is at peace now here in Córdoba,' he said softly, crossing himself and kissing his fingers.

'You talk of this as being sad my friend, but I will tell you what is truly sad.

'Manolete did not want this *corrida*, he wanted to retire but was persuaded to take this one last fight because the critics said that the young Dominguín who was to appear with him, was as good even at his young age as Manolete was in his prime.

'I do not think that the great man took this fight to prove that he was better than Dominguín, I think he took the fight because he was under so much pressure from the promoters and he was just too tired to argue any more. We have a word here in Spain which is "*superstición*". Many people still say that Manolete's *cuadrilla* and his friends should have taken notice of the signs that day and not allowed him to fight.'

I nodded. 'We have the same word. It's when someone has an irrational fear of ordinary things, or of things he feels he should avoid. In England the number seven is thought by many people to be a lucky number, personally I don't believe in things like that, I don't see how any number can be either lucky or unlucky.'

The young bullfighter gripped my arm.

'What you have just said about a certain number is extraordinary,' he exclaimed. 'When you have heard what I have to say you may wish to change your mind.

'When I spoke of Manolete's friends and *cuadrilla* taking notice of the signs that day and should have tried to persuade him not to fight, you too should think again when you say that to believe in numbers being either lucky or unlucky is stupid.

'When Manolete first agreed to "*los toros*", it was to be his twenty-first corrida in a row. The contract for those fights was signed on August the twenty first, and the number twenty one was the number of Manolete's hotel room. Also, the brand number which Islero carried was twenty one, and the number plate on the car used by the *cuadrilla* on that day began with the number twenty one.

'Well, what do you think now? Do you believe that all of these numbers were just a terrible coincidence, or do you think that the devil played a part in his death?'

For several seconds I was stunned and couldn't think of anything to say.

'That is unbelievable,' I said. 'I've never heard of anything so bizarre in my life. Perhaps you are right and there are things that we don't understand after all.'

He again made the sign of the cross before continuing.

'Believe me my friend. On the life of my mother, I would not lie about something so serious as this.'

For some time we sat there quietly wrapped up with our thoughts until suddenly the guard's whistle brought us back to the present, but it was several minutes more before the young man spoke again, his eyes clearly showing the grief he again felt at the recounting of what had occurred so many years earlier.

Clearly not understanding what had been said but having noticed the young bullfighter making the sign of the cross, the couple opposite discreetly averted their gaze, continuing to quietly enjoy the contents of their paper bags, both drinking copious amounts from a leather wine skin which they passed from one to the other.

Desperately trying to re-ignite the enthusiasm of moments before, I struggled to find something to say to alleviate the sombre mood which now hung like a heavy storm cloud above us.

'What was Señor Manolete's first name?' I asked innocently. 'I would like to find out more about him.'

It was if a light had been switched on somewhere in his head as his dark eyes flickered back to life, his amazingly handsome face breaking into a smile.

'Manolete was not his given name,' he said. 'I do not know how you would say this in English, but this was the name he chose for himself. His given name was Manuel

155

Rodríguez y Sánchez. His father and his grandfather were also *toreros* and were called Manolete so he was very proud to take this name also. I am known as El Huracán de Toledo, or sometimes Zorro because of my skill with the sword. These too are not my given names but names I fight under, my given name is Jaime Granero.'

He reached into the inside pocket of his jacket and produced a postcard-sized photograph which he handed to me.

'This was taken when I fought in Mexico,' he said.

I looked down at the picture and in big letters it proudly announced 'ESTES ES el ZORRO DE TOLEDO', and in the centre of the card was a picture of him standing in the middle of an arena holding a rabbit in one hand and some flowers in the other. I turned over the card and on the other side was another picture of him clutching yet another rabbit in one hand, but in the other he was holding what appeared to be a big box of groceries held together with string.

'Is this all you get paid for putting your life on the line?' I asked.

He laughed at the expression on my face at what I thought might be his wages.

'No,' he laughed. 'Sometimes when I have fought well, the crowd throw things into the ring for me, at this place they honoured me with the food and the flowers which I share with my *cuadrilla*.'

Taking the card from my hand, he took a pen from his pocket and with a flourish signed his name together with his best wishes, handing it back to me saying, 'Here, this is for you. When I become really famous, you will be able to show people this and tell them that you knew me before I took the *alternativa* in Sevilla.'

Gratefully, I put the card in my pocket and began to think what fate may possibly have in store for me. He most probably would become a great matador and fight all over the world, while my future did not look nearly so exciting with the prospect of National Service being all I could look forward to for the next two years.

With the train rattling through the dry hot countryside, we continued to talk of bullfighting and of bullfighters, my interest and curiosity increasing as he talked of great fights and of not so great fights where even some of the better matadors were found wanting when it came to standing their ground to receive the charge. He also criticised some for their inability to perform the '*estocada perfecta*' when the time came to despatch their opponent, relying instead on flamboyant and showy *adorno*.

Glancing at a slim gold wristwatch, made even more eye catching against his deeply tanned skin, Jaime stood up and reached for his big leather bag on the rack above.

'We will be arriving in Sevilla shortly; do you have someone there to meet you when we arrive?'

I nodded.

'Yes. I'm staying with relatives,' I answered. 'They should be waiting for me at the station.'

He shrugged. 'I was going to suggest that as I am to be met we would be happy to take you to where you want to go, but if you have made arrangements it is OK.'

The elderly couple opposite continued to munch on their bread, olives and various other goodies as they watched Jaime check his big leather holdall, the man taking a final drink of wine from the leather drinking vessel before having it snatched unceremoniously from his grasp by his wife who began hurriedly packing things away in preparation for their departure, the train beginning to slow down as if on cue.

Taking my case down from above, I placed it on the seat and lowered the window, excitedly peering down the length of the train towards the platforms which were slowly coming into view. Although in the distance I could see people waiting, we were still too far away for me to identify any individuals.

As we inched our way into the station I scrutinised the faces of people waiting there but all to no avail. An uneasy feeling began to bother me as I began to ponder the possibility of needing to avail myself of Jaime's offer. If Pam and Nick were not there, I knew their address but unfortunately had no telephone number.

As I pulled my head back inside, Jaime sensed my concern.

'Are your people not there?' he asked.

'I can't see them,' I answered. 'I told them when we would be arriving and they said they would be at the station waiting for me.'

'I shouldn't worry,' he replied patting me on the shoulder. 'They've probably been delayed in the city somewhere; I will of course wait with you until they arrive.'

He glanced at his watch.

'We are a few minutes early so there is still time. As I have said, my uncle and cousins will be here so if for some reason your own people do not arrive, it will give me much pleasure to take you to where they live. Do you have their address?'

I nodded, reaching into my pocket for the last letter they had sent, opening it to reveal the address at its head.

He glanced at the letter and nodded.

'This will not be a problem, my uncle has lived here all of his life and he will be happy to take you to wherever you wish to go. He will know of this address.'

Reassured by Jaime's promise, I nevertheless continued to scan the sea of faces waiting on the platform until finally the train ground to a halt. Picking up my case I swung open the door and dropped down on to the platform, stepping aside as Jaime did the same, moving my case as he dropped his big leather bag on to the ground.

As I straightened up and looked about me, I heard a voice heavily laced with an American accent from somewhere nearby quietly say, 'Hi buddy, what have you done to your head?'

Wheeling around, I was confronted by two casually dressed and extremely suntanned people, both wearing sunglasses and huge smiles on their faces. I would not be needing that lift after all.

Happily hugging my cousin and shaking Nick's hand I finally remembered my newfound friend who stood patiently just behind me, a relieved smile on his face at seeing our joyful reunion.

'Pam, Nick. I'd like to introduce you to El Zorro de Toledo.'

The surprised look on their faces was a revelation as they stared at this handsome young man by my side, Nick in particular as Jaime took Pam's hand and lightly kissed her fingers, my cousin quickly overcoming her surprise by thanking him for his courtesy, telling him how delighted she was to meet him.

As we talked, I explained how Jaime and I had met, proudly announcing that he was a bullfighter, telling them that he had noticed my magazine and that he had spent the time from Puertollano explaining the history and the intricacies of the corrida, also mentioning also that he had kindly offered me a lift should they not arrive. Nick apologised for not being there earlier, explaining that there had been some sort of incident involving a donkey cart and an American serviceman's car. The driver of the car had been unable to speak Spanish whereby both Pam and Nick had both acted as interpreters and peacemakers until the police had finally arrived.

Never having heard either Pam or Nick speaking any language other than English, I was hugely impressed as they conversed quite easily with Jaime until suddenly the conversation came to an abrupt end as we were surrounded by an elderly man together with three youngsters who whooped with joy as they embraced the young bullfighter, almost knocking him off his feet with their enthusiastic greeting. Finally deciding that he had had enough of the exuberant hugs and the backslapping, Jaime reached into his jacket and produced a similar card to the one he had given me earlier, and taking out a pen, scrawled something across its front.

Handing me the card he pointed to the elderly man. 'This is the address of my uncle and it is where I will be staying. Here is his telephone number and if you would like to speak to me please call, I would be happy to keep in touch with you and hear of how you are getting on in this lovely city.'

Taking the card from me, Nick stared at the picture on the front, turning it over to study the picture on its reverse.

'I am to fight in a small town called Castillo de las Guardas in two weeks' time,' Jaime continued. 'If you feel that you would like to see this as your first corrida, I would be honoured if you and your family would be my guests.'

As I thanked him and shook his hand, he threw his other arm around my shoulder as if we had been friends all our lives, and with a final firm handshake strode off down the platform with his admiring relatives, two of the younger ones fighting for the honour of carrying his huge leather case.

A City of Culture and of Hope

From the moment we left the Santa Justa station and walked out into the bright sunshine, I felt instinctively that this was to be my time, a period in my life during which I would change forever, that transitional period where I would reject youthful pleasures and become a man. No longer would embarrassing self-doubt, coupled with the inhibitions that post-war poverty placed upon people, become a reason for not reaching out for the things that my parents never had the opportunity to achieve.

Happily describing my journey and attempting to answer questions about my newfound friend, I was shepherded from the station out into the searing heat to be confronted by a huge American car parked at the side of the road, around which a small crowd of shabbily dressed children had gathered. I had seen American cars on cinema screens and a few on the base at Chicksands but the reality of seeing this monster with its white walled tyres and white steering wheel glittering in the bright sunlight made my jaw drop, this glistening leviathan appearing to have more chromium plate than you could possibly fit on five average size Vauxhalls.

After tossing my suitcase into the cavernous trunk, Nick slid behind the steering wheel while I opened the front passenger door to allow my cousin access, sliding in on to the back seat as several of the waiting children held out their hands in the hope of receiving a few small coins. I had never witnessed anyone begging before and I regretted having given all of my small change to the coffee and cake vendor at the station. I was surprised to hear Nick mutter something uncomplimentary under his breath as he started the car and quickly pulled away from the kerb in a cloud of dust.

'Why did you not give those kids any money?' I asked as we headed away from the station.

Pam turned in her seat as she answered.

'It's very difficult,' she said. ' Everywhere you go here you will find people begging and had we given those kids a few pesetas, in no time at all we would have been surrounded by dozens of others. It's like magic, one minute there might only be two or three but as soon as you put your hand in your purse you're surrounded.'

I related the story of the coffee seller in Madrid explaining that he only had one leg, saying that I felt that if people didn't help in some way he would probably starve.

'That's different,' Nick said. 'That old guy probably lost his leg and everything else he owned during the civil war, but it's different with kids like those. You see them all over the city and they're probably sent out by their parents as full-time professional beggars. They know where to go to get the best action; they'll hit on American servicemen in particular because they know that we're a soft touch.'

'Forgive my husband, he's all heart but unfortunately he's right, you have to be very careful who you give money to here.'

The journey across this beautiful city was like a journey back in time as I stared at the majestic old buildings and the fountains which were made even lovelier by the bright sunlight which sparkled and danced through the cascading water. Shaded flower-bedecked alleyways beckoned enticingly to passers by to come and rest and sit beneath colourful parasols which shielded small intimate café tables.

Dressed not that differently to people living over two hundred years ago, I was amazed by a sight that was more in keeping in the pages of history books as men urged painfully thin donkeys to pull wooden carts, on which were stacked enormous piles of bulging sacks and boxes. Some of these ancient carts literally groaned beneath the weight of piles of vegetables. Cabbages, potatoes, lettuces and other produce either hung in great bunches down the outside of the carts or were balanced precariously behind the drivers who continually flicked their long whips in an attempt to hasten these poor animals along the shiny cobbled streets.

As Pam and Nick continued to question me in respect of my journey, I became slightly more reticent with my answers as I became absorbed with the activity and the scenery outside. Not wanting to miss anything during the journey across the city, my head swivelled from one side to the other as I tried to absorb everything going on around us, not really listening or concentrating on the things they both asked.

Sensing my reluctance in answering their barrage of questions, Nick took on the role of unofficial tour guide, pointing out places of interest and slowing down at times to almost walking pace as we crawled along the historic thoroughfares.

'This is pretty much the centre of the old city where most of the places of interest are. I guess it's a lot like London where the heart of the city is on one side of the river with Westminster Abbey, the Houses of Parliament and Buckingham Palace, but on the other side of the river there's still a whole bunch of interesting things but they're more spread out. This part where we are now is on the eastern side of the Guadalquivir River, and just over there on the other bank is where we live in Triana.'

Triana... Jaime had mentioned Triana when he had talked of Manolete and I visualised a place where even if it was on the 'wrong' side of the river, it had to be the 'right' place to live. If Pam and Nick had chosen to live there then it had to be a bit special, and as I was soon to find out, my assumption proved to be correct.

'This is El Arenal,' he continued. 'This whole area dates back to the early fourteenth century, and that tower you can see over there, was built by one of the Moorish kings to help protect this part of the city from any sort of invasion by an army trying to creep up here in boats.'

'What was the king's name?' I asked, looking out of the open window to where he was pointing.

'Hell, I don't know, King Hasan something or other I guess. There were a few Hasans around then so I guess it could have been one of them. King Paco sure as hell doesn't ring too many bells so I reckon you can rule him out.'

I grinned at Nick's reply staring at this wonderful and historic building bathed in sunlight, its beauty causing an involuntary shaking of my head as I stared in disbelief.

'It looks as if it's made of gold,' I gasped.

'You're not far wrong,' Nick said. 'It's actually called the Torre del Orro which means the Tower of Gold. This whole district is where the Moors stored all of their munitions; it was also the main area for shipbuilding.'

He grinned and slapped Pam lovingly on the thigh.

'I'm reluctant to talk about soccer as I'm under strict orders from your cousin here not to get you going, but if you insert the letter "s" into the name Arenal, you come up with the name of a certain football club based in London.'

I saw him glance back at me in his rear-view mirror and laugh as Pam smacked him on the back of his hand, forcibly indicating that he was not to pursue the matter any further.

Disregarding the slap on his hand he continued with his analogy.

'Do you remember the arguments we used to get into about the merits of soccer as opposed to American football? Well, you once mentioned that your London Arsenal football club when they were founded were called Woolwich Arsenal because they were in an area of London where munitions were made so don't you think it's a hell of a coincidence that the two names are so similar in view of what they manufactured there?'

Again he received another reproachful slap as Pam continued with her threat.

'I warned you what would happen if you two carried on about football; and that goes for you as well Pete. I don't want to hear another word about football all the while you're here, otherwise we're back down the station and you can say *adiós* to any sort of prolonged stay.'

'Wow,' Nick laughed. 'I guess that's you and I told buddy.'

As we slowly passed an enormous oval-shaped building which appeared to have no windows but had numerous doorways and entrances, Nick pointed to where several lines of people queued to buy tickets from several portable wooden kiosks set up outside this huge arena.

'This is where your newfound friend is going to put his life on the line when he takes his *alternativa*; this is the Plaza de Toros de La Maestranza. Believe me buddy, that's one great bull ring. Guys have been fighting bulls and getting killed in there since it was built in the eighteenth century.'

Nick's casual off hand reference to people dying in pursuit of achieving greatness in the ring shook me as I gazed at this magnificent structure and the peeling posters that adorned its walls. The glossy photograph on the front cover of the magazine lying on the seat beside me didn't do justice to its golden stone façade which shimmered and gleamed in the early morning sun, its ancient buttery coloured walls offering little shade to those who offered lottery tickets for sale from the small kiosks.

As I watched, the weirdest feeling of déjà vu suddenly swept over me as I felt a desperate urge to get out of the car and pay homage to this historic amphitheatre. It was as if I had returned to where a previous dramatic episode had occurred in a past life, and staring at its walls I felt a shiver run through me. Maybe I had stood in the centre of that very ring and destiny had now brought me back once again to cleanse my subconscious mind and to put what may have happened in the past to rest.

I tried to shrug off this eerie sensation as Nick continued talking about the date of its construction and of the matadors who had been killed there; he also sang the praises of others who had emerged triumphant in their pursuit of bloody glory.

Suddenly, without warning, Nick brought the car to a skidding halt, swerving to avoid a would-be matador who had leaped in front of the car, using his tattered jacket as a cape to execute an elaborate but suicidal pass across its bonnet.

'Bloody lunatics,' Nick snarled, after shouting something which didn't exactly sound like 'have a nice day' in Spanish at the man who grinned and strolled away.

'These clowns all think that they're Belmonte or Arruza here. They know damn well that if they get knocked down by an American he'll probably hand them a couple of hundred pesetas rather than run the risk of being hauled in by the Guardia Civil and spending a few hours in the local jail. Some of those guys actually make a living by doing that, to them it's more money than they would ever earn if they worked on the roads or in the fields somewhere for a whole year.'

Pam nodded her agreement.

'Nick's right, you have to be so careful. Some of these people are so poor that it's surprising that they survive at all. The other day we were down town and this poor chap fell from the top of a tall building he was working on and all they did was drag his body into the shade and cover him with some dirty sacks until they had finished work for the day, they didn't even call for an ambulance. It's horrendous to see some of the conditions that these guys are forced to work under.'

'I thought that this was a land of plenty,' I ventured. 'I understood that when you Americans arrived here, Spain became a pretty prosperous country.'

Nick gave a contemptuous snort.

'Don't you believe it, buddy. It's certainly better now than it was, but the Spanish Civil War and that good old boy Franco cost this country plenty. You have to keep this whole ball game in perspective, Pete, we're not here having some sort of holiday in the sun, we're here because our government is using this country because of its strategic position in the world and fat Frank is sure making us pay for that. Do you understand what the civil war was all about?'

'I think so. Franco is a fascist isn't he and he overthrew the elected government and tried to crush everyone who opposed him?'

Giving a short laugh, Nick nodded as he stared at me in the rear-view mirror.

'There was a bit more to it than that but I guess that sums it up pretty well. Bearing in mind who the common enemy is these days and remembering Franco's political persuasions, we are here, as our own politicians so elegantly put it, to preserve world peace.

'We needed a couple of bases here in Spain to do that and when we go on base you'll see a little of what it's all about. It's not really top secret spy stuff or any of that crap, but it's better if you keep some of the things you might hear or see to yourself.'

Thoroughly intrigued, the sights outside were momentarily forgotten.

'What sort of things?' I asked eagerly.

'Well amongst other things, we're here to eavesdrop on what's going on in the world, you know the sort of stuff, who's talking to who and why. All of the air force guys you see in uniform who work on base and those wandering around the city here belong to SAC, or Strategic Air Command to give it its proper title, although having said that, you won't see too many guys walking around in uniform off base, it's not the smartest thing in the world to do.'

'What do you mean?' I asked. 'Why, what's the problem with wearing your uniform away from the base?'

'Let's just put it this way,' he answered. 'There are some people in this town who are still true to the nationalist cause and remember what happened between nineteen thirty six and nineteen thirty nine. Wearing some uniform that's not a dirty green colour in some parts of this town isn't going to endear you to the locals. There's been some trouble down town at times so it's safer not to risk it. Franco's bully boys are still pretty active and a few of the local population still disappear from time to time.'

'Disappear?' I gasped. 'What do you mean, disappear?'

He shrugged. 'You know what "disappear" means. There's a knock on the door one night, the guy in the house answers the door and it it's bye-bye blackbird.'

Barely able to believe what I had just heard, I continued to ask questions.

'I thought all of that finished at the end of the war. Are you saying that Franco is still killing people that fought against him?'

'No question,' Nick replied. 'There are a lot of mass graves out there and there are a lot of missing people filling them. One of these days someone will dig them up.'

'Pete doesn't want to hear you getting on your high horse about Franco and all that stuff,' my cousin said. 'We get enough of that on poker nights when you and Bishop have drunk too much beer, let's talk about nicer things, why don't you take us home via the Barrio de Santa Cruz and Pete can see the cathedral and the Giralda Tower, it always looks its best at this time of the day.'

Sensing that Pam was ill at ease about discussing Franco's brutality and the whole war scenario, I reluctantly changed the subject.

'Is the base here still an operational base or have things changed?'

'No,' he replied. 'We're still operational, both here and out at Barajas just outside Madrid. We fly B-52s, which are in the air around the clock and when the rest of the air crews are not in the air they're on permanent standby on a shift basis. A big part of what we do here is to listen to the world's encrypted traffic so we can be ready to hit some homers if it looks as if the brown stuff is going to hit the fan.'

'While you're here we'll go on base sometimes. I work with military computer systems but you'll probably see some of the ordnance that the ground crews load up. Those big old birds we have down here carry atomic payloads, and both the aircraft and the warheads are programmed to head out to hit specific targets should some overenthusiastic, sabre-rattling bastard decide to hit the wrong button.'

I whistled quietly between my teeth thinking that this holiday now had an entirely new and different dimension to it. Not only did it look like being the greatest holiday ever, I might also get to find out things that the newspapers didn't tell you. Mulling over the things that Nick had just said, I suddenly realised what it must be like to spend time in a foreign country that was still under military control, also I had the added bonus of being here with two of my favourite people as well.

'When we drive out to the base you'll see huge fields filled with earth moving equipment, bulldozers, cranes and stuff like that, well that's all part of the deal. Not only did our government pay Franco hundreds of millions of dollars to let us use this country for military purposes, we also agreed to supply him with enormous amounts of equipment for civil engineering projects. You might think that all of the people's birthdays have come at once but the truth is that Franco wants to keep the peasants in their place so he won't let them use it, so it just sits there rusting away.

'There's no doubt that it will be a good thing for Spain and the rest of the world when El Caudillo, or fat Frank as the guys on base call him, goes to meet the main man behind the golden gates to have his entry visa stamped.'

I burst out laughing at Nick's somewhat blasphemous description of the Almighty and his derogatory comments by calling General Franco 'fat Frank'.

Lighting a cigarette from the lighter on the car's dashboard, Nick tossed the opened packet of Lucky Strike over his shoulder which landed on the seat beside me.

'I hope you didn't waste your money buying cigarettes on the boat, you can keep those; we've got plenty more for you back at home.'

I knew that both Pam and Nick smoked, but my cousin had always favoured the taste of the longer and milder Pall Mall over the stronger Camel and Lucky Strike that Nick always smoked. I knew also that the cost of cigarettes at the P.X. was ridiculously cheap, so I gratefully accepted his gift without argument, lighting one from the car's lighter which Pam handed to me.

As we slowly turned a corner, Nick pulled over to the kerb and switched off the engine.

'What do you think about that for some sort of church?' He said, pointing at the magnificent cathedral. 'There's probably more gold and silver in there than in any other one place in Spain.'

He opened the car door and stepped out, opening my own door as he leaned against the shiny bodywork.

I stepped out into the blazing sunshine, craning my neck and squinting as I gazed up at the cathedral's enormous gothic towers and buttresses, marvelling as the sun danced and sparkled from its stained glass windows, its reflected glory turning the whole building into a creation of such awe inspiring splendour that surely God himself must have had a hand in its construction.

Pam climbed out of the car and came around to where we were standing.

'Amazing isn't it?' she said. 'You wait until you see the inside, it's just incredible. Some of the things that are housed in there you just wouldn't believe. On the high altar there is an effigy of John the Baptist's head on a solid gold platter which must be at least a quarter of an inch thick. There are also works of art and a wonderful pair of gold candlesticks which are thicker than your leg.

'Even if you're not particularly religious I guarantee that you will leave there thinking about things in an entirely different light. This is still a poor country as Nick said, yet people come from all over Spain on pilgrimages to donate every peseta they can towards its upkeep. Crazy isn't it when half the population are starving?'

Nick gave a cynical laugh. 'You'd better believe it. Most of the people who give all of their money to the church couldn't get much poorer if they tried, but the priests in there who collect it live off the fat of the land. Mostly they're all little fat guys who look like Sancho Panza, you know the guy I mean, Don Quixote's little buddy? It's the same the world over Pete, the rich get rich and the poor get poorer.'

Pam gave him an affectionate slap with the back of her hand.

'Take no notice of old grumpy here, he's suffering from a severe lack of caffeine, he's always the same until he's had his tenth cup of coffee.'

Tearing my gaze away from the cathedral, I looked towards shady whitewashed alleyways which led from this beautiful building, where patios and flower-festooned terraces and small intimate balconied houses jostled for position among inviting tapas bars. Everywhere I looked houses and apartments were awash with colour from wrought iron hanging baskets, each overflowing with multitudes of magnificent flowers still dripping water after having been given their morning nourishment.

'This whole area around here is the Barrio de Santa Cruz which used to be the old Jewish quarter of the city,' Nick continued, pointing towards the maze of narrow streets and alleyways.

'If you wander down through there you'll come out into another square where one of the Moorish kings had a huge tower built, it's called the Giralda Tower, and it really is something else. He built the thing so he could ride his horse right to the top and look out over his domain, we really have to take you to see that but I guess that will have to wait for another day, we'd better get you home, you must be beat.'

Despite my eagerness to see as much as I could, I knew Nick was right, not only was I tired but I was also starving hungry as well.

Climbing back into the car, we slowly drove through this magnificent and exciting city, each tree-lined square and flower-bedecked boulevard looking more beautiful than the one before as both Pam and Nick pointed out more sights and landmarks, continually promising that, 'If we go nowhere else, we've got to take you there before you leave'.

As the impromptu guided tour continued, we approached a bridge, beneath which a wide flowing river slowly ran, the pavements on both banks home to more bars and cafes. Even at this time of the morning several men sat outside, talking and laughing as they drank from small cups containing what appeared to be coffee, beside which empty balloon-shaped glasses stood which had once undoubtedly contained brandy.

As if reading my mind, Pam pre-empted my next question with a cynical and disdainful sniff.

'Don't tell me that it's not a man's world. You'll notice that there aren't too many women just sitting there in the sun shooting the breeze. Those guys may plead poverty but they can always come up with the price of a brandy or five.'

Nick laughed, letting her cynicism pass without comment, leaving me with the distinct impression that this was an observation that had been made before.

'This river is the Guadalquivir; the city was built around the river because of the trade it generated. Shipwrights and merchants had their businesses at El Arenal, and from there they could literally sail off to anywhere they chose. I guess it's like London, the River Thames offers access to all of the city, and the docks there were important for loading and unloading cargoes to feed and clothe the population.'

Until that moment, I hadn't been aware that we were driving on the opposite side of the road to that in England, but as we began to cross the river, the absence of buildings on either side of the car made it glaringly apparent. As we neared the centre of the bridge, another huge American car approached coming from the opposite direction, and as both cars pulled up along side each other, both Nick and the other driver called out in greeting.

At the sound of Nick's voice, a small Jack Russell dog with only one eye, a ripped ear and numerous bloody scratches criss-crossing its face leaped up on to the back of the other driver's front seat, sticking its head out of the open window and barking furiously. The barking ceased abruptly to be superseded by a sharp yelp as the driver swatted the animal from its precarious perch.

'Stupid dog never learns,' said the driver of the other car.

'Got himself all ripped up by the commissary cat yesterday. Damn fool dog stuck its stupid head into the cat's basket while it was snoozing in the sun; took me and McKeaver nearly five minutes to get the darn cat off him. Poor old McKeaver had to go and see the medics to get himself a tetanus shot for all the scratches that lousy cat gave him. He's got so many Band-Aids stuck all over him he looks like one of my old momma's patchwork quilts.'

With a parting shot of 'Catch up with you guys later,' the laconic driver of the other car headed on across the bridge.

Both Pam and Nick roared with laughter at the picture the other driver had painted of both McKeaver's and the poor dog's predicament.

'That's Bishop,' Nick said when he had finally finished laughing.

'He's one hell of a character. It could only happen to him that he got to inherit the only dog in Spain with one eye and a passion for sniffing armpits, you'll meet him later, Bishop I mean, not the dog. We told him you were coming over so I reckon now that he's seen us he'll probably drop by later on today.'

Choosing not to ask questions about Bishop and his dog but to wait until later, I sat back to enjoy the ride as we crossed to the other side of the river.

'Not far now Pete, we're just coming into Triana where we live. That bridge we just came over is the Puente de San Telmo and this is the Plaza de Cuba. I'm just telling you this in case you decide to go walk about on your own and you get lost.'

I smiled at the prospect of me wandering about in a strange city on my own, thinking that being driven around in a big plush American car was, by far, a much better option.

Driving with one arm out of the open window, Nick enthused about the area.

'We live down here in Los Remedios, I think you're gonna love it, it's a great place to hang out and watch some local action. This whole area is a haunt for gypsies, bullfighters and flamenco guitarists. If you want to see the real Spain you've come to the right place, it doesn't get much better than here.'

Soon, the wider avenues disappeared as narrower streets and alleyways took their place, the seemingly obligatory small bars and cafes all festooned with dazzling displays of cascading flowers.

Slowing down to a walking pace, Nick slowly eased the nearside wheels of the car up on to the pavement, gently coming to a halt as he pulled on the parking brake, switching off the ignition as the car came to a standstill.

'Here we are buddy, welcome to Casa Dumas.'

Opening the door, I slid across the seat and stepped out on to the pavement.

Directly in front of me was a wide, open fronted bar with half a dozen small tables placed strategically on the narrow pavement outside. Covering each of the tables were bright yellow and white check tablecloths, on which stood small vases of fresh flowers, and from inside the bar itself a mouth watering smell of cooking, heavy with the pungent smell of garlic, wafted out on to the street.

Open mouthed, I followed them both inside, staring at a long counter which stretched the length of the room. On top were bowls of delicious looking food, each one protected by glass covers which shielded the food beneath from the circling flies which circled above like tiny vultures searching for a free meal, but it was what was displayed on the walls which grabbed my immediate attention.

Brilliantly painted bullfight posters, some of them advertising fights of more than thirty years earlier adorned the walls, and between many of the posters, stuffed and mounted heads of long dead bulls gazed down in icy and indifferent silence, the macabre sight of these once magnificent fighting animals causing Pam to shudder before she spoke.

'Well, what do you think?' she asked.

'It's amazing,' I stammered. 'Is this where you really live?'

'Yes, but not down here in the abattoir,' she laughed, 'we have an apartment upstairs.'

At the sound of our voices, a man's head popped up from below the counter, a wide grin covering his face as he threw his arms out wide in a welcoming gesture.

'*Buenos días Señora y Señor Dumas, Cómo está usted?*'

Stepping out from behind the bar, a tall good-looking man emerged, wiping his hands on a cloth as he came to greet us, his smile widening even further as he took Pam's outstretched hand. Bending from the waist in a theatrical bow, his lips lightly brushed the backs of her fingers.

'It always gives me great pleasure to greet you *Señora*, my day would not be complete if I were to miss seeing your beautiful face.'

Nick grimaced before speaking.

'Pete, this is Señor Paco Ortega, he owns this miserable establishment, and apart from all the other pies he has his greasy little fingers in, he is also our landlord. You will also notice that his eyesight ain't that good either.'

Placing his hand over his heart the bar owner breathed a deep sigh, and with mock resignation said, 'Señor Dumas, you do both myself and your lovely wife a deep injustice and, if I were thirty years younger, I would be forced to take you into the street and give you the beating you deserve.'

Turning to shake my hand he said, 'You would do well to ignore this ignorant American; in this country we appreciate great beauty and honour and respect ladies such as Señora Dumas.' He waved his hand dismissively in the air as if brushing away a troublesome fly. 'This ill-bred excuse for a human being is what we call here in Spain a "*campesino*", a peasant, a person who is beneath contempt.'

I grinned at Nick being mockingly described as an ignorant American and a peasant, recalling previous arguments where I had staunchly flown the flag, jokingly belittling brash American attitudes by using Nick as an example.

Gently putting his hand on my shoulder, the bar owner ushered us back towards the tables outside.

'I am very pleased to meet you Señor, please come and sit outside where it is cooler and I will fetch coffee and brandy.'

As I made myself comfortable beneath a large parasol which carried the logo of a brand of local Spanish beer, Nick walked back to the car and opened the boot, taking out my suitcase.

'I'll get this upstairs and come back and join you in a couple of minutes,' he said, before slamming shut the lid.

Carrying a tray on which four cups of coffee, cream, a bottle of brandy and four glasses were delicately balanced, the bar owner placed it on the table and proceeded to pour a very generous measure into each glass before sitting down to question me about my trip. As we talked, it was clear that he was more than just the owner of a local drinking establishment, his questions about things I had seen and his command of the English language set him aside as a knowledgeable and much travelled man.

As we talked, Pam explained that Señor Ortega had once been a very accomplished matador, who during his career, had been one of the most popular and dedicated bullfighters ever to come from this part of Spain. During his much feted career, he had taken the leading role in many great corridas both in Seville and in other parts of the world until a serious goring had finally forced him into retirement.

At the mention of his bullfighting career, the bar owner shrugged, explaining that although he had experienced the pain of the *cornada* many times during his career, it had come to an abrupt end one day while fighting in Mexico. He further explained that one afternoon, whilst fighting a very difficult adversary, a sudden gust of wind had wrapped the cape around his legs and he had been badly gored as a result.

I listened enthralled at the details he gave with regard to his career and his ultimate enforced retirement, asking where he had learned to speak such excellent English. With almost child like reticence, he explained that he had fought in South America, Mexico and even over the border in Texas, while being fortunate in having a good *empresario* who had taught him English. This man, who had also gone on to become a great friend, had insisted that he put away money for the day when he could no longer fight, never imagining that this 'retirement' would not be long in coming.

With a cry of 'damn, it sure is hot,' Nick reappeared, minus his shirt and wearing just a T-shirt and light fatigue trousers. Pulling up a chair from a nearby table, he sat down and picked up his glass, raising it in a toast before putting it to his lips.

'Here's to good times Pete, it's great to see you again.' Taking a sip, he exclaimed, 'you old horse trader, you've finally got out the good stuff. How is it that you never get this out when we're here on our own? You'd better stick around

Pete, this is the first time I can ever remember him excelling himself like this, we usually get the stuff he wipes the bar down with.'

Pretending to be deeply hurt by Nick's insult, the good natured banter began all over again with Paco again winning the battle of words by stating that yes, it was his best Fundador brandy, but why would he waste it by giving it to someone who has the palate of an uncivilised peasant.

Again, I laughed out loud at Nick coming off worse in these exchanges as Paco generously began to refill the glasses, Pam refusing the offer after explaining that it was much too early in the day for her and she would need to be thinking of getting us something to eat. On hearing this, I felt rather disappointed as I had been looking forward to sampling some of the wonderful smelling treats sitting on the bar.

'You appear to show interest in the matter of the bulls, have you witnessed our fiesta before?'

Before I could reply, Nick said, 'I think he may be getting the bug, tell Paco about your new buddy Pete, I'd be interested to know if he's ever heard of the guy.'

Sensing that I was in danger of becoming embroiled in a subject about which I knew absolutely nothing and making a complete fool of myself in the process, I attempted to make light of my meeting with Jaime on the train.

'Oh, it's nothing,' I stammered. 'It's just that I bought a bullfight magazine from a kiosk on the station in Madrid and I happened to meet someone on the train who says that he is a bullfighter and he has come here to fight.'

At the mention of my meeting, Paco smiled indulgently and put down his glass.

'There are many young men here in Spain who wish to become matadors. They come here to simply jump into the ring in the hope that whatever little talent they may have will be appreciated by an *empresario*, someone who will recognise that they may have a future as a *torero* and take them under his wing and turn them into good money making matadors. I should not take too seriously what this man has told you.'

No doubt feeling that the bar owner's somewhat offhand and dismissive attitude had put something of a damper on my enthusiasm, Pam leaped to my defence.

'Show Paco the photograph he gave you and tell him what he said.'

I reached into my pocket and withdrew the picture, handing it across the table and relating the whole story.

Studying the picture and reading the card several times, his whole attitude changed as he read the name El Zorro de Toledo, the expression on his face instantly changing to one of curious interest.

'You have been fortunate indeed to meet this young man. I have read much about his skill and have followed his career with interest and I think that he may possess that which is required if he is to reach the top of his profession. He will be fighting here in the Maestranza when he comes to take his *alternativa*.'

Happy now that I felt I could add something relevant to the conversation, I mentioned Jaime's invitation for us to go and watch him fight in Castillo de las Guardas, adding that it would be nice if he would care to join us to see what would be my first bullfight.

Reaching towards me across the table, Paco shook me warmly by the hand.

'I would consider it a great honour to join you my young friend. I have long looked forward to seeing if it is true that this young man really has the skill and the courage that they say he has.'

Revelling in the ambience of the company and the mellowing effect of the brandy, I sat back in my seat thinking what the young bullfighter had said as he had related stories of great bullfights and of brave matadors. Sitting up with a start, I suddenly remembered a name that Jaime had excitedly mentioned while listing some of his heroes, in particular that of Ortega. I looked across at our genial host with a new interest. Nick had introduced him as Señor Paco Ortega, could this one time matador be the same person that Jaime had mentioned in such deferential terms?

'Señor Ortega, while on the train with Zorro, he talked of great matadors including a man named Ortega, your name is Ortega, was it you he was referring to?'

The man opposite smiled, leaning forwards and grasping both my hands in his own as he looked at both Pam and Nick.

'I think that our young friend here is destined to become a true aficionado, maybe even an *aficionado practico*. It also occurs to me that you have never asked this question Señor Dumas, yet you too profess to be a lover of the *fiesta brava*, but this young man is already seeking the history of the *corrida*.'

Feeling flattered by the compliments being paid to me but having no idea what an *aficionado practico* might be, I eagerly awaited the answer to my question.

'Regrettably, my friend, it was not me to whom he was referring. There are two great, great matadors with whom I have the honour of sharing the same name, one was Domingo Ortega and the other was Rafael Ortega, sadly I am not related to either. I wish that I could have matched both their skills and their courage, but I'm afraid this humble man you see before you was a simple *novillo* by comparison.'

At the mention of the word 'humble', Nick gave a derisory laugh, again seizing the opportunity of attempting to belittle the bar owner by saying that he was certain that Paco had no idea of the meaning of the word 'humble', telling him that if he knew what it meant he would not have the temerity of applying it to himself.

Ignoring both the laughter and the unflattering comment, Paco continued to pay tribute to the name of Ortega.

'Your friend was not mistaken in referring to these men in such terms, both were truly remarkable matadors. Domingo Ortega himself invented a pass called the *orteguina* that demands the greatest skill and courage. This pass, because of the great skill it requires and the danger involved, is seldom executed, but if you are ever lucky enough to see it performed properly it is something you will never forget.'

Feeling slightly disappointed that I was not sitting in the presence of one of the revered Ortegas, I asked about the term '*aficionado practico*'.

'You already know of the term *aficionado*', he answered, 'Well, an *aficionado practico* is a person who loves the corrida to such an extent that he also wants to fight the bulls, but doing this as one who is not paid but doing it purely for the love of this ultimate form of true art and the thrill of the encounter.'

After more coffee and light-hearted banter, we finally shook hands and took our leave of our genial host, promising to see him later as we made our way through the rear of the bar towards a flight of beautiful Moorish tiled steps which curved upwards towards the apartment above, the cool airy atmosphere coming as a relief to the heavy heat below.

Flamenco and the Bitter Taste of Fear...

Since first meeting Nick I had tried to visualise what it must be like to be sent all over the world in abeyance of military orders as he had been obliged to do. I was also aware that 'living in' on any military base was not something he chose to do and knowing him as I now did, I was confident that any accommodation he may have discovered for himself and Pam off base was bound to be different.

I felt that over the years I had come to know him pretty well and it had soon become obvious that, as far as possible, his intention was to treat his military career as a 'nine to five job', avoiding many of the restraints that military life inevitably placed on them both. To Nick, kissing my cousin on the cheek before leaving for work in the morning and striving to be back home again for lunch was top of his list of priorities, but obviously because of the complex nature of the work he did, this was not always possible.

With this in mind, I could barely contain my curiosity having already had a brief glimpse of what I might expect after my introduction to Paco and the bar downstairs. What I had already seen was typical of the way Nick embraced the unusual and I could barely wait to see the apartment itself, but nothing could have prepared me for what lay ahead as Nick turned the key in the lock of an old heavy iron-studded oak door, ushering me in as he stepped to one side.

Immediately, the cool air from inside the apartment washed over me as I stepped into the hallway. The floor had been laid with deep red earthenware tiles and they glowed like burnished copper in the light from the open but still shuttered windows, while thin shafts of sunlight filtering through the closed shutters picked out sumptuous heavy looking leather furniture, giving the room a homely comfortable feel while still retaining a traditional Spanish feel.

Standing in what was clearly the sitting room, my gaze took in three large leather armchairs complimented by soft tasselled cushions which faced a low antique-style Moorish coffee table, while in its centre stood a large brightly coloured pottery fruit bowl filled with large juicy looking oranges. On the opposite side of the table facing the armchairs, a matching dark leather sofa covered with cushions similar in design to those on the chairs, gave the impression that this was a room in which several people could comfortably stretch out and relax.

On one of the white rustic stuccoed walls, a large tapestry depicting a battle between Moors and Spanish knights in full armour hung from a twisted and turned wrought iron pole, the finials on each end representing the basket-type handles on a heavy fighting sword, this tapestry completing the picture of a room decorated by someone who was sympathetic to the designs and fashions of the country.

'Come on through buddy, I'll show you your room.'

Nick escorted me through an arched doorway into another large cool and airy room in the centre of which a long, heavily carved table stood, around which, six matching high backed chairs stood as if awaiting a feast to be placed before them.

'Wow,' I breathed, 'I love it, what a great place.'

'You should have seen it before Pam got to work on it, it was just a bunch of storerooms, full of boxes, crates and junk, but good old Pammy saw its potential and did some straight talking with old Paco downstairs and we rent it for an absolute song. Mind you, she'll be gutted if I get posted anywhere soon.'

I couldn't quite believe what I was hearing.

'Do you mean that you'll have to leave all this if you have to move on?'

Nick gave me a grin and winked.

'We're working on it. It may well be that, as the furniture and the rest of the stuff here is ours anyway, we might just make Paco an offer for the place. Just between the two us, if we make him a decent offer and he accepts, we'll hang on to the place. If I do get posted, Pam will stay here and follow me out later after renting it out to perhaps an officer and his wife who have just arrived and are looking for a place.'

Nick shrugged before carrying on.

'Who knows? Pam and I have talked it over and we might even come back here to live when I get out of the service, I don't know yet. I've still got a bunch of years left to go before I either get out or re-enlist, but I also have an option of working from here for the government and doing what I'm doing now as a civilian but with a military rank. Like I said, I've got a bit of a way to go yet but it's an option.'

Looking puzzled, I asked, 'How does that work then, how can you be a civilian with a military rank?'

'I can't tell you too much, but there's a whole bunch of guys currently hooked up with the military doing the same sort of stuff that I do, so when it's time for me to call it a day, I might apply to transfer to the DIA, that's a government outfit which is allied to the military, their real John Hancock is the Defence Intelligence Agency, I would still be dealing with computers, but like I said, I can't say too much.'

From somewhere behind me, Pam called out saying that she was just about to make coffee and she would do some angel toast and then, if I wasn't too tired, we could go out later to eat.

With a shout of 'good idea hun', Nick pushed open the door to what was to become my bedroom and pointed to a large, heavy oak wardrobe, saying that it was all mine while I was here and that there were some T-shirts and light coloured 'fatigue pants' which I could wear for just slobbing around the house, adding that there was no rush and that I should come and eat when I was good and ready.

As I was about to open my case which lay on the bed, I listened to the various sounds which drifted up from the street below, and walking over to the open French windows, I opened the shutters and stepped out on to a pretty, black painted, wrought iron balcony overlooking a fairly narrow alleyway, where on the pavement below, additional small tables presumably also belonging to the Bar Ortega were placed.

Leaning over the balcony rail, I looked up and down the narrow shaded street, watching two small children playing with what looked like an old-fashioned whip and top, enjoying their childish shrieks and screams as the top careered across the uneven cobbles with both in hot pursuit.

Glancing across to the building opposite, I noticed an elderly man and woman sitting on an identical balcony to the one on which I was standing, both watching me with interest. Smiling, I gave a brief wave, simply expecting a similar wave in reply, but to my dismay the man began speaking rapidly in Spanish. Not understanding one word of what was being said, I offered the odd '*sí*' and 'no' in halting Spanish, finally ending the one-sided conversation with a heartfelt '*adios*', stepping back inside and hoping at least that one or more of the yeses and nos I had uttered fitted appropriately into the conversation.

As I flipped open the lid of my case, I had the sensation of being watched and, quickly turning round, I saw sitting in the open doorway, a large ginger and white cat, its face and in particular its ears, bearing testament to many previous won and lost battles. As soon as it noticed me looking at it, it arched its back as it got to its feet, spitting defiantly as it backed from the room, never taking its eyes off my face. It was, without doubt, one of the most battle-scarred and hostile cats I had ever encountered.

Choosing to ignore its antagonistic behaviour, I squatted down in an attempt to pacify and make friends with the animal, but the cat would have none of it. With a final defiant hiss and a slashing of the air with its bared claws it turned and dashed from sight.

Returning to the task of emptying my case, I soon had my clothes stowed away in the wardrobe, and shutting the lid, I carried my dirty and bloody shirt into the kitchen to where Nick was helping out by preparing a crisp green salad, while Pam concentrated on frying some delicacy on the top of the stove, something which I took to be the mysterious 'angel toast' my cousin had mentioned a few moments before.

As I entered the kitchen, Nick turned and pushed a bottle of ice cold beer across the work surface, not the local brand that I had seen in the photograph they had sent with the letter, this one bore the logo of Budweiser, an American brand that, amongst several others, was soon to become very popular with me.

As we clinked bottles in response to him wishing me a great holiday, his eyes switched to the bloodstained shirt I held in my other hand.

'What in hell happened to you? I noticed your head when you got off the train, did you get mugged or something?'

Rather shamefaced, I related the story of how I had smacked my head while boarding the ferry, following that by mentioning my experience in Paris and the two men who had attempted to mug me. When I had finished, Nick shook his head.

'I don't think it's a good idea to let you out on your own while you're here, and while we're on the subject, remind me to not let you and Bishop get too chummy, he's also another accident waiting to happen. Between the two of you and that stupid dog of his you could turn this place into a potential disaster area.'

Opening a cupboard beneath the sink, Pam took out a bucket and filled it with cold water before taking the shirt from me and dropping it in.

'If we leave that to soak for a couple of days before I wash it properly it should get most of the blood out. Now, sit down while I take a look at your head.'

Gently parting the hair from around the wound, she finally said, 'You certainly gave it a smack. You've got five stitches in there but it seems to be healing nicely, we'll get you down to the base hospital and get you checked out just to make sure. Did the guy on the boat tell you when the stitches needed to come out?'

I replied by telling her that the doctor who had sewn me up had said that the stitches needed to come out in about ten days time, protesting that there was no need for me to go to the hospital, insisting instead that I would go and see the local doctor if there was one nearby rather than bother anyone at the base.

Handing me a second beer, Nick laughed saying that there was no way he would take me to the local doctor, adding that he was probably the right guy for neutering the cat or treating flamenco dancer's ankle or castanet player's wrist, but he wouldn't trust any local guy to take out stitches or anything like that.

Sipping the beer, I spoke of the more pleasurable memories of Paris, describing in detail my taxi ride around the city and the wonderful paintings and other works of art I had seen in the Musée d'Orsay. As we talked, I remembered the sweet face of Avril as she bent to kiss my cheek and my own slightly more passionate response, feeling a warm glow as I remembered this brief interlude. I thought back to what I might have done with the piece of paper on which she had written her address and telephone number, relieved when I remembered that it was tucked safely away in my wallet.

As I continued to relate what had happened in Paris, Pam ushered us both into the dining room, carrying plates of wonderfully fresh salad, together with the angel toast she had been preparing, setting everything down on the table as Nick mixed her a large Cuba Libra before flicking the tops off two more bottles of beer.

Biting into the angel toast, I realised that it was simply beaten egg and Worcestershire sauce, into which slices of bread had been dipped and then fried, but with the addition of the cold crisp salad it was absolutely delicious, and two further slices later, I finally put down my knife and fork.

After clearing the table and taking our drinks into the lounge, we stretched out and began reminiscing about things and people at home, with me supplying answers in respect of the health of our respective families together with who was doing what with who or how that person was getting on. Suddenly the sound of music drifted up from the bar downstairs, warm emotional guitar music interspersed with a rhythmic beat of booted feet on the tiled floor, all accompanied by the staccato chatter of castanets.

'The cabaret has started early tonight,' Nick said as he nodded his head in the direction of the open door behind us. 'They don't usually start until much later than this.'

'A cabaret?' I asked. 'Do they have a cabaret downstairs in the bar?'

Both Pam and Nick chuckled at my question.

'It's not exactly a cabaret,' Nick laughed. 'It's like I told you earlier, this whole area is alive with flamenco dancers and singers, and there's always guitar players hanging about downstairs waiting to play a few chords and drink a few beers.

'It's a real hangout for musicians here; they come from all over to play. We'll slip down later if you like and you can get the feel of the place, although you might get fed up with it after a while. These guys never seem to get tired and sometimes they go on until dawn so I shouldn't get too excited too soon.'

Listening to the vibrant and earthy sounds coming up from the bar below, I knew that getting fed up with it was never going to be an option. I instinctively knew that the music and the culture of this extraordinary country with its colourful and charismatic people would always remain with me and become a huge part of my life.

Today, nearly sixty years on, even second-rate dancers and musicians masquerading as authentic gypsies pandering to tourists in places like Torremolinos and Fuengirola still stir in me vivid memories of a Spain which was once both far more romantic and wild. However second rate the playing or the dancing, the unique and haunting sound of a traditional acoustic Spanish guitar sends my soul on a magical journey which takes me back to the heady and exciting days of my early adulthood, back to wine-fuelled encounters in bodegas and bars throughout Spain.

Classical guitar music played by virtuosos such as Segovia, Pujol or Manuel Cubedo has always given me an extraordinary feeling of déjà vu as I close my eyes to recall some of the great renditions I've heard played both inside and outside the walls of the wonderful Alhambra, the beautiful Moorish palace in Granada. Today, the more modern and flamboyant hot-blooded melodies played by the Gypsy Kings and the wonderful Tonino Baliardo and his flamboyant band of brothers continue to excite and enthral me, re-igniting the tastes and smells of Spain as if it were only yesterday.

Curiously, I often dream that, in a previous life, Don Quixote, Sancho Panza and I were once travelling companions, tilting at windmills as the Man of La Mancha had done, sleeping under the stars while listening to the far-off strains of a flamenco guitar being played to serenade a loved one. To quote one of my mother's more philosophical homilies when pondering on the imponderable, she would nod her head knowingly before saying, 'The Lord surely works in mysterious ways'.

An hour later, Nick hauled himself out of his chair and suggested that we drop into the bar downstairs for a nightcap. My cousin, who had by this time been giving a visibly poor impression of someone pretending to be interested in the intricacies of Rugby Union as opposed to those in American Football, declined the offer. Apologising, she said that she was tired and if I didn't mind she would get an early night, but encouraging Nick to take me down to show me what it was all about.

Needing no further encouragement, he slipped his bare feet into a pair of soft leather moccasins, and wearing just a white T-shirt and light-coloured American issue fatigue pants, he grabbed his wallet from a nearby table and beckoned me to follow.

'Come on buddy, the hell with modern day stress and the problems that go with it, I'll show you some people who have the right idea about life and follow the maxim of *mañana*, people who don't have that much but still live in the old traditional way.'

Stepping inside the bar was like being transported into the pages of Kenneth Tynan's excellent book *Bull Fever*. In it, his account of a journey home to Madrid after watching Pedres and Jumillano fight in Segovia includes a wonderful descriptive narrative of him having dinner on a café terrace with five total strangers, one of whom ended the evening by giving him his shoes. His wonderful account of that scene mirrored what I now saw and smelled when eloquently describing '*gazpacho*' as the stinging cold soup of the south being accompanied by glasses of metallic tasting Spanish champagne, all of this coupled with paella, sticky with lobster oil.

In addition to mirroring his extraordinary perceptive description of that scene was something else, the pungent smell of Spanish tobacco hanging in the air and stinging the eyes, all combining to create a dramatic backdrop for the throbbing sensual sound of flamenco which reached out to embrace the senses. I stood in the doorway in wonderment as the atmosphere of this heady cocktail bombarded and stunned me.

In one corner of the room, perched high on a bar stool, a young man with jet black shoulder length hair and a heavily pock marked face caressed the strings of a guitar. As he played, his head and shoulders were bent over the instrument; his eyes closed as he lovingly stroked and plucked the strings, oblivious to anything else going on around him as he became totally absorbed in the playing of the intricate rhythms.

The man's black shirt was unbuttoned to the waist and loosely tucked into a pair of narrow-legged black trousers, exposing his olive-tanned skin. On his feet, soft, black leather calf-length boots completed the romantic picture I had always held of Spanish gypsy men. As he played, his long hair cascaded down on to the instrument, perspiration occasionally dripping from his brow. While one foot supported his weight against the bottom rail of the stool, the other tapped out an accompanying rhythm, his face portraying the agony and the ecstasy of his heartfelt emotions.

Sitting at his side was an older man also clad entirely in black, but instead of the shoulder length hair, this man's hair was much shorter and scraped back from his face and tied in a small ponytail at the back. The two men could not have been more different in appearance, one being lithe, slim and muscular while the other having the paunch of one who enjoyed both the fruits of field and vine, but in spite of the difference in their appearance, they both shared one obsession as he too, unashamedly, lost himself in the passion of the music.

The older of the two men was seated on an upturned beer crate, and between his legs, he cradled something which looked like an ordinary plywood packing case about eighteen inches square on which he beat out a staccato rhythm, his stubby fingers performing unbelievable acrobatic movements across the surface of the box that produced an amazing accompaniment to the guitar. From around the crowded room an appreciative audience nodded its approval, sometimes calling out an enthusiastic '*olé*' while others joined in with complicated clapping routines in time to the music.

Not wishing to disrupt the performance by walking across the bar, Nick and I stood watching from the doorway. Señor Ortega who was busily snapping off tops from bottles of beer, caught sight of us from behind the bar, his face breaking into a craggy smile as he saw us. Pointing to two tall bar stools which stood in front of where he now stood, he held up two fingers and pushed the opened bottles across the bar towards where he had motioned us to sit, putting two half pint glasses by the side of the opened bottles.

With our arrival into the bar going completely unnoticed, we slipped around the rear of the room and sat down on the stools, Nick acknowledging Paco's greeting by shaking hands before pouring some of the beer into one of the glasses and taking a long pull of the cold frothy beer.

Suddenly, amid rapturous clapping and shouting, the music stopped, the two musicians smiling and nodding in appreciation of the generous applause, their faces damp with perspiration as they left their seats carrying their instruments as they made their way to where we were sitting, two beers already sitting on the top of the bar awaiting their arrival.

Standing by my side, the guitar player spoke to the bar owner who appeared to be congratulating the two men on their performance, at the same time pushing two small plates of delicious smelling tapas towards them as they gratefully sipped at the opened bottles of beer.

Trying not to appear like some star struck teenager gazing upon his current pop idol, I glanced at the man by my side as he picked up the small fork which lay by the side of his plate of food. Noticing me watching him, the man turned and nodded, greeting me with a muttered '*hola*' before beginning to eat.

As I desperately tried to think of some word of greeting in Spanish, Nick leaned across in front of me and spoke to the two men, emulating Paco's congratulations on their performance.

'*Muy bien*', he said, continuing to talk to the two men in Spanish as he raised his glass and motioned Paco to give the men two more beers.

Still holding their forks in their hands, both men reached for their bottles of beer, acknowledging Nick's toast with a brief '*muchos gracias*', before resuming eating.

Despite the many hours I had spent travelling, I still felt eager for more of this wonderful spontaneous entertainment and I was not to be disappointed as other musicians and singers all took their turn, sweeping my tiredness aside as I listened to the pulsating rhythms which spilled out on to the street as yet more people arrived to watch and enjoy this extravaganza of passionate, hot-blooded music.

With the music and the dancing growing noticeably more intense and heartfelt, more and more people began to arrive until the already crowded bar reached saturation point where late comers were obliged to squat on the kerb outside. More and more musicians and dancers arrived and, with nowhere to sit, had no alternative other than to perch themselves on the doorsteps of the houses opposite.

Sipping my beer, I watched as the occupants of the houses opposite began to appear on their balconies to watch the proceedings. Two elderly ladies wearing black lace shawls around their shoulders sat rocking backwards and forwards in cane chairs, their grey hair swept back and held in place by tall tortoiseshell combs while they cooled the air by fanning themselves with elaborately decorated fans. Even young children, despite the lateness of the hour, clung to balcony railings to peer down into the street below.

The deep-throated refrains of flamenco being sung by two men drew my attention back to performers out in the street as they were joined by a trio of raven-haired women of differing ages who suddenly flounced into the centre of the circle of tables and chairs. As the three women all dressed in colourful full-length, tight-fitting dresses stamped and gyrated to the rhythm of the men's voices and their clapping, I became aware of the change in tempo as it took on a different fervour and urgency, the women plunging themselves into graceful and balletic dance, their castanets clicking to accompany the sound made by the heels of their shoes as they swirled and pirouetted despite the uneven surface of the cobbles.

Staring in amazement at this remarkable and moving scene being performed before me, it was as if I had been transported back in time to become an explorer visiting a parallel universe, witnessing what Bizet had undoubtedly seen before composing his evocative and colourful opera, *Carmen*.

With a final swirl of their beautiful costumes and shouts of '*olé*', the dancers dropped down on to one knee, their arms held high above their heads and their wrists curved and arched in graceful splendour while their faces portrayed the arrogance and disdain befitting such a breathtaking performance as they bathed in the rapturous applause.

Without realising it, I found myself leaping to my feet to join in the adulation being exhibited, clapping and shouting as the dancers drew the attention of the audience to the two singers who smiled and bowed in appreciation. As I stood cheering and clapping, I felt myself being patted on the shoulder from someone standing behind me.

'Well, what do you think of our humble attempts at bringing Spanish culture back to the people?'

Feeling genuinely at a loss for something to say, I stammered out some incomprehensible reply as I turned to stare into Señor Ortega's smiling face.

'That was unbelievable,' I stammered. 'It was so moving and full of passion, I've never seen anything like it in my life. Are they all professional dancers and singers?'

The bar owner shook his head.

'Some of them earn a little money by singing and dancing in some of the bigger hotels in the city, but you were right when you said it was so full of passion. Music is in their blood and they love what they are doing, they just want to share that passion with others whether they are paid or not.'

He shrugged. 'I will give them a little money when they leave but that is not why they do it, they live for this music and culture just as their parents did before them. They are "*gitano*", people who roam the country playing, singing and dancing.'

He turned around and snapped his fingers at two young men I had noticed earlier serving drinks and food, issuing them with instructions on what he wanted doing before continuing.

'They will be resting now and my sons will serve them so we can talk without me having to leave suddenly.'

Dragging another stool from behind the bar, Señor Ortega sat down and began to explain about the origins of the music and the dance I had just witnessed, calling for a beer as he wiped his hands on a small, wet bar towel.

'What you are seeing is a very old and complicated form of music, even the clapping which accompanies the instruments and the dance is something which has been handed down over the centuries and is very difficult to follow and perform.

'Spain, as you probably have learned from school, is a country that has been constantly fought over, and our history, just like your own, dates back to when the Romans arrived here and attempted to use us as slaves, but like you we fought them and eventually drove them from our lands.'

Before continuing he took a sip of his beer.

'Originally, it was people from the north of India and then the Moorish invaders who have had the most influence over us, particularly with regard to the music you have just heard. It is thought that flamenco music originated in India and if you listen very carefully to their own music you can hear many similarities between that and what we now call traditional Spanish music. Even though the Spanish word for the music you have just heard is called flamenco, men more clever than you and I have discovered that this word is derived from the Arabic word "*Fellahmengu*" which, literally translated, means "peasant without land"'.

After about another half an hour, I reluctantly decided that my need for sleep far outweighed my desire to find out more about Spain and its culture, and before the music began again, I mentioned that I was feeling pretty tired and needed to call it a day, and after shaking hands all round, we both headed back upstairs.

As we walked into the lounge, we found that Pam had already gone to bed, but not before leaving a note addressed to me which read.... 'Hope you enjoyed yourself and that you sleep well. There's no rush to get up in the morning so get some rest and if you're up to it we'll go out later'.

Refusing a nightcap, I bade Nick good night, and after brushing my teeth, gratefully slipped into the comfortable bed before blissfully dropping off to sleep to the soporific strains of the music downstairs, the sounds acting as an accompaniment to one of the most memorable days of my life.

* * * * *

'Come on buddy, rise and shine.'

From somewhere deep within me I seemed to recognise a small persistent voice which was seriously cramping my style. Until that precise moment, I had been whispering sweet nothings to one of the most beautiful women imaginable, so what would a vaguely familiar voice be doing intruding in such an untimely manner?

'Come on buddy, let's see some action here.'

There it was again, only this time sounding more insistent.

Grudgingly, I slowly opened my eyes, groaning as I saw Nick standing at the side of the bed, a broad grin on his face as he placed a mug of coffee down on the bedside table. For several seconds I couldn't take in where I was or what was happening as I stared up at him, my mind reluctantly ridding itself of the remnants of my dream as I rubbed my eyes and became reacquainted with my surroundings.

'What time is it?' I mumbled, propping myself up on one elbow and feeling the roughness of the stubble on my chin.

'It's time to be up and doing buddy, we have to go down to the commissary. Pam needs to get a couple of things and if you feel up to it and you're not too pooped we'll grab a couple of beers and some lunch at the NCOs' club.'

As Nick left the room, I fell back on to the pillows, coming to the conclusion that I was feeling much better than I was probably entitled to after everything that I had eaten and drunk the previous day. Reaching for the mug of coffee, I glanced towards the window where already the sun was streaming through the shutters, making interesting patterns of contrasting light and shade on the stone floor.

I slid out of bed yawning and stretching, wiggling my toes on the cool stone tiles before walking over to the window. Pushing open the shutters, I stepped out on to the balcony and leaned on the already warm wrought iron railing as I sipped my coffee. Down below in the street it was hard to visualise how it had been the previous evening where the impromptu flamenco performances had taken place, all the tables were now neatly back in place and it was as if nothing had ever occurred there.

Already, the business of the day was beginning to get underway as two men sat at one of the tables drinking coffee and reading newspapers, occasionally speaking to one another as some item of news caught their eye, noisily arguing when differences of opinion stirred each of the men to voice their feelings more forcibly.

As I flopped down into the wicker chair wearing only a pair of pyjama bottoms, I put my feet up on the balcony rail enjoying the warmth of the sun on my bare feet. Stretched out with my eyes closed, I listened to the sounds drifting up from the street below as people went about their daily business, among them Señor Ortega, who I could hear giving orders to someone, who was from the tone of his voice, issuing a stern reprimand to him for either doing something he shouldn't have done, or conversely getting chewed out for not doing something he was supposed to have done.

Blissfully sipping my coffee, I pondered on what could possibly be in store for me if I failed to report on the allotted date of my conscription, already certain that, however dire the consequences might be, I was here and I was going to spend as much time as humanly possible with Pam and Nick, and if that meant a prolonged stretch in some sort of guardroom or being confined to camp for the next two hundred years, so be it.

Pushing aside thoughts of National Service and the comparative tediousness of my life in England, I gulped down the remainder of my coffee and made my way back into the bedroom where I was surprised to see the battered and scarred ginger cat that I had seen yesterday sitting just inside the door. As I looked, it rose to its feet and arched its back as it had done previously, spitting and hissing as it backed away.

Squatting down, I put out my hand offering whispered words of encouragement in the hope that it might pacify the animal. Immediately, it leaped into the air, its claws slashing at me before turning tail and rushing out of the room, its feet desperately seeking some sort of purchase on the tiled floor as it made its escape. Seeing its rapid departure, I knew for certain that this flea-bitten creature and I were never going to become bosom friends, and if I was to avoid becoming another of its torn and bloody victims, we would both need to avoid each other.

Wearing a white towelling dressing gown that barely covered my 'essentials', I padded into the kitchen carrying a towel which I had also found hanging in the wardrobe to where Pam stood whisking eggs in a large earthenware basin.

Hearing me enter the room, she turned to greet me, suddenly bursting into uncontrollable fits of laughter when she looked at what I was wearing.

'Did you find that in your wardrobe?' she asked in between fits of giggling.

'Nick must have left it in there by mistake. That's my robe; I was looking for it this morning when I got up and when

I couldn't find it I figured that it must still be in your room but as I didn't want to disturb you, I left it.'

Embarrassed at my mistake, I looked down at my white legs sticking out from the bottom and at the sleeves which barely reached passed my elbows. Self-consciously, I pulled the belt tighter in the vain hope that it might miraculously gain several more inches in length and cover any further indignities.

'I'm sorry,' I said. 'I saw it hanging in the wardrobe and thought you had left it for me although I did think it was a bit on the short side when I put it on.'

In between further fits of hysterical giggling, Pam pointed down to my exposed legs.

'Come on Pete,' she spluttered, 'It's hardly big enough for me, so it's not likely that I'm going to leave it out for you to wear is it?

'You may not get embarrassed that easily but I can assure you that if I see very much more of you, I sure as hell will.

'Would you mind just keeping it on until Nick gets back,' she laughed, 'He's just going to love seeing you in that.'

'No, I'm certainly not going to keep it on just to give him a few cheap laughs,' I stammered. 'I didn't think that you had left it for me to wear for all of my stay, I just thought that it was just for this morning until I got myself sorted out.'

Still unable to control her giggling, Pam finally managed to stop long enough to usher me down the hall towards the bathroom.

'Look, in the bathroom hanging behind the door you'll find two or three clean bath robes, find one which is more your size and use it while you are here. I don't think I could stand seeing you wandering around dressed like that anymore, I'd have a heart attack.'

Still chuckling, she said, 'Why is it you never have a camera handy when you want one, can you just hang on there for a couple of minutes while I go and get mine?'

With her laughter still ringing in my ears, I turned and hurried down the hallway, tugging down the back of the robe as she fired her parting shot.

'I can't make up my mind if I like it better from the front or the back, but I have to admit that it looks pretty raunchy from where I'm standing right now and that colour matches your legs perfectly.'

As I gratefully closed the bathroom door behind me, I heard her crash down on to one of the kitchen chairs helpless with laughter, and with the sound ringing in my extremely red ears, I turned and dropped the bathrobe on the floor and stepped into the shower cubicle, turning on the shower and turning my face upwards into the stinging jets of cool water.

Carefully washing my hair to avoid getting too much shampoo on the cut on my head, I towelled off and tried on one of the clean bath robes which I took to be Nick's, ensuring that there wasn't going to be a repeat performance of earlier by twisting and turning in front of a large mirror to make sure that I was decently attired, pulling the belt tightly around me as I exited the bathroom.

Closing the door, I inwardly groaned as I heard laughter coming from the kitchen. Nick had obviously returned and Pam was gleefully relating the details of my earlier gaff, their laughter leaving me in no doubt that the next ten minutes or so were going to get pretty unbearable.

'Listen, I know that you two are related, but wandering around the house half naked in front of your own cousin is not exactly what I would have expected. Where's this old English reserve I was told to expect and all that stiff upper lip crap? Come on buddy, I know that this is the fifties and we're more liberated than ever before but you have to draw the line somewhere.'

'Go on,' I retorted. 'Get it over and done with; let's hear a bit more of that good old American homespun humour you're so famous for. It's a shame that the Marx brothers aren't looking for another stooge, you'd have no trouble at all with the audition; you're perfect for the part.'

Leaving them both convulsed with bouts of uncontrolled laughter, I beat a shamefaced retreat back into my bedroom, denying them the pleasure of seeing my burning face. From behind the closed door, I could still hear them laughing, their spluttered remarks questioning my lack of physical attributes which would undoubtedly hinder my progress in following the path to become an exotic dancer.

Half an hour and a few more odd ribald comments later saw us driving back across the bridge out of Triana, the same bridge we had crossed when I had first arrived, the sun once again sparkling and glistening on the water below.

Already, the heat from the morning sun had virtually emptied the streets of casual shoppers and sightseers, leaving only small oases of cool shade beneath gaily striped awnings pulled down to provide shelter for coffee drinkers and early diners who were already frequenting the city's tapas bars and restaurants.

The cool breeze through the open windows of the car made travelling a delight as we drove slowly through the beautiful old thoroughfares towards the city centre. With my head turning first one way and then the other, Pam and Nick pointed out streets and alleyways of particular historical significance and I began to look forward to the time when maybe I could do some exploring on my own.

Gently easing the big car around a particularly narrow corner, Nick skilfully avoided a man bent almost double as he struggled to push a handcart covered with cut flowers along the uneven cobbles, while from somewhere nearby I could hear the shouts and cries of both men and women as they urged potential customers to buy.

Slowly following the direction taken by the man with the cart, we turned into a magnificent plaza in which dozens of flower sellers had set up stalls. Not all of the vendors however had the luxury of stalls, some simply sat at the kerbside calling out to passers by, while the more permanent traders sat behind tables literally awash with flowers of all description, the scent from which was hanging heavy in the breezeless air. Looking beyond the flower sellers, I could see a line of open horse-drawn carriages, each one bedecked with coloured ribbons and tassels as they patiently awaited customers wishing to be taken on guided tours of the city.

As I stared at these beautiful painted carriages, it was obvious that each one had been lovingly restored and decorated by its owner in an attempt to outdo the splendour of the others, but it was the attendant horses which stood patiently in the cool shade of overhanging trees that almost guaranteed customers. How could anyone resist wallowing in the hypnotic atmosphere of this magnificent city and not indulge in a journey back in time by being transported in a carriage being pulled by a horse wearing a straw hat, docile and patient animals which simply stood and dozed, several with one front leg bent at the knee as if resting their aching feet.

Pulling the car over to the side of the cobbled roadway, Nick switched off the ignition and pointed in the direction of one of the bars across the square.

'We thought that you might like to get a coffee here before we head off downtown?'

Opening the car door, I inhaled the warm heady aroma of the flowers, their perfume acting as a drug as it enveloped the whole area to numb the senses with its intensity.

Pam slipped around the side of the car and stood next to me, placing her hand in mine and squeezing my fingers as she smiled up at me.

'We thought you would like it here! This is my very favourite place in the whole of the city, Nick and I come here all the time. This is where we took the photograph we sent with our last letter, it's called the Plaza Virgen de Los Reyes and at night it really is so beautiful and atmospheric. Most of the flower sellers leave late in the afternoon but some will stay and come to your table to offer their flowers while you are eating or just having a drink.'

'It's a bit like Triana with the gypsies coming into the square here to sing and dance, but much prettier. This is the best show in town at night and all it costs is the price of your meal or maybe a few drinks and a couple coins for the musicians.'

'It really is beautiful,' I said, watching everything that was going on around me. 'Thanks so much for inviting me to come and see you both.'

'It's a pleasure,' she said, reaching up to kiss my cheek, 'It's great to see you. Living abroad, as we do, I miss seeing family and friends so we've got some catching up to do, even if you are prone to a little cross dressing every now and again.'

'Please don't start that dressing gown thing again,' I laughed, 'I thought we'd done with all that. If you carry on and he hears you, you'll start him off again and I don't think I can stand any more humour from Uncle Sam over there.' I nodded towards Nick as he headed off to find us a table in the shade.

As we sat beneath the shade of a large coloured parasol, I watched the comings and goings of people visiting the square to buy flowers, slowly sipping the strong black coffee laced with brandy which Nick had ordered for me, while Pam slowly stirred a creamy looking coffee which appeared to be thickened with condensed milk.

'How do you like your coffee, Pete?' Nick asked. 'It's called a *carajillo*. That's good coffee guaranteed to set you up for the rest of the day and put hairs on your chest, although, from what I hear, you can do without any extra hair.'

'Oh God,' I exclaimed in mock despair, putting down my cup and turning to my cousin. 'Look what you've done now; you've started him off again.'

Dropping her spoon on to the cobbles, Pam laughed as she fought to stop herself from choking, finally recovering her composure as she dabbed her eyes with a handkerchief before managing to splutter, 'Right, that's it, enough is enough. I've just nearly wet my pants, so please, let's all forget about this morning; I don't want to hear anymore about Pete and his predilection for women's clothes.'

Laughing out loud at my cousin's close call, I watched several women dressed completely in black, their heads draped in black tasselled shawls moving from table to table quietly offering flowers to people sitting there, the waiters delivering food and drinks seemingly oblivious to their presence.

'Are those ladies selling the flowers in mourning?' I asked
Nick nodded.

'They'll wear black like that for the rest of their lives or until they re-marry,' he explained. ' There's a big shortage of eligible men of their age in Spain these days, the civil war took care of all that, so the chances of the thousands of other women who are in the same position ever re-marrying is pretty remote.'

'As we go around, you'll see lots of little kiosks dotted around the city called *"Tabacs"*, they're run by women like those, they're another of fat Frank's generous little vote catching gestures to the widows of this country. All you needed to do to get one is to have had your husband slaughtered on his behalf during the war.'

At Nick's derogatory mention of General Franco, Pam slapped his arm.

'Shush, someone might hear you, keep your voice down.'

After apologising, Nick continued quietly with his story.

'When the civil war was over, Franco decreed that as a sort of recompense to the thousands of women who had lost their husbands during the struggle, he would allow them to run those little *tabac* kiosks, no men, only war widows. Good of him, or what? I reckon that's a form of compensation these ladies could have well done without.'

After listening to this tragic little story, I watched people in the square enjoying both the food and the wine, people whose situation and lifestyles were so far removed from these poor women struggling to survive that I began to feel somewhat guilty at my own position. Had I too become guilty of exploiting these people or was I contributing in some small way to their very existence however pitiful that might be?

As I pondered on what Nick had just said, I watched one of the flower sellers approaching our table. I looked into her eyes and at her deeply furrowed and careworn face, noticing too her bowed back, but despite her appearance I guessed that she couldn't have been much older than fifty, but in her eyes there still burned a passion and a dignity that her current situation had failed to extinguish.

Smiling slightly, but not speaking, she held out several different coloured roses and small bunches of flowers, not saying anything but simply standing there in silence.

Taking a five peseta note from my pocket, I chose a small bouquet and handed the flower seller the money, waving away any change which might be due as I turned to present the flowers to my cousin who sat watching the proceedings with curious interest.

A sharp tapping on the table startled me as I looked back at the lady who stood with the change from the small denomination note in her hand. Slowly and deliberately she counted out my change as she laid it on the table in front of me, the frown on her face replacing her initial smile as she turned and hobbled away.

Feeling slightly dismayed by her abrupt attitude, I watched as she headed off towards another table. Pam, noticing the look of surprise on my face, quietly pointed out that one had to be careful when offering tips to the gypsy flower sellers and other vendors, explaining that, in offering money other than that which is due, could be interpreted as charity and was likely to cause offence.

As we finished our coffee, Nick dropped a few coins on the table as we stood up to leave.

Seeing the disappointed expression on my face, Pam touched my hand.

'Don't worry about it Pete, there's no harm done, the flowers are lovely and it's very sweet of you. Although the lady may have looked a bit put out she made a sale that she probably wouldn't have done, so in the long term that's what it's all about.'

'She's right Pete, forget it, you weren't to know. It was a nice gesture and you did it for the right reason and, like Pam said, there's no harm done. Drink your coffee and we'll go and get your head looked at and maybe get some lunch at the club.'

Despite the imminent prospect of being prodded and examined by a strange doctor and that I had also inadvertently managed to insult a proud and defiant lady flower seller, the welcome drive through the city soon began to have a calming and soothing effect and it wasn't long before I began to feel like my old self again.

I had been on an American air force base several times before when Nick had been stationed at RAF Chicksands in Bedfordshire, and although that was a fairly large base shared jointly by the RAF and the Americans, I had never seen anything quite like this. The moment we drove past the armed guards and through the camp gates nothing could have prepared me for the scene that unfolded before me, it was as if I had gatecrashed an enormous and surreal scene being shot for an MGM movie spectacular.

In the distance were several huge menacing Boeing B-52 bombers, each with eight enormous engines standing row upon row in front of cavernous hangers, the engines of each aircraft weighing so heavily that the wings themselves drooped towards the ground. Around each aircraft, groups of technicians and armourers clad in light tan boiler suits with rank and insignia on their sleeves toiled in the hot sun, some wearing baseball caps while others wore the more conventional blue air force headgear.

As I sat spellbound in the back of the car, Nick pointed to several strange looking vehicles which raced to and fro between the aircraft while carrying ominous looking missile-shaped devices, while others returned empty, scurrying back towards what appeared to be heavily fortified bunkers, the high reinforced walls of the concrete outer buildings being guarded by heavily armed men wearing camouflaged uniforms and steel helmets.

'You see those long jeep-like vehicles?' Nick said, pointing out of the window, well they're carrying the ultimate future of warfare my friend. You are looking at the latest form of nuclear weapons that are destined for the Kremlin and all other points east of Zurich if our Russian counterparts are stupid enough to start anything.'

'And God help us all,' Pam said solemnly.

As we skirted around the hangers which clearly housed the aircraft, Nick explained that that the bombers we had just seen were not only intercontinental, but were capable of carrying a nuclear payload of five hundred thousand pounds each... How unaware were we then of the international incident which was about to unfold which would send a shiver down the spines of governments all over the world when one of these very aircraft crashed while carrying just such a nuclear weapon.

Driving past a maze of huts, offices and administrative buildings, I was flabbergasted at the overall size of the place, it looked to all intents and purposes like a small self-contained town constructed within the confines of the airfield.

Stopping at an intersection which allowed a huge fuel tanker the right of way, I looked across to what I took to be the base high school where young men and women sat on the grass outside, some reading or just chatting, while several others clad in baseball jackets and caps, wearing catcher's mitts, pitched a ball to one another amid shouts of encouragement from some of the onlookers.

From a flagpole high up on a wooden church-like steeple, the stars and stripes fluttered proudly from its masthead and, completing the picture of what I imagined to be small town America, the ubiquitous bowling alley also announced its allegiance by also flying its country's flag.

It needed no sign to tell me that we had arrived at the base hospital as Nick pulled into a parking bay in front of an impressive, white three-storey building. A steady stream of both men and women clad in pristine white uniforms entering and leaving, indicated that this was either a real life medical centre, or the set of some fictional, glamorous and totally over the top second world war hospital drama.

As I watched this continuous column of whiter than white individuals going in and out, it was laughably noticeable that they all wore the same aviator-style sunglasses, these Hollywood 'must have' accessories obviously being as typically American as the legendary Jeep motor vehicle. I smiled as I was reminded of the movie *It Came from Outer Space* as the large elliptical lenses reflected the bright sunlight, the overall effect giving the wearer an alien bug-like appearance to their faces.

Entering the building and walking up to the reception desk, behind which sat two strikingly attractive uniformed women, we were greeted by the whitest and most magnificent tooth-filled smiles I had ever seen. Smiling back with my own mouth firmly closed to hide my own lack of dental brilliance, I now realised that this was probably another reason why everyone was wearing those ridiculous sunglasses, encountering such glistening splendour outside in the bright sunshine would almost certainly cause one's eyesight to suffer serious and permanent damage.

Introducing me to one of the 'Playboy of the Month' receptionists, Nick explained the situation, asking if there was a doctor on hand who could take a look at the cut on my head to make sure that everything was as it should be, asking also would it be possible for someone to remove the stitches at the appropriate time.

With totally over the top southern geniality, the woman behind the desk picked up a telephone which, coincidentally, perfectly matched the colour of her teeth and spoke into the mouthpiece, all the time smiling up at me indicating to anyone who may have been watching that it was obvious that we had been lovers for years.

Finally replacing the receiver, she leaned across the top of the desk and pointed down the corridor, this wanton and alarming act offering an unrestricted view of an enormous bosom which stretched the fabric of her uniform jacket and blouse to startling proportions, a bosom which could only have been held in place by some major feat of engineering.

'Well, now. If you all go down the corridor and take the fourth door on the left,' she drawled, 'Lootenant Richards will be glad to take care of you.'

Once again, we were treated to another dazzling smile as she sat back and adjusted the clothing on her substantial upper body, levering it back to its previous precarious and, no doubt, strict regulation position, her parting remark becoming something I was to hear with sickening and monotonous regularity during the rest of my stay.

'You all go and have a nice day now, you hear?'

Less than twenty minutes later and we were once again back in the car and heading for the NCOs' club after having been reassured by a young, good looking officer that my head was 'looking good' and if I cared to come back in about ten days' time he would be glad to take the stitches out, this being followed once again by the seemingly obligatory phrase, 'You all have a nice day now.'

Like most people, I suppose I have at times been guilty of jumping to conclusions without being fully aware of all of the relevant facts, and from where I now stood it was clearly obvious that I had done it again. Having had only a small and very myopic insight into the lives of American servicemen and their families, I should certainly have known better than to surmise what life would be like for off-duty American servicemen when serving overseas, but nothing could have prepared me for what I was now seeing.

Before entering the NCOs' club, my preconceived idea of what it might be like had been that of having to queue at long food counters to be served something which resembled traditional school dinners by women wearing aprons and brandishing ladles who slapped something unrecognisable on to your plate as you shuffled past on your way to a cash desk, a further soulless wilderness staffed by pimply, gum-chewing adolescents... How wrong can you be, and how stupid could I have been to think that Americans would be prepared to suffer the indignities that we English were forced to accept in post-war Britain?

Absolutely amazed at the scene before me, I could only mutter a surprised accolade for both the décor and the ambience of the place.

'Wow, this is really nice,' I said. 'You lot certainly know how to look after yourselves, I wasn't expecting anything like this.'

Pam laughed at the surprised expression on my face.

'Why do you think I married him?' she joked.

'You were at our wedding; don't you remember all the food and the drinks Nick and his buddies brought in from the base for our reception?'

I cast my mind back to the day Pam and Nick married. Rationing hadn't long ended and the village hall just behind the pretty little church in Stopsley had never played host to such a spectacular spread. Every imaginable type of food, together with accompanying drinks, was laid out before the astonished guests, most of whom had never set eyes on such an abundant banquet, and coming so soon after such times of deprivation, every morsel was to be talked about, drooled over and savoured.

There were meats of all description followed by a multitude of different desserts, and to wash it down, American beer. There was also whisky and American bourbon, rum, gin and vodka, an incredible array of drinks which some of the guests had never seen before, all waiting to be mixed with Coca-Cola, tonic water, ginger ale and tomato juice, a banquet which would be talked about for many, many years.

For people like my father and mother, together with uncles and aunts, living in a country that had literally faced starvation since nineteen forty, it must have seemed that the good Lord himself had been instrumental in sending down such a feast as a reward for our diligence and abstinence.

For the sober members of our family, the journey home was a walk of about two miles, but far more for my father and uncle who had increased the distance quite considerably by staggering from one side of the pavement to the other. For curious passers-by it must have resembled a badly performed Lambeth Walk by two men who had forgotten the steps. To his eternal credit, this was the only time I ever saw my father the worse for drink, a rare occasion my mother never ceased to remind him of at Christmas when parties around the festive table began to get over-exuberant.

Looking around the large room at the comfortable surroundings with its leather upholstered chairs gathered around each table, I was glad of the pleasant coolness after the stifling heat outside. Although Nick usually had the air conditioning on in the car unless the windows were wound down to enable him to point out various points of interest, the short walk to the entrance of the club in the blazing sunshine had been one which caused my shirt to cling damply to my back, and to feel this cool air blowing gently against my skin was wonderfully refreshing.

As we obeyed the instructions written on a large, ornate, tasselled card bearing the crest of Strategic Air Command placed on a lectern asking us to wait to be seated, a shout from someone seated at a table at the far side of the room caught our attention.

'Hey, Pam, Nick; over here.'

Looking across, I saw that it was the man we had seen earlier on the bridge.

Pam waved back in acknowledgment as Nick headed in their direction.

'It's Bishop,' he said. 'Let's go join him.'

As we approached the table, the man stood up, a broad grin on his face.

'Hi Nick, hi Pam, come and join us. We've only just got here so we haven't ordered yet.'

Sitting down in one of the unoccupied chairs at the table, Nick introduced me to the man he had referred to simply as Bishop, introducing him together with his wife as Robert and Marie, while she proudly introduced the youngest member of the Bishop household who, if the mood took him, answered to the name of Clifford.

It quickly became apparent why Nick had described Bishop as a 'hell of a character' as he voiced his laconic opinion on the state of the military, the Spanish dictatorship, the cost of cigarettes and beer and even the Pope's latest edict; his comments bringing guffaws of laughter from us all, all that is with the exception of his wife who had presumably heard it all before.

While we talked, a pretty young American waitress arrived at our table to take our orders, introducing herself by saying, 'Hi, my name is Candy and it will be my pleasure to serve you today, how may I help you all?'

Inwardly cringing at this sycophantic introduction and offer of help, I buried my head in the menu which she handed me, deliberately choosing not to notice the way she favoured me with her whiter than white smile, her all too perfect teeth appearing to illuminate the rest of her face like some religious halo.

Reading through the huge list of meals on offer, I finally chose a fourteen ounce T-bone steak which appeared to be the smallest portion of meat of any description on offer, declining the offer of hash browns and grits by not wanting to draw further attention to myself by asking what in hell they were, choosing instead a salad which I felt might go some way in appeasing my digestive system.

Handing back my menu and placing my order with the delectable and dentally perfect Candy, I was treated to another flashing smile followed by a loud giggling comment of 'Oh gee, you're English. I've never met an Englishman before.'

As if orchestrated, every head within a radius of twenty or so feet turned in my direction, their obvious curiosity causing my face to change colour from my normal ashen white to an interesting and brighter shade of embarrassed pink.

With a huge grin on his face that left me in no doubt that I was about to undergo another prolonged period of leg pulling, Nick said, 'I think we'll have two pitchers of Bloody Marys if that's alright with everyone, or would you just prefer a cup of tea, Pete?'

His derision in respect of English etiquette and of me in particular, was, I felt, below the belt but I chose to ignore it as Candy the tooth fairy giggled, bending down to scoop up the menus saying, 'Don't you take no notice of him sugar, he's just jealous because you're so cute. If you all need anything at all, you just call.'

After enduring further torment about me being referred to as 'sugar' and being 'cute', I quickly realised that Bishop's homespun backwoods humour hid a more serious side than was immediately obvious. The more I listened to his more reasoned and studied arguments, the more I became aware that this was a man whose exaggerated country boy style was nothing more than a disguise that camouflaged a far more serious side to his personality.

Listening to them talking, it became obvious that Bishop's expertise also lay in computers as he and Nick discussed problems they had previously encountered, but after some time, both men were told in no uncertain terms that work-related subjects should be left at work as we were there to enjoy ourselves.

After a wonderful meal washed down with several Bloody Marys, the reality and the drama of everyday life in Spain for those who have, and those who have not, suddenly cast a long shadow over the proceedings as Bishop announced that a young boy had been killed during a local corrida that had been staged in a nearby town. He explained that the young man had been hidden by the crowd and shepherded to the front before leaping over the barrier into the ring and confronting the bull with his homemade cape and wooden sword. According to several news broadcasts, the young man had shown great style and panache as he performed three very accomplished and successful passes with his pitiful little cape; an act which, despite a few isolated boos from the crowd, had earned him rapturous applause. Then, suddenly, disaster struck as the boy attempted an almost impossible pass, the bull goring him to death as he made a futile dash for the safety of the barrier.

Love Me, Love My Cat...

Long, leisurely days of discovering more of this beautiful city began to slip by and in my quieter moments I began to think more and more about the date of my enlistment. It was approaching the end of June and I had already been here for nearly three weeks, and the thought of being due back in England in just over two weeks' time to serve Queen and country was something I was certainly not looking forward to.

It had been on a night when Robert, Marie and two more of Nick's friends from the base had arrived for one of the regular poker sessions that the subject of military call-up had crept into the conversation. Bishop had questioned me by asking if serving in the armed forces was still compulsory in England to which I had replied that it was, an answer which prompted him to ask if I was of eligible age for conscription and, if so, when would I have to go? This was a question I had feared might crop up, and was one on which I had rehearsed several evasive but non-committal answers.

Nonchalantly shrugging my shoulders in a dismissive manner, I made light of the situation and replied that I was due to go into the RAF sometime later in the year but I didn't know exactly when. Fortunately, my cousin stopped further questions being asked by gleefully leaning forward to scoop up the pile of chips on the table in front of her after revealing a craftily concealed winning hand, something which evoked several uncomplimentary comments which questioned the morals of innocent looking foreigners whose aim in life was to steal money from susceptible Americans.

My reason in wanting to avoid further questions was perfectly simple. Although Pam and Nick had insisted that I was free to stay with them as long as I wished, I knew that by revealing the date of my incarceration they would behave as responsible surrogate parents and quite rightly advocate that I meet this deadline. It had been difficult enough at home to be 'economical with the truth', and the last thing I wanted was to go through all that again. This was to be my great voyage of discovery and introduction into manhood and nothing was going to stand in its way.

One of the players sitting at the table had been introduced to me as Sergeant McKeaver, the same Sergeant McKeaver who had been savaged by the commissary cat while attempting to help separate Bishop's dog Chico from its feline attacker, his hands and face still bearing vivid testament to the damage his entanglement with the cat had caused. Each time I looked at his torn face and hands, I desperately tried to stifle a smile as I recalled Bishop's account of the incident, but had I have known what was shortly to follow I may have been far more tolerant to his discomfort.

Discarding my cards after another fruitless and disappointing hand, I leaned back in my chair with my hands behind my head to watch the ensuing play, unaware that the battle-scarred ginger cat I had attempted to befriend earlier had silently entered the room and was sitting unnoticed in the open doorway. Suddenly with a howl, the cat launched itself at me, spitting and scratching as it landed squarely on my shoulders, digging its claws into the back of my neck as it gouged and clawed, hissing and spitting before leaping back down and rushing out of the room.

Jumping up out of my chair, I spun round in the direction of the doorway but the cat had made good its escape which was lucky for the cat and also beneficial for the continuation of American and British relationships, because had I have caught it I would have happily strangled it there and then. Tentatively touching the back of my neck, I withdrew my hand and saw the blood on my fingers; great I thought, now I've got the full set, first I whack my head and now I've been savaged by the family cat.

'Welcome to the club', Nick laughed. 'Pam and Marie are the only ones the cat hasn't attacked. I don't know what's wrong with the stupid thing but it does that once in a while. I should have told you to watch out for it, I guess it just has a thing about men.'

'Thanks a bunch,' I muttered amid howls of laughter. 'It would have been nice if you had just thought to mention it, or were you just sitting around waiting for the moment when the cat could get the taste of English blood as well?

'Why do you keep the rotten fleabag anyway if it does things like that? It could have someone's eyes out.'

Getting up from the table, Pam took my arm.

'Come into the kitchen, I'll put some antiseptic on it just in case, you never know what else it has had its claws into today.'

As we walked into the kitchen, I again asked why they would want to keep such a crazy animal.

'It isn't exactly our cat,' she explained, 'I think it's feral. When we first moved in here we thought it belonged to the bar downstairs but Paco says it isn't his either. Nobody seems to know where it comes from so we just put food out for it once in a while and it comes and goes as it likes, otherwise it would probably starve.'

Thinking that would be the best thing that could happen to it, I vowed that this wasn't the end of the matter and a day of atonement for the wretched animal would not be long in coming. However long it took, I made a solemn promise to myself that I would teach that flea-infested excuse for a cat a lesson that it would never forget.

Several days later, Nick had left for work and Pam and Marie had arranged to go out to the PX together to do some girlie shopping, and as this was an area on the base that was strictly off limits to me, I happily agreed that I would stay home and probably wander off to explore some of the city nearer to home which I had previously only seen from the rear seat of the car.

Waving them both off from downstairs, I stopped to pass the time of day with Paco, telling him that I intended to go out and do a bit of exploring on my own and, after having a cup of coffee with him, I left the bar and made my way back upstairs. In front of me I noticed my feline adversary also making its way up the stairs, and giving it a head start, I quietly followed as it entered the apartment through the open door.

Pretending that I hadn't seen it, I walked casually into the kitchen, taking a large jug from inside one of the kitchen units, and filling it with cold water I took it into the room where I had been attacked. It would have been simple just to hurl the water in the direction of the cat but I wanted more than that and nothing was going to give me satisfaction other than complete and utter revenge.

As I returned to the kitchen, I could see the cat's attention firmly focussed on what I was doing. Unobtrusively, I watched the cat as I picked up a large jar of olive oil and some paper kitchen towel from on top of one of the work surfaces, taking it back to where I had left the jug of water. Casually whistling, I strolled into the bathroom, hoping that the cat would remain where it was until I was prepared, and picking up a large shaving mirror on a stand, I returned to where I had left the other things. Risking a quick peek around the doorway, I could see that the cat was still sitting there grooming itself just outside the kitchen door.

With the cat unable to see me from where it now sat, I quietly poured some of the oil on to the tiled floor just to one side and slightly behind the table, wiping it gently across the floor with the paper towel. Sitting down in the same chair I had occupied on the night the cat had pounced, I carefully placed the shaving mirror on the table in front of me, positioning it to enable me to see the open doorway behind. Finally, I strategically placed the jug of water immediately to hand and sat back in the chair with my hands behind my head, exactly as I had when the cat had attacked.

Carefully watching in the mirror, I didn't have long to wait as the cat appeared in the doorway, sitting down to watch me as I twiddled my fingers behind my head. Minutes ticked by as I patiently waited, watching intently in the hope that the cat would make its move, whistling quietly to hopefully instil a sense of ease and relaxation in the room for the benefit of my chewed and scabby adversary.

Suddenly, with a high pitched howl the cat launched itself into the room preparing to leap on my shoulders as it had previously done. It hit the oiled and slippery floor at maximum speed, all thoughts of an all out attack quickly disappearing as it vainly attempted to get all of its feet going in the same direction at the same time.

Picking up the jug of water, I laughed maniacally as I watched the hapless animal desperately trying to apply the brakes as it skidded past where I was sitting, slamming into the opposite wall at no less speed than that of its initial rush. With a look of undisguised panic on its face, the cat's feet flailed and thrashed as it tried desperately to get some sort of traction for a hasty retreat.

With a cry of 'got you, you bastard,' I happily and forcibly administered the *coup de grâce*.

The water from the jug hit the cat forcibly in its face, the impact knocking it back against the wall as it let out a howl of terror. Flinging the last dregs of water on to something that now resembled a drowned rat as it skated past where I sat; my joy knew no bounds as it banged into the leg of my chair in its desperate bid to escape.

After half an hour of diligent scrubbing and wiping, I finally removed all traces of the olive oil from the floor and mopped up the puddle of water. Carefully disposing of the wet and oily paper which if found would have clearly indicated that something untoward had been going on, I congratulated myself on the way my plan had worked, certain that the cat would now think twice before it came anywhere near me and that hopefully it had learned a lesson it would never forget.

Strolling into the bar downstairs, I was still grinning as Paco looked up from his newspaper and called for one of his sons to bring us both a beer.

'You look pleased with yourself *Señor*, what have you been up to?'

Barely able to stop myself from laughing out loud, I walked over to where he was sitting.

'Nothing,' I grinned. 'I was just thinking to myself what a great day it was and that I just might go out and have a little wander around the neighbourhood.'

Warmly shaking his hand I sat down, looking around in the hope I might see in which direction the cat had made its escape as it fled the apartment, hoping that it hadn't been noticed as it exited at full speed via the bar.

As I picked up the beer that had been placed in front of me, Paco pushed across the paper which was still open at the page he had been reading.

'This says that your friend is fighting in Castillo de las Guardas on Sunday,' he said, pointing to an article that gave details of the forthcoming corrida.

Looking at the paper, the handsome face of Jaime stared back at me, his flashing smile reminiscent of how he had looked on the train, only this time he was wearing his bullfight costume. As I struggled with the wording in the article I thought back to our conversation when he had invited me to come and watch him fight at this corrida.

'What does it say Señor Ortega?' I asked eagerly.

'It says that your friend is to fight two bulls from the Ganaderia of Dona Concepcion Concha y Sierra on Sunday at five o'clock. It also mentions that he has shown himself to be brave, very good with the cape and that his muleta and sword skills are exceptional.

'What does that mean, that thing you said about the Granada of Dona something or other, or whatever it was that you said?'

Repeating what he had previously read, he explained that Ganaderias were ranches where fighting bulls are bred and raised, and that Dona Concepcion y Sierra is one of the best known ranches in all of Spain where some of the best bulls have been bred since the 1880s. He went on to explain that this ranch is just outside Seville and it is considered to be a great honour to be given the opportunity to fight bulls from such a prestigious ranch.

'That's marvellous,' I said. 'Jaime gave me the address and the telephone number of his uncle here in the city and he said that if we would like to get in touch with him, he would arrange for us to obtain tickets to see him fight.'

'Do you remember that when I first told you of how I met Jaime on the train Señor Ortega, I asked that perhaps if you weren't too busy you might like to come with us as well; I hope that you will still be able to come?'

Señor Ortega smiled his thanks and inclined his head in a slight bow.

'Nothing would give me greater pleasure *Señor*, and afterwards perhaps you will all do me the great honour of having dinner with me at Los Corales.'

'That would be super, is that a bar near where he is to fight?' I asked.

The little bar owner smiled.

'No, this is not a bar,' he answered. 'Los Corales is a restaurant in the Calle de Sierpes here in Seville where many matadors like to go to eat after a corrida and discuss how bravely the matador has fought, or how badly the bull has performed. I often go there with friends so I am known there. I think you will find the food to be of the highest quality and hopefully we will have a good table where we can see who is dining. Perhaps you will also permit me to show you just a small part of my city, places that maybe the *senora* and the *senor* are not familiar with?'

'That sounds wonderful,' I said, barely able to conceal my excitement, 'I'll tell Pam and Nick when they get back and they can telephone Jaime's uncle and make the arrangements.'

Hardly able to suppress my excitement at the prospect of being able to watch Jaime fight, I questioned Señor Ortega further at what we might expect to see and whether the ring in which he was to appear was as beautiful as the one here in Seville, and although he said that it was not in the same league as the Maestranza, it made no difference as I excitedly thought of what was to come.

Gulping down the remainder of my beer, I offered my apologies in wanting to rush off and explore, adding that if he happened to see either Pam or Nick before I did, I would be grateful if he would mention our conversation.

When I first arrived, I had noticed a few small fascinating looking local shops tucked away in small shaded alleyways not far from the bar, not large shops with well lit windows and interesting displays, but small cluttered shops with dark inviting interiors whose exteriors were festooned with baskets, local knick-knacks and other small bits and pieces that definitely demanded closer inspection.

After having visited a couple of shops and failing to find anything of interest, I stepped inside a darkened cavern of a place, standing stock still and not daring to move until my eyes became acclimatised to the darkness after the glaring brightness of outside. The first thing I became aware of apart from the immediate blackness was an all encompassing earthy, leathery smell; the second and more importantly, was the vast array of things for sale. Everywhere I looked I could see that every nook and corner was crammed with various consumable items.

In amongst rickety wooden shelving, boxes were haphazardly strewn across the floor from which spilled earth-covered potatoes together with the odd neglected onion. Piles of open crates containing oranges, apples and peaches all mingled quite naturally with cabbages and cauliflowers, while long strings of garlic hung from nails banged into wooden posts which appeared to be the only support for the ceiling above, this local produce casually forming the shop's fruit and veg department.

Suspended from the ceiling, all manner of shirts, blouses, jumpers and other items of workaday clothing were loosely attached to wire coat hangers, all looking like large colourful bats waiting for nightfall when they would undoubtedly release themselves from their restrictive moorings to flap around the shop to feast on the flies which buzzed and circled around everything. Elsewhere, cabinets containing warped and twisted shelves sagged alarmingly beneath the weight of hundreds of dusty items, sufficient in quantity to furnish and decorate an average sized town.

Hardly daring to touch anything, I gazed around this Aladdin's cave, my immediate attention drawn to two round wooden plates on which were painted scenes from a bullfight. One featured an exquisitely dressed matador performing an elaborate and flamboyant pass with a huge blood-red cape, while on another, a *banderillero* leaped high in the air to plunge a pair of barbed darts into the shoulders of a charging bull. To my naïve and gullible mind, I thought that these two beautiful works of art would not have been out of place if displayed alongside many of the more traditional paintings I had seen exhibited in the Louvre.

Carefully taking down the two plates from where they were precariously balanced, I blew off the dust that had obviously been on them since their introduction to the shop and ran my fingers over the thickly painted figures. I was in no doubt that these two items were, without doubt, worthy of gracing the walls of the most discerning person's home, definite 'must haves' for anyone with a sense of style and good taste. Admiring them again after having brushed off the remainder of the dust together with a long dead fly that was suspended from a thin cobweb, they looked even more spectacular, instantly reassuring me that if any form of appeasement present was necessary on my return to England, these would do the job admirably.

Handing my works of art to an elderly lady sitting behind a rustic wooden counter, I wondered if her choice of clothing had been deliberate, blending in as she did with the dark interior of the shop, her all black clothing making her virtually invisible. Putting my change into my pocket, I watched as my bargains were 'wrapped'.

Clutching my purchases which had been simply bundled up in newspaper and pushed into a brown paper bag, I left the shop smiling secretively to myself as I recalled the cat's mercurial exit from the apartment, wondering if it had dried out by now and had subsequently returned after its skating debut and unscheduled bath.

When I got back, Pam and Nick were already home, Pam unloading groceries from long brown paper bags while Nick lounged on the sofa, perfecting his much practised leisure activity of drinking beer.

'Hi buddy,' he called. 'Get yourself a beer and take the weight off.'

'I spoke to Paco when we got back and he showed me the article in the paper. He also told me what you had said so I rang your bullfighting buddy but he wasn't there, but I did get to speak to his uncle and we're definitely on for Sunday.'

A derisive laugh came from the direction of the kitchen as Pam appeared in the doorway.

'I shouldn't pin your hopes too high on old Pancho there, he was actually having to speak Spanish to your friend's uncle, and from what I heard it could well be that we might be getting a new set of tyres for the car plus some new chairs for the balcony.'

Despite feeling slightly apprehensive at the prospect of Nick getting it wrong, I laughed at my cousin's interpretation of Nicks attempt at conversing in Spanish.

'Get back in that kitchen, woman. Me and old Pepé there, or whatever his name was got on real well.'

'Oh that's all right then,' she sneered. 'Is he going to deliver the new tyres and chairs or do we have to go over there and pick them up?'

Skipping back from the doorway, she narrowly missed being hit by one of the big cushions Nick hurled in her direction.

'Take no notice, Pete; a jealous streak like that in a woman isn't too pretty.'

Nick pulled his wallet from his back pocket and took out a slip of paper on which he had scribbled down some of the details and times.

Quickly skimming through what he had written, he looked up and said, 'We need to be there in plenty of time to catch this one guy who's working at this particular "*sombra*" entrance and he'll have the tickets all ready for us to pick up.'

'Is that as well as our new tyres and furniture?' was the shout from the kitchen.

Laughing at my cousin's final sarcastic remark, I asked, 'What's all that about when you said the *sombra* entrance?'

'Well, at bullfights, you get to either sit in the sun which is called *sol*, or in the shade which is *sombra*'.

'Where is it best to sit then?' I asked. 'Is it better if you sit in the sun?'

'Hell no,' he retorted. 'It's the other way round. If you've ever sat for about three hours squinting into the sun you'll know why it's better to sit in the shade.'

As I sipped my beer and thought about the coming Sunday, Pam came into the lounge and flopped down on the sofa next to me, picking up my bag of recent purchases and peeping inside.

'Paco said that you were off on some sort of mission, what did you buy?'

'You can have a look if you like. I found them in this super little shop that sells absolutely everything and I thought that Mum and Dad might like them.'

Taking the plates out of the newspaper and holding each one at arm's length, Pam cocked her head from side to side as she studied them.

'Yes,' she said at last, although not very convincingly. 'They're quite nice but not exactly my cup of tea, but they are nicely painted. They'll look even better when you've wiped all that crap off them.'

Nick took the plates from her and ran his fingers over them, just as I had done in the shop.

'Yeah, I think they're pretty neat. Where did you say you got them? I wouldn't mind a couple of those for in here.'

'Hold on Pancho,' Pam snorted. 'We see and hear enough old bull downstairs.'

Sunday dawned as every other day had dawned, the sun shone through the half-closed shutters making intricate patterns of light and shade across the tiled floor of my bedroom, but today it was different, today I was going to see my first bullfight.

Although we had stayed up pretty late playing poker with the usual bunch, I had barely slept with the prospect of today's adventure uppermost in my mind. I had looked again at the photos in the magazine I had bought in Madrid in an attempt to translate some of the wording in the hope that I could familiarise myself with the names of some of the passes and the sequence of events for the afternoon. Trying to remember what I had read and what I had been told, I was beginning to wonder if the complexities of what lay ahead might be all too baffling. Not only that, would I find the spectacle of an animal being ritually slaughtered completely abhorrent?

Pam had also expressed concerns at what the afternoon might have in store, but tempted by Paco's enticing offer of dinner in a restaurant which offered not only fine dining, but also an insight into the more glamorous world of the matador, she had agreed to go.

With breakfast finished, I poured myself another cup of coffee from the always 'on the go' percolator and took it out on to the balcony where I sat in my usual position with my bare feet resting on the rail, my mind wrestling with various aspects of the conversation Paco and I had had earlier.

I had popped down to the bar below to find out what time we should be thinking about leaving for Castillo de las Guardas, and during the course of our conversation I asked about some of the less obvious aspects of the fight. What happened prior to the matador's entry into the ring and what sort of preparations would Jaime be making in preparation for the afternoon ahead?

Explaining what went on behind the scenes, Paco explained that at midday the bulls that would be taking part in the afternoon's corrida would be taken to the arena and driven into a holding pen where the ritual called the *sorteo* would take place. He explained that this procedure would be witnessed by each matador's representative who would draw lots to see which animals each would fight. Explaining that it was done in this way to ensure absolute fairness, he said that in some of the smaller towns which hosted bullfights, there could be considerable differences in the characteristics of each animal. One bull may be bigger, another might have a wider spread of the horns and also the ages of the bulls might differ drastically so the animals are paired together with differences like that in mind.

After the pairings had been carried out to everyone's satisfaction, the brand numbers of each bull were then written on small pieces of paper which are placed in a hat and drawn out by each matador's representative. He explained that this simple ritual had begun in the very early days of the corrida and had been used ever since to ensure that everything is fair and above board and that no matador has any choice in respect of any of the animals he is to meet in the ring.

Calling on his own past experience, he explained that for some matadors this was the worst time of all. Some he said, surrounded themselves with friends to joke and enjoy light-hearted conversations that have little to do with what lay ahead, while others preferred to remain alone, preparing themselves for the forthcoming struggle.

As I listened, it became obvious that he was reliving his own past, explaining that if ever there are moments of doubt and fear prior to when the big wooden gates were swung open and the bulls enter the arena, it is then that even the bravest of matadors would willingly exchange places with the most humble employee in the stadium.

There was a slight pause before he continued as he took a sip from his coffee, a dreamy faraway look in his eyes suggesting that this was a situation he had faced many times.

'Every matador is aware that from that point on there can be no turning back, this is that time and he is now on his own. He will be helped to change into his *traje de luces* by his dresser who might be a close friend, someone who has been with him throughout his career, or perhaps a relative. Some matadors will give this honour to their sword boy who they literally trust with their life, but it will be given to someone who is capable of putting him at his ease, someone who will calm and reassure him.

'Many matadors,' he said, 'are superstitious and will go through an identical ritual each time they are to fight. Each item of dress must be laid out in precisely the same order before they go into the chapel to pray, for this is the time when they must conquer their fear and not think about what might happen if things go badly wrong.'

I listened enthralled as he painted a picture in words of those final moments before the *torero* enters the ring, my mind leaping ahead and picturing the scene in which, even at that moment, Jaime was preparing to be one of the leading characters.

As I got up to leave, the little bar owner laughed dryly as he told me the name that is often cynically applied when describing the red and yellow national flag of their country, a name derisively given in respect of what is invariably seen at a bullfight.

'Do you know, my young friend, what we who have the '*afición*' call our national flag here in Spain?'

I shook my head and grinned as I waited in anticipation of some ludicrous name that he might be about to apply to the flag. As he leaned forward slightly in his seat as if he were about to whisper some private joke that no-one else was entitled to hear, his dark eyes staring intently into mine.

'We call it Old Blood and Pus.'

At that moment, despite the warmth from the afternoon sun, his cold blooded definition sent a shiver down my spine as I recoiled in shock from those terrible words. Until now, all I had to draw on were glossy and romantic images of brave young men and equally brave bulls pictured in a magazine, a Hollywood portrayal, if you like, of the heroic struggle between man and beast, but now it was different as those four words suddenly encapsulated the primitive struggle for life itself.

Deep in thought, I failed to hear Nick's entry into the room and jumped as he stood by my shoulder.

'Man, where were you buddy? You were miles away, are you getting homesick?'

I shook my head and laughed.

'No, I was just thinking of something Paco said.'

It was Nick's turn to laugh as he said, ' I shouldn't take too much notice of what that old horse trader says, he's got more crap in him than what's in those bull pens down at the Maestranza. By the way, have you seen that darn cat today? Pam says she hasn't seen it since we went out yesterday.'

'A Sport it Ain't.'

Since my arrival, I now felt that I was pretty well versed in who had built what and when it had been built, or which king or Moorish dignitary had used which particular building for what purpose. I had thought Pam and Nick were pretty well clued in to the history and the geography of Seville, but in sitting in the front seat of Paco's big black Mercedes, it became a whole different ball game as I listened to his descriptive and sensitive interpretation of this wonderful city. Here clearly was a man passionately in love with the city in which he had been born. Even Nick who was sitting in the rear of the car began to enthusiastically question our host about places of historical interest, questions which Paco proudly answered by going to great and detailed lengths to eloquently describe.

It was however, when passing the great Gothic cathedral that Nick's usual sarcastic banter was completely silenced when Paco laughingly pointed out that if Christopher Columbus or Amerigo Vespucci, after whom the United States of America is named, hadn't first knelt in prayer in front of the great altar, neither Nick or any other of his 'new world' countrymen would be here at all.

As we crawled past the Maestranza, described by many as the most beautiful Plaza de Toros in the world, it buzzed with activity from lottery ticket vendors and souvenir sellers as our tour guide continued with his informative dialogue.

'I'm sure that since you have been here you have seen this beautiful arena, but did you know that it is also the second oldest. The arena here was built in the year 1761 and it is only in the lovely city of Ronda that you will see one which is older. Before the Maestranza was built, bulls were fought by men on foot in the public squares, but as with all things, someone soon realised that there was much money to be made from charging people to watch and as a result, wooden arenas were erected in cities and towns and people paid to watch, when the fights were over, the arenas were taken down and moved on to somewhere else. The word "sand" in Spanish is "arena" and this was just thrown down to cover the cobbles. It was here that the first wooden arena was built, and then in 1743, another was built in Madrid and then a third in Ronda.

'Although we fought with the Romans and the Moors before finally driving them out of Spain, it was the Romans who left us this heritage as it was they who built the first amphitheatre here to show off their Roman circus. Their arenas were built to hold chariot races but men also fought to the death with wild animals, so it can be argued that our modern arenas are copies of what they first built.'

'I know that Spain is actually the home of bullfighting and there are some arenas in Mexico and South America, but are there any elsewhere?' I asked.

Paco grinned from ear to ear as he answered.

'Has Señor Dumas not mentioned his valiant American countrymen who have tasted the ecstasy of the corrida? I am surprised that he has been so reluctant to sing their praises, or can it possibly be that he does not know of them?'

Sensing that this was to be the start of a further round of good humoured banter between them, I went along with what he was saying and kept a straight face as I waited to hear what he was about to say.

'No,' I replied. 'He hasn't mentioned any Americans apart from Ernest Hemingway, but he wasn't a bullfighter was he?'

'You are quite right my young friend, Señor Hemingway was truly an aficionado and of course he wrote that great classic, *Death in the Afternoon*, in 1932 just four years before the start of the civil war, but he did not face the bulls.'

I turned and looked at Paco as he glanced in the rear-view mirror to where Nick sat stoically awaiting the next inevitable dig at his ancestry.

'Are you seriously saying that Señor Dumas has never told you of Harper Lee and of Sydney Franklin,' he said, sounding seriously aghast.

'No,' I answered, trying hard to stop myself from laughing out loud as I entered into the spirit of Paco's feigned surprise, eager to know what was coming next.

'You never said that there were American matadors Nick, did you not know?'

I was enjoying Paco's barbed jibes and the inference that Nick's knowledge of American bullfighting history might be sadly lacking, but I also revelled in this as recompense for his derision at my embarrassment in respect of the earlier episode with the dressing gown.

Before Nick could answer, Paco, who was clearly enjoying this game of one-upmanship, delivered the coup de grâce.

'Surely he must have mentioned the beautiful Bette Ford and Patricia McCormick, I cannot believe that he hasn't told you about these brave and exciting women?'

'No,' I gasped, momentarily dismissing this game of partisan pride as I tried to imagine a woman pitting her courage against a bull, an alarming host of images causing me to stop in midstream as I struggled with the whole concept.

'You can't be serious?' I said, 'women matadors?'

'Oh yes,' he replied. 'I have heard that not only are they very beautiful but they are also very good. I have never seen either fight but I have read much about them.'

Intrigued by the prospect of any woman having sufficient courage to fight a bull, I questioned the bar owner further.

'You said "are" very good; do you mean that they are actually still fighting now?'

'Yes, very much so. They fight mainly in Mexico and in the towns which run along the Mexican-American border but not here in Spain. I have spoken to others who have seen them perform and I understand that they both possess great skill.'

I shook my head at the thought of a woman putting her life on the line in such a fashion.

'How can women pluck up the courage to do something like that? I would think that it's only men who have the strength and the heart to do that sort of thing.'

'What makes you think that it's only men who have a capacity for being stupid?' Pam snorted from the back. 'No disrespect Paco, but you don't just need stamina and heart to become a bullfighter, I think you need to be crazy as well. Mind you, having said that, they probably look more like men than a lot of actual men I've met recently.'

'On the contrary Señora, I have seen photographs of them and they are both very beautiful woman. Bette Ford in particular was once a model and also a fine actress before she took up the muleta.'

'OK Paco, you've got me, I have to admit that I've never heard of either of them,' Nick chipped in. 'where are they from, do you know?'

'Bette Ford is from New York and Patricia McCormick was born in St. Louis. I understand that they get top billing wherever they fight and that they are already rated extremely highly in Mexico, but whether either of them will take the *alternativa* here in Spain is a different matter. From my own limited knowledge of them I have to say that it is, as you Americans say, a very different ball game over here.'

Satisfied with his verbal victory, Paco squeezed the big car into a street that appeared only large enough to accommodate an average-sized wheelbarrow and slowly brought the car to a gentle halt. Pointing across the narrow road in the direction of a small but very exclusive looking shop, there in the centre of the window was an object that caused my jaw to drop in astonishment. Carefully fitted on to a tailor's dummy was the most unbelievably beautiful costume imaginable, the traditional suit worn by both matadors and *banderilleros* alike, the incredible *traje de luce*, or in English, 'the suit of lights'.

This breathtaking example of the tailor's art was made from pure silk and dyed a rich deep pink. The short bolero jacket was adorned with heavy gold and silver wire which had been fashioned into flowers, this ornamentation following the line of the jacket down each breast to where exquisitely fashioned lapels flowed like a river of silver and gold from around the neck to adorn its back and arms.

On each shoulder, heavy epaulettes, also fashioned from gold and silver wire, overlapped on to each arm, and as one final glorious tribute, small tassels made from the same rich materials hung like small shimmering bells, each one catching and reflecting the sunlight like small glittering torches.

To accompany the jacket, superbly tailored skin-tight three quarter length trousers made from the same coloured silk were adorned on the outside of each leg with the same beautiful design, echoing precisely that of the sleeves and back of the jacket. Finally, replicating those which hung from the shoulders of the jacket, two small tassels hanging from the bottom of each leg completed this fantastic work of art.

'This is the shop of Señor Manfredi, the creator of the finest *traje de luces* in the world. The jacket is called a *chaquetilla*, and because it is made using pure gold and silver wire thread, it is extremely heavy. Only the very top matadors can afford a suit such as those made by Manfredi, it is like owning the very best car or the very best pair of shotguns. When you wear the suit designed and made by this man, people will recognise you as being the very best.'

'What would something like that cost?' I asked.

Paco shrugged.

'A suit such as the one in the window costs hundreds of thousands of pesetas and will have been made especially for a matador who will have agreed to let Señor Manfredi display it for a short time. If you were to go closer, you will see who it has been made for, but be assured that it will have been made for the very best.

'Each and every suit made by Señor Manfredi is something very special and will have been made from the finest materials. Each stitch and every thread will have been sewn by hand and it will have taken many months together with many fittings to create something so beautiful. If you were to sit here long enough and watch, you would see the greatest matadors the world has ever seen pass through those doors.'

Paco glanced at his watch as he pulled away from the kerb.

'I think that we should leave for Castillo de las Guardas now, I am very curious to see how generous your new friend has been in his choice of tickets for us.'

Shrugging his shoulders philosophically, he gave a wry laugh.

'I think even if we find ourselves sitting in the sun today we must accept this inconvenience and be grateful for his generous gift.'

From the back of the car, Pam snorted at Paco's acceptance of this worst case scenario.

'I'm sorry,' she said. 'I don't care how generous you think his offer is, there's no way I'm going to sit in the sun for three hours watching some dumb animal being slaughtered.'

She continued with a wry laugh as she said.

'I still won't be ecstatic if he's given us the best seats in the house, but as far as topping up my tan by sitting staring into the sun all afternoon, no way José, so you guys will have to excuse me while I slip off and find a nice little bar somewhere and you guys can catch up with me later.'

To be honest, my first sight of the bullring in Castillo de las Guardas was somewhat disappointing, but to be fair, after seeing the glorious edifice that is El Maestranza, any other bullring in the world is likely to pale into insignificance and bearing that in mind it would be unfair to make a comparison between the two.

The stadium itself is constructed mainly from stone, gathered and carved from the surrounding areas and dragged into position by teams of mules and put lovingly into place by skilled local artisans, men who fashioned the arena with both love and pride. Although never acclaimed to be one of the most beautiful arenas in the world, it was on this unfashionable sand that the great Juan Belmonte once performed brilliantly to a capacity crowd of more than six thousand delirious spectators.

Carefully steering the vehicle between throngs of excited people already heading for the entrances to the arena, a few continued to walk down the centre of the road, stepping aside at the last moment to peer curiously into the car.

'What the hell is wrong with these people, are they trying to get themselves killed?' Nick asked as more and more people began to gather around the car.

Giving a brief toot on the horn in an attempt to clear the way ahead, Paco explained that they were just curious, saying that it was usually matadors and their entourage who arrived in vehicles such as his, and they were simply eager to catch a glimpse of the afternoon's combatants.

Slowly inching his way forward, a path suddenly opened up in front of us as two uniformed Guardia Civil officers began to use their heavy batons to clear the way, pausing only to beckon us forward through the dispersing crowd.

Although the blows the two men were administering weren't delivered using all of their might, I was shocked at this show of brutality.

'That's a bit much isn't it?' I muttered, 'I don't think there was any need for that. They only wanted to see who we were, they weren't doing any harm.'

'They don't need much of an excuse to lay into people with those clubs, most of them are just a bunch of thugs,' Nick growled. 'They're not like your local downtown cops, they're Franco's civil guard, and you don't mess with those guys if you know what's good for you.'

I looked back through the rear window half expecting to see some sort of protest at the treatment which had been meted out, but it was as if nothing had happened as the crowd carried on towards the stadium, meekly accepting the beatings as being nothing out of the ordinary.

Pulling up near to one of the entrances to the arena, Paco switched off the engine, quickly glancing back to where the incident had occurred.

'Señor Dumas is correct in what he says. Here in Spain during our civil war, men wearing uniforms similar to those behaved worse than animals.'

He shrugged.

'Although those days are now virtually over, it is unwise to think that people like those we have just seen are simply policemen; they are much more than that.'

Still feeling slightly uneasy at what we had just witnessed, Pam and I followed Nick and Paco as they made their way towards one of the entrances, around whose stone archways posters advertising the afternoon's corrida were pasted.

While the two men disappeared from view into one of the entrances, I stood looking at several posters depicting matadors performing their elegant and dangerous art, beneath which were names of matadors who had previously fought in the arena, one of these names leaping out at me, that of the great Juan Belmonte.

'I don't believe it,' Pam laughed as a shout from ahead caught her attention. 'We've either got tickets for the show or we're now the proud owners of a new set of tyres for the car and some balcony furniture.'

I remembered her earlier derogatory comments when she had questioned Nick's ability to converse in Spanish with Jaime's uncle and started to laugh.

'I think he's pretty good,' I argued. 'I wish I could speak Spanish.'

'So does old Pancho over there.' She grinned. 'I bet he's never told you of the time when he and I ended up having to drink twelve beers between us when we first got here because he tried out his Spanish on a waiter and got it wrong?'

'You're having me on,' I spluttered. 'What did he say?'

'Who? Nick or the waiter?'

'Nick.'

'Well instead of saying *dos* which is Spanish for two, my bilingual husband actually said *doce* which means twelve. I don't know who was more surprised, Nick when the beer arrived, or the waiter when he took the order. Ask him if you don't believe me, mind you, knowing what he's like he will probably tell you that he was just trying to save the waiter from having to go backwards and forwards all the time.'

'What did you do?' I laughed. 'Don't tell me that you actually drunk them all?'

'You'd better believe it,' she said. 'There was no way old Pancho there was going to admit that he'd got it wrong. I think, if I remember rightly, I only had three and Nick drank the other nine. Not only that, we had to leave the car where it was and get a taxi home and he spent the rest of the day nipping in and out the toilet.'

Practically doubled over with laughter as I imagined Nick struggling to drink nine beers, we walked over to where he was standing, a broad grin on his face as he waived a handful of tickets in our direction.

Pam raised her eyebrows and heaved a huge theatrical sigh as she saw his face.

'Oh my God, look at his face, he's going to be unbearable.'

Happily waving the tickets under my cousin's nose, Nick cashed in on his moment of triumph.

'There you go honey, how's that? Not bad for a guy, who according to some can't speak the language, practically the best seats in the house. Four tickets, three rows from the front, with cushions and in the shade, what do you have to say now my little transatlantic bride?'

Looking at me, Pam shook her head sadly.

'What did I tell you Pete? Unbearable, bloody unbearable.'

There was no doubt that we could not have been given much better seats if the president himself had been responsible for the choosing. To me, it was like being in front of the royal box on cup final day. We would be sitting comfortably in the shade just three rows above the barrier which separated us from where the matadors would be standing before entering the ring; it could hardly have been better.

I could barely contain my excitement as we took our seats, Paco who was sitting next to me pointed to the gate from behind which the bulls would be released from their pens to hurtle into the sanded arena, also pointing towards the entrance through which the procession, or '*paseillo*', would also enter.

Immediately above and behind us, the president's box, which was decorated and adorned with the Spanish flag, jutted out to form a segregated area, the first few rows of this enclosed area obviously designated as being where honoured guests would be invited to enjoy the afternoon's spectacle.

As I stared at the large flag, I was reminded of Paco's chilling words when he had described the colours of the national flag as being 'old blood and pus', his description now having a far more sobering effect now that I was about to witness the reality of blood being deliberately spilled for the first time in my young life.

'Is that Franco in the president's box?' I whispered as I stared up to where a group of men, some in uniform were sitting talking.

'No,' Paco laughed. 'It is probably the mayor of the town or perhaps someone who has donated money to the local hospital and is trying to gain favour for some political reason, Franco would not come here unless it is for a very special occasion. El Caudillo prefers to be seen in Madrid or Seville and would consider that this place is of little importance and not grand enough for such a great man as himself.'

As we talked, Paco described how the arena was designed, pointing to the barrier behind which the matadors and their assistants could safely stand. This *callejón*, or passageway, containing openings from where the matadors would enter the ring, each opening protected by a wooden barrier called a *burladero*, designed in such a way to deny access to a charging bull. On the other side of the barrier, a shelf called the 'stirrup' ran around the entire circumference of the ring where a matador, if he found himself in trouble, could launch himself from there over the barrier to safety.

Suddenly aware of a growing feeling of expectation that quietened the noise from the crowd, I glanced at my watch. It was as if looking at the time had been some sort of signal as the hush was shattered by the shrill strident sound of a single trumpet. Seconds later, the brittle sound of the instrument faded away on the soft evening breeze to be replaced by the passionate and vibrant strains of a *paso doble* which heralded the entry into the ring of a magnificently costumed procession. I felt my breath become caught in my throat at the majesty and the splendour of the scene below, it was as if I had been transported back in time to a different civilisation and was witnessing the procession of gladiators entering a Roman coliseum.

At the head of the majestic and colourful procession rode two men, both exquisitely attired in black doublet and hose wearing matching black hats decorated with red and gold plumes and white gauntlets of the period of King Felipe II. Paco explained that these were the *alguacilillos*, both sitting proudly astride high stepping horses, harness and bridles matching exactly the colour of the riders' gloves.

Behind these came the *cuadrillas*, or teams of participants marching in time to the music, these *cuadrillas* being led by the three participating matadors, their heavy and elaborate ceremonial cloaks wrapped tightly around their bodies.

I could scarcely breathe as I watched enthralled at this magnificent procession making its way towards the centre of the ring. Climbing to his feet, Paco enthusiastically applauded as he pointed down at the colourful scene in front of us.

'What you are seeing now has not changed for hundreds of years. The matador you see on the left of the procession is always the senior matador and next to him in seniority is the man on the right, and today of course your new friend Jaime is the most junior and his correct position is in the centre of the *cuadrillas*.'

Listening to Paco's explanation of these formalities, I realised with a start that I had become so enthralled by the spectacle unfolding before us that I had not noticed that the matador in the centre of the procession was indeed Jaime.

Leaping to my feet, I thrust my fingers into my mouth and whistled as loudly as I could, oblivious of the glares of people around us as I shouted and called his name, Paco joining me in my noisy salute as he too clapped and cheered our current hero.

As the procession made its way around the arena to pass directly in front of us, Jaime's eyes scanned the crowd, his handsome face breaking into a broad smile as he nodded in our direction. If I had been given a knighthood by Her Majesty herself, I could not have felt more proud as I frantically waved both arms in response.

Behind these modern day gladiators marching in single file came the *banderilleros*, etiquette and custom dictating that they too paraded in order of seniority, and behind them four mounted picadors, each of their horses swathed in what appeared to be red mattresses designed to offer protection from the bull's onslaught. On the backs of the horses, picadors sat squarely on traditional heavy leather saddles. Wearing the traditional broad-brimmed, round felt hats, they were clad in tight three quarter length trousers and short decorative bolero style jackets, their legs protected by steel leggings, while their feet rested in heavy protective metal stirrups.

While less flamboyant than the high stepping horses leading the parade, they added their own brand of pageantry as they easily bore the burden of their riders. Each one of these rather burly and somewhat rotund men were armed with the necessary tools of their trade, long spiked poles called 'picas' held erect, the less formidable end of these lances resting easily in one of their armoured stirrups.

As I stared at what can only be described as modern day gladiatorial knights astride their war horses, I noticed that all of the horses wore blindfolds and were dutifully following the instructions being given by their riders by means of judicious prodding of heels and tweaking and tugging of the respective reins.

'Why are the horses wearing blindfolds?' I asked Paco tentatively, remembering reading in my magazine the role of the picadors, but at the same time thinking that I really didn't want to hear his explanation.

'It is so that the horse does not see the bull,' he answered. 'If they do not wear the blindfold when the bull makes his charge, they may panic and the rider may be thrown, then he would be at the mercy of the bull as he lies on the ground.'

Looking back at the picadors as they passed in front of us, my gut feeling was that if they were to fall then they should take their chances on the ground in the same way that the matador has to.

'But surely,' I continued, 'the horse can smell and hear the bull so why not let him see what he is up against. If the horse sees the bull coming towards him he could step to one side so he doesn't have to take the hit?'

Patiently, Paco carried on with his explanation.

'The horse does not always receive the charge because the picador, if he is good, will hold the bull off with the pica. Sometimes the bull will not receive the pica at all and he will have to be fought without such wounds. There is only a limited time in which the picador has to do his job, and when the trumpet sounds, if the bull is untouched, the matador must continue the fight while it still has all of its strength, and trust me when I say that is not something you look forward to.'

I sensed that Paco was not entirely thrilled by my questioning of the age old rituals and his final answer when it came caused our conversation to cease abruptly.

'You must understand that the picador has to be allowed the opportunity of using his pica to bring down the head of the bull. If the horse were to see the bull when it charged, it may be that it would not stand squarely to receive it, and if this were to happen, not only could the picador be thrown to the ground, but the horse may also be injured as it turns away. Also, if the horse were to rear up on its hind legs it would expose its stomach and present an easy target and that could be fatal to both the horse and the rider.'

Realising that it would be crass to continue with my argument, I watched as the lesser mortals of the bullfighting fraternity also proudly played out their role in the procession as a pair of mules decorated with plumes and tassels led by their handlers brought up the rear. I knew from seeing the pictures in my magazine that it was the job of the mules and their handlers to drag out the bodies of the dead bulls, while finally, four men carrying what appeared to be long wooden rakes for raking over the sand, brought the elaborate procession to a close.

The colourful troupe of both men and animals crossed the arena to stop in front of the president's box, each matador doffing his *montera* as gladiators might have also done in saluting the emperor in ancient Rome. I cynically imagined that this salutation might be similar to that of 'we who are about to die salute you'.

With the ceremonies completed, each man took up his required position behind the barrier in front of us, each of the matadors swapping their heavy dress capes for their working capes or the muleta, a smaller red flannel cape supported by a short wooden pole. It is his skill with the muleta and the cape on which the matador's performance is judged. However thrilling, it is relatively insignificant how accomplished or flamboyant he might be if choosing to place his own banderillas, it is his work with the capes that his courage and ultimate skill will be judged on. It will be his performance with the 'cloth' which will either be his passport to fame and fortune, or alternatively the medium on which his obituary is written.

Watching the matadors below practising the passes they would be performing if they are to escape being impaled on the animal's lethal horns, the feeling of tension became palpable around the hushed arena as the keys to the *toril*, or bull pens, were thrown down from the presidential box to the keeper, the man allotted to this task deferentially bowing and hurrying away to attend to his deadly charges.

Suddenly, the blood tingling sound of a high-pitched trumpet ripped through the still air as the big wooden gates to my right swung open to reveal a cavernous blackness. Nothing could have prepared me for what came next. For several seconds nothing happened, then, like an express train roaring out of a darkened tunnel, the most magnificent animal I had ever seen hurled itself out into the bright sunlight.

As the crowd roared, the bull startled by the sudden and unexpected noise skidded to a halt, sand flying from beneath its hooves as it shook its huge head from side to side, foaming saliva flying from its mouth in all directions as the animal took in its surroundings, snorting and pawing the ground with its front feet as it searched for something or someone on which to vent its fury.

It is no exaggeration to say that I was horrified as I stared at this awesome creature, the photographs in my magazine instantly paling into meaningless caricatures of what I was now seeing. How was it possible that anyone in their right mind could even contemplate confronting such an animal? The beast that pawed the sand in front of me was not some docile farmyard creature whose sole function in life was to tamely chew grass and perpetuate its bloodline through its progeny; this was a dangerous killer, as dangerous and lethal as anything kept behind bars in a zoo.

Unable to believe either the size or the speed of the animal, I turned to speak to Paco and heard him gasp as he said, '*Madre Dios*, it's a cathedral!'

It could not have been described in a more appropriate way.

The deadly looking horns were at least four and a half feet from tip to tip, while the hump of muscle on its neck and shoulders rippled and shivered as it continued to swing its huge head from side to side seeking anything that moved.

Pawing the ground, the bull stood nearly as tall as any man at the shoulder, its tail slashing angrily against the brand mark and number on its flanks. Suddenly, its attention was drawn to a movement as one of the matadors' *cuadrilla* stepped out from behind one of the *burladeros* where he had been observing the bull's mannerisms. The crowd roared as the man stepped forward brandishing his cape and shouting to attract the bull's attention, the animal needing no encouragement as it raced towards him with an astonishing burst of speed.

I hardly dared breathe as the man stood his ground, sweeping the bull past with an elaborate swirl of his cape, the wicked looking horns slashing upwards as its front hooves completely left the ground, its horns ripping past the man's chest. As the bull skidded to a halt and whirled around to resume its attack, the man dodged back behind the barrier, the bull's horns slamming into the woodwork sending jagged splinters flying into the air. Looking bemused at how it had managed to miss its intended target, the bull snorted as it backed slowly towards the centre of the ring, shaking its head and looking towards where the matador had made his escape.

As it stood snorting and pawing the ground, the man again left the sanctuary of the barrier, this time from its other side to repeat the process, flourishing his cape in a breathtaking pass as the bull hurtled past, ending the movement by dragging the cape along the ground with the bull following as it continued to rip at the cloth.

With the crowd clapping and cheering both the man's skill and also his courage, Paco turned and shouted to me above the roar of the crowd.

'He is testing the bull for the matador who is to fight. This is done so that his *Jefé* can see if the animal has courage, also to see if it has good eyesight or hooks to the left or the right. He will be looking for the slightest thing that might tell him that the bull will not fight honestly and will cause him to be caught on the horns.'

To me, as someone who had never previously witnessed a bullfight, there was no doubt that this bull certainly had immense courage, the only doubt in my mind was did the matador have sufficient courage to remain in the ring with such an opponent?

There was another huge roar from the crowd as, once again, the bull's horns ripped into the woodwork as the man retreated behind the barrier, the cheers increasing in volume as the most senior of the afternoon's matadors stepped out to face his adversary for the first time.

If I had any doubt in respect of the man's courage it vanished in an instant with his first extraordinary and flamboyant pass. I gasped as he lured the bull away from the barrier, watching its fearsome horns scything terrifyingly close to the man's stomach as he executed pass after pass, the cape appearing to be an intrinsic part of his body as he inched even closer to the bull's massive shoulders, ending his astonishing display as he arrogantly turned on his heel and slowly walked away.

With sand flying in all directions, the bull skidded to a halt as it turned in an instant to repeat its charge, the matador calmly reacting as he turned to face the animal again. Executing two more dangerous and flamboyant passes, he again turned his back on the bewildered animal to stroll calmly back to behind the barrier.

With the bull's attention firmly focussed on the barrier, behind which the matador now stood, a single shrill blast from a trumpet heralded the entry into the ring of one of the picadors. As he cajoled his obviously nervous mount into position close to the barrier, he leaned forward and braced himself with the pica beneath his right arm in readiness to receive the inevitable charge. He did not have long to wait as the bull spotted the movement to its left, quickly lowering its head to race into the attack, hooking viciously with its horns as the picador thrust himself forward in the saddle to drive the long spear into the hump of muscle behind the bull's head.

Ignoring any pain that it might be feeling from the impact of the long steel-tipped wooden lance, the bull continued to bore forward, its immense strength forcing both the horse and its rider back against the wooden barrier, the picador fighting desperately to retain his seat in the saddle. Just as it seemed inevitable that both horse and rider must fall from the furious onslaught, all three matadors stepped out to execute a series of passes to lure the bull away, Jaime showing flare and panache as he finished the sequence with a magnificent pass in which the cape was swept both high above the bull's head and his own, the manoeuvre earning him a huge cry of 'olé matador' from the enthusiastic crowd.

Enticing the bull once again towards the blindfolded and padded horse which stood braced to receive a further onslaught, Jaime stepped to one side, avoiding the animal's charge with another pass so close to his body, that in passing, the bull left a wide bloody smear across the front of his suit. I looked on horrified as I saw the blood, believing for a moment that Jaime had received an injury before realising that it was in fact blood from the wound inflicted on the animal moments before.

As the three matadors stood with their capes held in front of them, they watched as the picador once again prepared himself to receive the bull's charge. The animal barely paused before resuming its attack, ignoring the pica which glanced from its shoulder without causing further wounding and slamming into the protective padding which covered the side of the horse. The weight of the bull coupled with the speed of its attack sent the horse and its rider crashing against the barrier, the ferocity of the charge sending the picador tumbling from the saddle and down on to the sand.

With the rider now lying helpless on the ground the angry bull turned its attention to this unprotected target, the man trying desperately to crawl from its path. Slashing and hooking, the bull tried without success to skewer him as he scrambled for safety, one of its horns raking the sand inches from the man's head as Jaime leaped to his defence, standing with his back dangerously close to the barrier. Even above the roaring of the excited crowd I could clearly hear him screaming '*toro, toro brava*' as he bravely flourished his cape between him and the downed picador.

I could scarcely believe my eyes as I watched my new found friend courageously draw the bull back into the centre of the arena as three ring orderlies appeared from behind the barrier, one of them dashing forward to grab the horse's reins as it reared and pranced, the other two helping the picador back to his feet as he angrily snatched his arm away in a fit of undisguised temper. As Jaime performed three more sensationally brave passes, he succeeded in drawing the bull back towards the remounted picador; the senior matador stepping forward to attract the animal's attention, taking the initiative as he angrily drew it away from Jaime's flying cape.

Paco leaned towards me and shouted to make himself heard above the cheering of the crowd.

'Your friend demonstrated great courage and the senior matador is not happy now that he has become the favourite with the crowd. When he drew the bull away from the fallen picador in that fashion, his series of passes were some of the best I've ever seen. The senior matador knows that he has lost the affection of the crowd and he knows that he must perform even better if he is to win them back.'

Seemingly unaware of the matador's anger, Jaime smiled as he walked back towards the barrier, happily waving his acknowledgement of the crowd's rapturous applause.

Again Paco shouted in my ear, pointing down to what was going on in front of us.

'Did you see the way he took the bull from your friend? That did not go unnoticed with the crowd and they did not like it. I cannot believe he did such a thing and they are shouting because they see that as an insult.'

He pointed towards the barrier behind which there appeared to be a heated argument going on.

'I think his *cuadrilla* is also unhappy at what happened and I think we may see something very special here today if he wishes to regain their favour.'

Fascinated by the dangerous politics being enacted out in front of me, I watched as the senior matador performed a series of stunning passes as he led the bull back towards the picador who was now remounted and ready to receive the charge. Finally slipping behind the barrier, he glanced across at Jaime, but the young man appeared not to have noticed, his flashing smile remaining intact as he watched the bull being held off by ferocious thrusting of the pica by the mounted picador.

Feeling sorry to see the bull being treated so savagely by the vengeful picador, I was relieved to see the bull being lured away by the third matador, heralding the end of the first act.

Paco pointed back towards the president's box to where a large white handkerchief was now laying draped across the rail in front of him.

'It is time for the second act,' he said. 'As this is your first corrida I think that you may find this the most exciting of all, it is time for the placing of the banderillas.'

With the bull watching the departing picador, it now stood alone in the centre of the ring, pawing the ground obviously deciding on what it should do next. It was not to be confused for long as Jaime appeared from behind the barrier carrying two long wickedly-barbed poles, one in each hand and decorated with what appeared to be yellow and red ribbons.

With both arms outstretched and the two banderillas pointing directly at the bull, he shouted to attract the animal's attention. I held my breath as the bull lowered its horns and charged. Standing directly in the bull's path with its horns inches away from his chest, he raised the banderillas and leaped high in the air, slamming the two spiked sticks into the animal's shoulders, at the same time using the banderillas as supports as he pivoted his body to twist himself away from the wide pointed horns.

I could hardly believe what I had just seen as the crowd bellowed its applause at both his bravery and his skill as Paco shouted excitedly in my ear.

'Absolutely magnificent,' he shouted. 'I have seldom seen better; to place the sticks in that way takes the greatest skill and courage. You do not often see banderillas placed in that way because of the danger, it takes a very brave man to do such a thing. To place them in that way is called *poder a poder*, and it is where the banderilla meets the bull face to face without turning away. Magnificent.'

'Will he do that again?' I shouted above the roar of the crowd.

Paco turned to stare at the president's box before answering.

'Normally there would be three pairs, but I think because of the attention the bull received from the picador there may only be two, the president may even decide that he will only allow one pair.'

We both stared up towards the box to see what his judgement might be, and although I didn't want to see this brave animal injured further, I hoped that I might get the chance to again witness such courage.

The president rose slowly to his feet, clearly deliberating on what the crowd might want, at the same time considering sparing the animal further distress. Watching with bated breath, I saw the president raise just one finger.

'He wishes to see one more pair,' Paco explained. 'I think that is wise. I think he is aware that this bull is something special to show such great courage and he wants to see this animal given every chance.'

Seeing the signal, the other two matadors made ready by practising several passes over and over again behind the confines of the barrier while Jaime again stepped confidently into the ring.

As before, he stepped slowly forward calling to the bull and waving his arms, preparing himself to replicate his previous act of supreme courage, or, as my cousin later put it, his act of 'sheer stupidity'. This time the bull didn't rush forward to attack but stood staring as if trying to work out where it had previously gone wrong.

Still calling, he inched his way forward towards the bull, his back arched and his hands held high above his head as before, still no response. Slowly moving even closer, he called again, this time more urgently. The bull stood and stared, pawing the ground as it watched the man getting closer.

'*Toro, toro,*' he called, this time stamping his foot, sending up a puff of dry sand and dust to float up in the still evening air.

The crowd was hushed as if hardly daring to breathe, sensing that they were either going to witness something incredibly spectacular or a bloody death.

'*Olé toro,*' he called, louder this time, as he edged nearer and nearer until they were barely six feet apart.

Without warning the bull charged, the blood from its wounds colouring the flying saliva as it threw itself at the waiting man.

It was as if I was watching the whole drama being played out in slow motion as he leaped acrobatically into the air between the horns of this huge animal, slamming down the two banderillas into the bull's shoulders before somehow managing to draw in his torso to narrowly avoiding being impaled. For a split second there was silence and then the whole arena erupted into a huge roar as the bull skidded to a standstill, the man slowly walking away, his back arrogantly turned towards the bull as it stood watching him, unable to comprehend what had just occurred.

Looking down towards the barrier, I watched the senior matador take the offered muleta in his left hand and the slightly curved sword in his right before striding out into the centre of the ring to stand directly in front of the president's box. Taking off his *montera,* he looked up to where the president was now on his feet, mouthing his dedication as he requested the honour of being allowed to complete the final act. After receiving a brief acknowledgement, he turned to face the crowd, making a theatrical gesture by sweeping his arm to encompass the whole arena, indicating that this act was for them. Receiving what I thought was no more than polite applause rather than rapturous acknowledgement; he tossed his *montera* towards one of his entourage who deftly caught it before placing it on the barrier in front of him.

With the muleta being supported beneath the cloth by its short wooden stick, the matador walked towards the bull which watched his approach with curious interest, its front feet again pawing the ground as it geared itself up for another attack; suddenly, without warning, it charged.

Standing motionless, the matador steered the bull past with a nonchalant, almost careless, pass, the muleta sweeping the animal's back, its bloody shoulders brushing the man's body as it thundered by. Turning in an instant, the bull repeated its ferocious charge, the matador again sweeping the bull past while this time exposing his back towards the enraged animal.

While the audience roared its approval, the bull again turned to renew its attack, the matador performing an amazing act of bravery by snatching the small piece of red cloth from in front of the animal's nose, sweeping the muleta high above his own and the bull's head, the manoeuvre causing the bull's front feet to leave the ground as the impetus of its charge carried it into the air. Along with the entire audience I leaped to my feet, clapping and shouting my congratulations to the matador as he arrogantly turned from the animal, walking back in the direction of the barrier while completely ignoring the bull which stood as if mesmerised at what had just occurred.

The warning screams from the crowd came too late to alert the matador as the bull covered the distance between them in an instant, one of its huge horns spearing the man in the top of his right thigh as he desperately tried to use the muleta to divert its charge. Tossing its head, the man remained impaled on the bull's horn as he was lifted from the ground, his body spinning on the horn before a further shake of its head sent the injured man flying through the air to land sprawled on the sand several feet away. Suddenly, where only moments before, we had been applauding a magnificently choreographed ballet, we were now screaming in horror at the drama now being played out before us.

Immediately, as if by magic, the ring now seemed to be filled with people, each one desperately trying to lure the bull away from the injured matador who lay curled up in a foetal position on the sand, helpless against any further attack. As I stood horrified, waiting for the bull to inflict further injury on the injured man, I became aware of Jaime standing inches away from the horns of the bull bravely brandishing his cape while another of the matador's assistants desperately hung on to its tail as he tried to pull the huge animal away.

Between them, the matadors drew the bull away from their injured colleague while three of the injured man's *cuadrilla* half-dragged and half-carried him from the ring, jets of blood pumping from his wound to mingle on the sand with that of the bull until only Jaime was left in the arena to fend off further charges.

With people now still on their feet clapping Jaime's cape work, Paco shouted in my ear.

'I think it will now fall to your friend to have the honour of killing this very brave animal.'

Standing perfectly still, he called to the bull, executing three more breathtaking passes before finishing the *faena*, standing to face the bull before strolling casually back to the barrier, returning seconds later with his muleta and sword to where the bull stood watching his approach. Unbelievably, he tapped the bull lightly on its nose with the point of his sword before walking towards the president's box to make the same dedication as his injured predecessor, bowing before taking off his *montera*. Receiving permission to complete the final act,

Jaime replaced the *montera* on to his head, taking care to make sure that it was firmly in place before continuing.

Paco placed his hand on my shoulder as he leaned across to make himself heard above the roar of the crowd.

'The first matador was allowed to fight without wearing the *montera* after the dedication, but as he has been injured, the matador who is to make the kill in his absence must replace and wear the *montera* following the dedication.'

I nodded, thinking back to my questioning of the rules with regard to the picadors, now beginning to realise that these traditional rules which have lasted over the centuries are vitally important to the whole ethos of bullfighting and for me to even think about questioning the logic of such rules must have seemed crass and insensitive.

If the terrible wounding of the first matador was uppermost in Jaime's mind, he certainly didn't show it as he performed three magnificent passes with the small piece of red cloth. Each time the bull charged, he drew the animal past his body with barely any movement of his feet, the final pass leaving the bull standing with its front feet together, totally confused as it contemplated how it might deal with this new and elusive tormentor.

Slowly and coolly, Jaime changed the muleta from his right hand to his left, taking the sword in his right hand to stand bolt upright facing his adversary, lifting the slightly curved sword to just below his chin as he sighted down the blade.

A hush descended over the entire crowd in anticipation of what was to come, and despite not wanting to miss even one second of this final act, I found myself looking at the faces of the people around me as they awaited the bull's execution. Some were standing, their attention riveted on the final scene being played out before them while others sat calmly, ready to declare their approval or to vent their anger for a badly performed kill.

Quickly looking back, I watched my newfound friend as he sighted along the blade of the sword to a point on the bull's back behind the hump of muscle to where the animal's spine ran back towards its tail. Suddenly he stepped forward, sweeping the muleta across the lower part of his body in front of the bull's face, the animal's head following the movement of the cloth to the right as it brushed the ground. As the bull ripped at the muleta, Jaime leaned across between the animal's huge horns to plunge the sword deep between its shoulders, the thrust carrying the blade into the bull's body right up to its hilt.

Feeling the steel entering its body, the bull's head arched upwards, its horns brushing the matador's chest as he pivoted to one side on the handle of the sword. Seconds later, the stadium erupted with a huge roar as the crowd screamed its appreciation at the perfection of the kill, the animal already dead as it crashed to the ground, its legs thrashing in a final farewell to life.

Barely able to comprehend what I had just witnessed, I flopped back down on my seat as people all around me stood clapping and cheering, wildly waving their hats and handkerchiefs in appreciation of what they had just seen. I looked across to where my cousin sat with her hands covering her eyes, her head bowed as if in prayer before getting to her feet and squeezing past Nick and Paco to stand at my side.

'That's it for me Pete, I can't take any more.'

'There's a bar just opposite the entrance where we came in and I need a drink so I'll catch up with you guys later, you stay and enjoy the rest of the show.'

I glanced at Nick who stood cheering and waving, obviously unaware of Pam's decision to leave.

As my cousin started to squeeze past me, I knew that I couldn't let her leave on her own but I hated the thought of having to do the 'right thing' and go with her, but as there was no indication that Nick was going to accompany her I knew that I had no other option and I would have to forgo the pleasure of seeing Jaime fight under his own name.

I looked again to where Nick was still on his feet cheering, still oblivious of my cousin's intention.

'I'll come with you,' I muttered half-heartedly, 'I can't let you go over there on your own. When Nick sees that you've left he's sure to come after you and I can come back.'

I turned as if to escort my cousin through the row of occupied seats to the exit.

She placed a hand on my arm.

'You stay here. The American version of the typical English gentleman over there won't even notice that I've gone, but thanks for the offer. You stay and enjoy the rest of the fights; I'll see you all later.'

She placed a restraining hand on my chest and turned to push her way through the crowd of applauding fans towards the exit.

I again glanced back to where Nick stood clapping and cheering, still obviously unaware that Pam had decided to leave.

Paco paused in his clapping and looked concerned at Pam's unexpected departure, a questioning look on his face as he turned to enquire what was wrong.

'Is everything alright?' he asked. 'Is the señora unwell?'

'She's fine,' I replied. 'She just wanted to get some air and something to drink. She wants us to stay and enjoy the rest of the fights and she'll meet us later in the bar across the street near to where we came in.'

Still feeling guilty at not leaving with her, but at the same time feeling upset that Nick had not done the right thing and accompanied her, I turned back to see what was going on in the arena below.

A pair of horses bedecked with plumes and tassels had entered the ring and the body of the dead bull was being ceremoniously dragged from the arena. As I stared at this somewhat macabre scene, Jaime, who was basking in the plaudits of the crowd, walked past where we were standing, a huge smile on his face holding aloft what appeared to be two ladies' leather purses, one in each hand.

Paco, who was still standing and clapping, turned and shouted in my ear.

'Your friend has been granted both the ears from the bull. It is a very great honour, and for what he has done here today he will have gained a great reputation for when he fights in Seville.'

The rest of the afternoon sped by with all five of the remaining contests exceeding my expectations, Jaime fighting and killing two more bulls and covering himself with further glory in the process. Not surprisingly, he was unable to better his performance of earlier when coming to the aid of the fallen matador; that one supreme act cementing his reputation with the assembled aficionados and critics for ever.

Sadly, the afternoon's performance came to an end with me wishing that I could turn back the clock and watch the whole breathtaking procedure all over again. On leaving the arena, we caught up with my cousin sunning herself in a small bar opposite and we joined her in what Nick described as an '*après* fight' libation. After apologising for not having left with her, he then expressed the opinion that, 'that sort of stuff was not really meant for women anyway,' and that he was surprised that she had chosen to join them in the first place.

Paco in his gallant manner had again aspired to become a latter day Don Quixote by placing his hand over his heart before stating, 'In my humble opinion I am amazed that a lady with such outstanding qualities as those of the Señora has bothered to bless the uncultured American with her presence at any point in her life'.

He also added that she would do well to consider leaving the ignorant 'gringo' immediately and spend the remainder of her life being adored by someone who truly appreciated her great beauty and intelligence. (Nick's reply to this is unprintable.)

Los Corales and Matadors...

With the relentless sun again turning any exposed railings and other metal objects into potential health hazards to bare flesh, I walked slowly through the bar to where Pam and Nick sat at one of the pavement tables drinking coffee.

'Well look who's finally decided to honour us with his presence,' Nick said with a grin as I slumped down on to a vacant seat. 'I wondered if you might feel up to putting in an appearance this morning, feeling just a little frail are we today?'

I answered his question with a weak sheepish smile, knowing that now was not the time for me to be entering into any sort of dialogue with him while he was in this sort of mood.

Not letting the matter go, he continued with his teasing in the hope that he would get me to respond.

'I told you not to order another bottle; I knew that it would get you in the end.'

Leaping to my defence as usual, my cousin turned on Nick as he laughingly asked if I would prefer a beer instead of coffee.

'Why don't you leave him alone?' she said. 'I noticed that you didn't put up any objections when the waiter kept topping up your glass. You were also pretty damn quick in raising your glass to Pete's health, Paco's generosity, American and Spanish relationships and the state of the peseta against the dollar if I remember correctly.'

We had left the arena, and after drinking a couple of beers in the bar in which we had found Pam, Paco had driven us back to Seville and introduced us to the joys of the wonderful restaurant called Los Corales, and it was while we had been enjoying several courses of magnificent food, copious amounts of wine had also been consumed which was the reason I was now feeling very much the worse for wear.

It would be fair to say that the reason I was unaware of the effect that the wine was having on me was because I had already become intoxicated by the atmosphere of the restaurant itself, Paco's brief description having given me no idea of what to expect.

Entering through the heavy, carved wooden doors was like finding oneself suddenly stepping on to the set of the opera *Carmen*. The wonderful aroma of chargrilled beef mingled easily with the heavy scent of garlic and herbs, while the thin veil of cigar smoke which clung to the ceiling like a shroud did nothing to take away the mouth-watering aroma emanating from the dishes of tapas and other assorted delicacies on display on the ornate and heavily carved counter, a counter on which a gourmet selection of fresh lobsters and langoustines rested on beds of crushed ice.

Around the walls of the traditionally furnished and discreetly lit restaurant were items of bullfighting memorabilia dating back to well over a hundred years, together with several mounted heads of long-dead fighting bulls which surprisingly blended in perfectly with rich velvet tapestries and large gold-framed oil paintings, portraits of both men and women, each painted in the style of the artist Goya.

We had barely crossed the threshold before being approached by a smiling head waiter who, after offering his hand in greeting, addressed our host in almost reverential terms by welcoming him on his return before respectfully beckoning us to follow as we were ushered to a table already laid to accommodate us all.

As we sat down and made ourselves comfortable, the man turned and called to another waiter standing attentively nearby who, after giving a slight bow, placed a large deep red leather menu in front of each of us.

I stared at Paco in undisguised admiration at the respect he obviously commanded, the unchanging expression on his face indicating that this was the kind of attention he was used to receiving.

'You weren't lying when you mentioned that you were known here,' Nick said. 'Just for a moment there, I thought that the waiter was about to kneel and kiss your hand.'

Paco shrugged dismissively.

'I think I am possibly remembered for my humble attempts at becoming a *matador de toros* here in Seville in my younger days. I think also that my reputation and a few minor triumphs here may have become slightly exaggerated over the years.'

Pam smiled at Paco as he shyly tried to deflect any further conversation away from himself.

'I think that you are a man who is honourable and sincere and I suspect there is much more to you than you would have us believe,' she said as she leaned across to lightly touch his hand.

Paco placed one hand over his heart.

'I am just a simple bar owner,' he said quietly, 'But I am honoured that you think this of me.

'I think you will find the food here very much to your liking,' he continued, glad to be able to move the conversation away from himself.

'I would recommend the meat dishes, particularly the beef. You will not find fresher anywhere in Spain than that which is served here, in fact what you see on the menu tonight was probably fighting in the ring this very afternoon.'

Pam visibly flinched on hearing what Paco had just said.

'I think I would have been a lot happier if you hadn't told me that, I might just have the fish or maybe a salad,' she said with a grin.

Sitting back in my chair, the conversation going on around me became a blur as I thought of everything that had happened over the past weeks, particularly how my values with regard to life had changed since leaving my job in Luton. I now knew that life had far more interesting things on offer than those which awaited me back in England. My relatively short time in Spain had opened up new horizons which pushed thoughts of home and reporting for duty even further to the back of my mind.

Clearly, staying in Spain indefinitely at this time wasn't an option, but I had nevertheless considered various ways which would enable me to continue with this exciting change of lifestyle allowing me to pursue a more rewarding career path than the one currently beckoning at home. Nick had been surprised when I had questioned him in respect of following in his footsteps and enlisting in the American military.

Overcoming his surprise, he realised that I was serious and we had talked long into the night with regard to what this entailed. He had explained that I would need to be domiciled in the States and apply for American citizenship, and if successful, I would then be drafted to do military service with all the ramifications that this involved. He explained that when my time came to leave the military I would then be free to follow whatever career path I chose. He had also emphasised that I should not become too influenced by the lifestyle that he and my cousin now had, he explained that his own situation was the result of many years of study coupled with dedication and hard work, and because of this, both he and Pam were now in a position where life had become far more satisfying and decidedly easier than when he had first enlisted.

The return of the waiter to take our orders jolted me back to the present, his intervention stopping me thinking further about what I might or might not do as I considered Paco's recommendation before finally accepting the tantalising offer of chargrilled fillet of beef with garlic sweet breads and fresh salad.

Revelling in the atmosphere of my surroundings, I sat enthralled by the sight of beautiful raven-haired women wearing traditional dress being escorted by impeccably dressed men in the style of that worn by actors who had starred in such Hollywood epics as *Death in the Afternoon* and *For Whom the Bell Tolls*.

Many of these strikingly impressive men appeared to be much older than their beautiful escorts. Already dark, their skin bore the unmistakeable signs of being subjected to countless hours spent in the blazing sun, presumably by either having fought bulls, breeding bulls, or being involved in other business transactions undoubtedly associated with the world of the corrida. Everywhere I looked, these elegantly dressed men and women oozed both wealth and confidence.

Without exception the men were dressed in traditional short black or grey unbuttoned bolero jackets with small neat lapels, these simple jackets further enhanced by white linen handkerchiefs tucked into small breast pockets, while snowy white shirts worn with thin black ties completed this picture of elegance and style.

Some of the shirts worn by the younger men were elaborately frilled at the chest, while the tailoring of the trousers appeared to have been completed while being worn by their owners, so tight were they around the buttocks. In every instance, these beautifully fitting trousers were elaborately flared at the ankle to reveal wonderfully soft, black, calf-length leather boots.

As I listened to the soulful sound of softly played guitars providing a haunting and atmospheric backdrop, I suddenly felt sad as, again, the prospect of leaving this wonderful country and going back to England threw me into turmoil. The one thing of which I was certain was that my future did not entail a nine-to-five job with only an old age pension as my ultimate goal. I wanted more from life than that, but was it in my power to achieve it? I had very little idea of what I wanted to do but I was absolutely sure that whatever decision I came to, I was going to live life to the full.

I felt a touch on my arm as I thought about my future.

'You appear to be sad my friend, is everything alright?'

I turned to see Paco looking at me with some concern.

'I'm fine,' I replied. 'I guess the music and the wine, together with being here with you all, has got to me a bit.'

I looked across towards Pam and Nick, hoping that they hadn't noticed my unaccountable mood, but they were oblivious to what was going on, enjoying themselves and happily chatting to each other.

'I think that you are a man who has the soul which searches for something more,' he continued.

'It is true that there have been many people who have come here and feel that they are re-born, they come and they never leave. Some may go away never to return, but their heart remains here; I think that you may be one of those people.'

I nodded slowly, certain that he was right, confident that even if I didn't choose to live in Spain on a permanent basis, I would spend much of my life enjoying the passion and the culture which I knew would remain within me for ever.

Raising his glass, he tapped my own lightly in a toast.

'Señor Dumas has said that when you return to England you are to go into your army, but when that is over if you wish to return you would be welcome. If the *señora* and the *señor* leave to go back to America I have business interests which you could assist me with. You would be able to learn our language and see more of Spain, there is much to see.' He shrugged, 'Maybe you will also fight the bulls, who knows?'

Raising my own glass, I thanked him.

'I'm honoured, but please forgive me,' I said. 'I'm just being stupid.'

'No *señor*, you are far from stupid, you have the *pasión*, I see it in your eyes. The music touches you and it is this that tells me that you and I are very much alike; you have the soul of a *gitano*, a gypsy, one who searches for truth and wisdom.

'This music you are listening to is peculiar to this area of Andalucia and to the gypsies who live here, its roots are very old and date to the Moorish occupation. It tells of the sadness and the hardships of the oppressed, it is known as *canté jondo*. I think because you have the soul it is this which is perhaps making you sad.'

I smiled. 'Thank you for your kind offer, I am very grateful and I will think about what you have said, but please, tell me more about the people here tonight.'

He looked around at the other diners, sometimes acknowledging a greeting by a nod of his head or a brief wave of his hand as someone he knew caught his eye.

'Of course,' he replied. 'There are people here who are known to me. Most of them are men who have faced the bulls at some time or other, some of them are breeders and also there are one or two promoters here as well. This place is where there is a lot of business done with regard to the bulls, also it is where many young bullfighters come in the hope that they can perhaps persuade an agent or a promoter to manage them and hopefully make them famous.'

He discreetly nodded towards a man sitting alone at one of the tables away from the main dining area.

'Look,' he whispered. 'Do you see that man sitting at the table in the corner near to where the musicians are playing? That is the Paco Corpas, and over there, the man sitting with those two beautiful women by the far wall, that is the incredible Luis Procuna.'

I looked at the man laughing and joking with two extraordinarily beautiful women, his flashing white teeth and darkly handsome good looks combining to make him what could only be described as 'God's gift to women', a man, who by anybody's standards, made Errol Flynn look fairly average.

'Is Señor Procuna a great matador?' I asked excitedly.

Paco shook his head. 'Not a truly great matador, but amazing for other reasons.'

'He is not from Spain; he was born in Mexico of a very poor family and started his career as an *espontáneo*. Do you remember I told you of the young boys who jump into the ring in the hope that they will be noticed and be adopted by an *empresario*?'

I nodded, recalling our conversation when we had first met.

'Well, he is a person we would call a *misterio*, an "enigma".' He looked towards Pam and Nick for a possible translation, 'I do not know how you would say this in English,' he said.

Nick nodded as Pam gave him his answer.

'You mean a "mystery", or an "enigma". It is the same in English.'

'Yes, that is what he is. He is a mystery, a very complex and troubled man who is difficult to understand. One day he would be the greatest fighter of bulls that you have ever seen and the next he may run from the ring. He had the talent to be even greater than Belmonte or even Manolete, but he has this thing in his head which seems to destroy his thinking.

'I have seen him do things with the cape which has made me doubt my own eyes, and some of the banderillas he has placed may never be bettered, but he is truly remarkable for another reason.'

I interrupted.

'You said, he had the talent, does he not fight anymore?'

'Oh yes, he still fights which is what makes him truly remarkable. Two years ago he was involved in a serious motor car accident and his back was broken. He was told by his doctors that he might never walk again, but such is the courage of the man that he swore that he would once again face the bulls, and a year later true to his word, he came back fighting in the same inspired way that he had always done. For that reason alone it is why he is so incredible.'

Nick, who had been listening, whistled under his breath.

'That's some story,' he said. 'Old Pammy here has to go to bed for a couple of days if she breaks a fingernail.'

His facetious remark was promptly rewarded with a sharp elbow in the ribs.

'Not so much of the old,' she said. 'I can remember not too long ago when a certain military hero who's sitting not a million miles from here practically passed out while I was plucking his eyebrows.'

'Oh that was different,' he retorted. 'You nearly took my eye out with those damn tweezers.'

As Paco and I laughed at this hardly comparable scenario, I steered the conversation back to Señor Procuna.

'Do you think that it might be possible for us to go and see him fight while I am here, I would really like to go and see someone who is as good as you say he is?'

Paco shrugged.

'I will make enquiries as to when he is to fight again. If he is to fight in this area I will try to obtain tickets, but I have to say that what we saw this afternoon from your friend, and that first pair of banderillas he placed were of the highest order and no matter how many other fights you see, you will not see better.'

As we continued to enjoy the excellent food and the finest of wines, the atmosphere around the table grew more and more light hearted and frivolous as the good-hearted banter between Nick and Paco became even more vociferous, Pam intervening every now and then to try to restore some semblance of order. Suddenly the music stopped abruptly as people began to clap while others jumped to their feet calling out "Olé matador".'

Looking in the direction of where several people now stood, I couldn't believe my eyes as I stared down at a smiling and slightly embarrassed El Huracán de Toledo as he stood shyly accepting the congratulations that were being showered upon him, the people accompanying him standing back as he bathed in his newfound celebrity status.

Jumping to my feet, I threw myself unreservedly into joining the applause which rang round the restaurant.

Accepting the plaudits of people who, in the main, were his peers, he waved his hand in recognition of their thanks, finally looking across to where we were now all on our feet clapping.

If I had been standing in front of the Queen of England receiving an accolade for some heroic feat that I had performed in the heat of battle I could not have been more proud, as with a huge boyish grin, Jaime nodded in our direction before making his way to our table, motioning the people with him to accept the head waiter's offer of an already prepared table.

'Was your first corrida all that you expected or did it disappoint you?' He asked, holding out his hand in greeting.

'You were magnificent,' I said, almost too tongue tied for words. 'I could not believe that you found the courage to stand and face such a huge animal, it scared me just watching you. When you fought the bull so close to the barrier when the picador was unseated, I nearly had a heart attack.'

'So my efforts this afternoon did not disappoint you?' he said almost shyly.

'Disappoint me?' I gasped. 'I think what you did today and the way in which you despatched the bull was incredible. I shall never forget it.'

Jaime smiled a huge smile of thanks.

'That is very nice of you to say this. Today I was lucky, he was a brave and honest bull and I could not have wished for a truer animal, particularly after he unseated the picador and tasted my colleague's fear when he gave him the *cornada*.' He crossed himself. 'Not all days will be like today, but today I am thankful.'

At the mention of the fallen matador, I asked about his condition.

'I am afraid it is not good. They have given him many blood transfusions but could not stop the bleeding. He has been taken to Madrid where he will be treated by one of the very best surgeons who knows much about such injuries.' He again crossed himself. 'Hopefully, he will recover fully and be fit to fight again soon.'

I suddenly realised that, in my excited and flustered state, I had forgotten to introduce my companions, hastily explaining that he had already met Pam and Nick at the station as he shook their hands, his eyes lighting up in recognition as I introduced him to Paco as someone who had also been a matador of some repute.

As the two of them happily conversed in Spanish, Jaime turned to me and explained that he remembered having seen Paco fight when he was younger, adding that it was an honour to meet a man of such stature, adding also that he was proud to receive the praises of a man so highly regarded both in and out of the ring.

Chatting light-heartedly for several more minutes, he finally bowed slightly towards Pam, expressing his regrets at having to leave, adding that he hoped that I would still be in Seville when the time came for him to take his *alternativa*.

Seeing him happily enjoying the company of his friends, I watched as a steady stream of people continued to visit his table to pay their respects, amazed as the head waiter delivered bottle after bottle of wine sent by other diners as congratulatory offerings, smiling at the thought that if things continued at that pace he would soon have enough wine stored in the restaurant's cellars to satisfy his thirst for at least the next twelve months.

As I thought about Jaime's comments with regard to me being in Seville to witness his *alternativa*, I contemplated my return to England and my imminent conscription, acutely aware that if I was to report on time I would have to be leaving in six days' time. I knew too that if I did return to England at the appointed time I would almost certainly not be there to see him fight on his big day and that would be devastating.

With the evening coming to a reluctant close, we all bade Jaime and his friends goodbye as I swore that some day following his inevitable success in the Maestranza, we would return once again to raise our glasses to him in this very restaurant, drinking to the inevitable fame and fortune that I knew in my heart would be his in the years to come.

****

Nick's irritatingly chirpy voice added to my discomfort as my head continued its agonising thumping, the wonderful memories of the previous day's fights and seeing Jaime again in the restaurant cruelly vanishing.

'What about it buddy, do you think you'll live? Listen, we've got a whole bunch of stuff to do today, people to see and fish to fry and all that crap. Don't you know what today is? We can't sit around all day waiting for you to recover. Like the man once said; let's get up and get at 'em, shoulders to the wheel and all that.'

Wincing at Nick's over-emphasised cheerful repartee, I looked despairingly at Pam.

'What the hell is he on about now?' I groaned. 'Why does he have to be such a pain in the backside in the mornings?'

'Take no notice,' she replied. 'He's been like that ever since you arrived. Once you've gone he'll be back in his usual "what the hell have I got to smile about" mode. Normally, he doesn't say diddly squat until he's had his sixth cup of coffee, and then it only amounts to him telling me not to forget to buy more cigarettes when I go to the commissary.'

'Woman, that's no way to talk about the breadwinner in this house, disloyalty like that in a wife is very unbecoming. Let's get your man here washed and scrubbed up and ready for today's big event.'

'What big event is this?' I asked with a groan, a feeling of foreboding suddenly descending on me like a dark shadow. The only 'big event' I felt like looking forward to at that moment was lying down in a darkened room until the pain finally subsided, then, and only then, I felt that it might just be possible for me to manage the proverbial 'lightly boiled egg' provided that it was served in complete silence.

'"What big event?" He asks. Do you really have no idea what goes on in the rest of the world outside of Luton? You need to get out more Pete, it's a big old world out there and you seem to be missing out on most of it. For your information, buddy – and you might want to put this in your diary for future years – today is Parents' Day in the "Land of the Free". We're all going to put on our best bib and tucker and get on down to the base to celebrate.'

'What in hell is Parents' Day?' I groaned. 'Please tell me he's making this up?'

'Sadly, he's not making it up. It really does happen to be Parents' Day today and, true to form, they always put on a show of what the Americans call flying the flag.'

'You've got to be pulling my leg,' I snorted. 'Only some intellectually challenged Yank with nothing better to do with his time could dream up something like that.'

'Well you know how sincere and caring these Americans are,' she added sarcastically. 'They don't need much of an excuse to wander about all day wearing daft hats and increasing the overseas sales of Budweiser beer.'

Smothering a grin, Pam continued with her derision of the American way of life.

'You wait until next week; it really kicks off then. Next Tuesday we get to celebrate National Toenail Clipping Day, that's when we all think back to that wonderful day when the

Pilgrim Fathers all sat around scratching their backsides and clipping their toenails when they first arrived.

'Oh, and let's not forget about next Thursday, that's a real biggy. It's the never-to-be-forgotten Get the Air in Your Tyres Checked Day, that's just about on a par with Thanksgiving and Christmas. I'm sure glad you're going to be here for that one, that's one real humdinger you wouldn't want to miss.'

Despite my lingering hangover, I laughed out loud at my cousin's derogatory remarks, waiting to see what sort of comeback Nick would throw her way.

I didn't have long to wait as he immediately replied in kind.

'You'll be sorry that you've been so cynical when you see what I've bought you. There's not going be too many wives on this base who'll be getting new nail scissors and a new foot pump for the car next week.'

Once again, I laughed at this unrehearsed double act as Nick lovingly squeezed Pam's hand.

'By the way, has anyone seen that darn cat recently? I haven't seen the thing for days; it's not like him to go missing for this long.'

'Oh, he'll turn up when he gets hungry,' Pam said. 'You know what he's like; he just likes doing his own thing. He's probably got some scrawny lady love around here somewhere and they're curled up in some little love nest.'

'Christ hun, I hope not,' Nick retorted. 'Can you imagine a whole bunch of kittens running around the place all looking like him? If that cat brings his flea-ridden offspring back here he's out on his ear. I guess old Paco there won't be too pleased about it either.'

Hearing his name mentioned, Paco stopped what he was doing in the bar behind us and called over.

'Are you talking to me, or about me Señor Dumas?' he asked, wiping his hands on a bar towel.

'Don't worry about it Paco,' Pam answered. 'We were just saying that we hadn't seen the cat for some time.'

'Oh, he was around here earlier Señora. He was sitting across the road just watching what was going on. He looked as if he was trying to make up his mind whether to come over or not, but I think he must have decided not to as I saw him walk off around the corner.'

Surprisingly, I felt a little relieved that he hadn't got himself run over; at least he had put in an appearance so he hadn't suffered too much from our earlier encounter.

'Right,' said Nick, easing himself out of his chair. 'Let's get this show on the road. There's beer to be drunk and good steaks to be barbecued, we can't sit around here all day waiting for old Noël Coward here to start feeling better.'

Realising there was no point in arguing, I reluctantly pushed back my chair, deciding that perhaps a cold shower might be the first step on my road to recovery vowing that today was going to be a day of total abstinence, there was no way that I was going to either drink or overindulge with food. Thinking back on it, that vow was just about as ludicrous as General Custer stating at the Battle of the Little Bighorn, 'Don't worry men, there's no bloody Indians within miles of here'.

Beer, Baseball and Horseshoes...

Although I had expected a typically over the top display of ostentation when it came to a presentation of little America at play, the transformation of what was essentially a twenty four hour operational air base on permanent alert was startling.

Driving through the gates and past the various huts and hangars in front of which some of the huge B-52 bombers still stood, we finally reached an enormous grassed area the size of at least two full-sized football pitches which had miraculously been transformed into a fairground.

On three sides of this huge field, row upon row of gleaming American automobiles stood parked side by side, the heat haze from which shimmered above these glistening behemoths like a metallic mirage in the desert.

Finding a space at the end of one of the ranks of cars, Nick slid the car neatly alongside an open-topped Ford Thunderbird, around which a group of teenagers were gathered, gazing in envy at its shiny red paintwork and its soft white leather upholstery.

As we stepped out of our own air conditioned vehicle it was like stepping into a blast furnace as the heat from the blazing sun hit us. Seeing me wince and shade my eyes, Nick reached back inside the car and pulled open the glove box and took out a pair of sunglasses.

'Here, put these on,' he said, tossing them to me.

'This sun ain't gonna help with your hangover much but you'll feel a hell of a lot better after a hot dog and a couple of beers.'

Gratefully, I slipped on the glasses, immediately feeling the benefit of the darkened reflective lenses, realising that all of the people I had silently ridiculed for their *They Came from Outer Space* appearance wore them as an essential part of their attire, not as some sort of fashion statement. I had never felt a burning desire to purchase sunglasses before, as living in

Luton was so far-removed from being one of the hedonist capitals of the world, it all seemed rather inappropriate. Lacklustre Luton was definitely a place which did not warrant such an extravagance, but now confidently sporting my new look, I vowed that these were definitely a must have for the future.

Strolling casually towards this extraordinary and recently constructed miniature Coney Island in the general direction of the tiered grandstand, I noticed several large open-topped refuse bins packed with ice and filled with bottles of beer dotted around the whole area, and from these bins, people appeared to be helping themselves.

Obviously having graduated in the art of being able to spot a cold beer at distances far greater than this, Nick noticeably increased his pace as he headed in the direction of the nearest of these containers. Watching him as he reached in, I saw him pull out three bottles, whipping off the caps in one fluent motion with one of the openers that dangled by cords attached to the side of the bin, and casually putting a bottle to his lips, he casually strolled back to where we stood in the shade of the terraced grandstand.

'Here you go, miserable wife of mine, here you go Pete, let's drink to a Happy Parents' Day,' he said with a grin as he handed my cousin and I a bottle each.

'Is he for real?' I groaned. 'I did vow that I wasn't going to have a drink today.'

'You can't celebrate Parents' Day without a beer and a hot dog,' he said with a look of horror on his face. 'That's like not having presents on Christmas morning.'

Despite my feeble protest, I took the offered bottle, marvelling at his resilience and powers of recovery after last night's reverie. I shook my head despairingly as my earlier resolution melted like the ice in the nearby containers.

'Just take it easy, Pete,' my cousin cautioned. 'He's in his element at this sort of thrash. Whatever you do don't be tempted to try and keep up with him, he cut his teeth on doing this sort of thing. He's got citations for drinking beer at ball games and barbecues and you know what he's like, he would love to see you drunk so that he could say that we English don't measure up.'

Pam's mention of the possibility of the English not measuring up was tantamount to throwing down the gauntlet. The idea of the British coming second in any respect to an American immediately drove all thoughts of my hangover to the back of my mind. However much I suffered there was no way that he was going to belittle me by drinking more of Mr Miller's, Mr Budweiser's or Mr Coors' chemically-enhanced liquid posing as beer than me. Didn't I come from a land where real men ate pork scratchings and drank real beer, the stuff you couldn't see through? This had become a point of honour and there was no way that I was going to let the side down.

I nodded briefly at my cousin's well-intentioned caution, vowing that whatever the outcome, he would know that he had been in a fight. If it was his intention to play any sort of mind games, he would need to be at his best to get the better of a determined Englishmen flying the flag on foreign soil. Hadn't we slugged it out alone during the Second World War before the Americans had finally decided to join the struggle? This was about national pride and, whatever happened, there would be no surrender.

Following Nick's lead, we slowly climbed up the terraced scaffolding, on to which planks of wood had been carefully fixed to form steps and bench seats. Reaching the top, I was relieved to see that large sheets of canvas had been fixed to the uprights to form a backdrop which offered welcome shade from the fierce sun as we gratefully flopped down to watch what appeared to be a very seriously contested game of baseball going on in the marked diamond-shaped arena below.

This was the first time I had ever encountered the inane complexities of this slightly advanced form of rounders, and to be perfectly honest, I hadn't the foggiest idea of what was going on. I could understand that the object of the game was for the hitter, or whatever he was called, to hit the ball as hard as he possibly could towards what I was reliably informed was something called the outfield and then run like hell as fast as he could towards something called the first base, but all of the other bits in between made absolutely no sense at all.

Nick patiently sought to explain the intricacies of loaded bases and the rule about three strikes and you're out, and homers, but after about twenty minutes of desperately trying to look interested, I felt that I was beginning to lose the will to live.

Several more beers and four innings later, I was seriously contemplating throwing myself screaming from the top of the grandstand. As a conciliatory attempt at bringing some degree of sanity to the situation, I turned my attention to the pantomime style antics of the people off the field of play, who, judging by the histrionics going on below, had clearly overdone the amount of beer they had already consumed, either that or they were seriously under the influence of tobacco containing some form of vegetable additive.

From what was laughingly referred to as the 'dugout', grown men wearing baseball caps back to front on their heads would emerge with monotonous regularity to scream instructions or abuse to those on the field. On occasions, it became so heated and demonstrative by these men rushing out and throwing their arms in the air while screaming abuse at the umpire, that he left his relatively safe position from where he held court from behind both the batter and the catcher, or whatever it is they are called, to confront his tormentors. Invariably, he would put on a great theatrical show of histrionics by ripping off his caged helmet in a fit of over-accentuated anger to hurl it to the ground, and, with much shouting and waving of his arms, he would physically drag the offenders back towards the dugout.

As I watched the moronic behaviour of so-called grown men, whose posturing antics appeared to be those of inmates recently released from a high security mental institution, it began to dawn on me that I was observing people from arguably the most powerful nation on earth getting increasingly hysterical over something akin to a game played by children in a school playground. If these were the sort of people on whom world peace depended, God help us all I thought.

Shaking my head in despair, I watched as yet another uneventful innings, which I estimated to be about the seventy third, came to an end. Suddenly, a loud brassy explosion of sound heralded the appearance of about one hundred young men and girls dressed up like toy soldiers marching into the arena, each carrying some sort of musical instrument and looking like escapees from the pages of *Alice in Wonderland*.

A huge roar followed by a standing ovation greeted these absurdly overdressed and hyper individuals, each one wearing a glittering star-spangled cloak and a tall, plumed hat. The girls all wore the skimpiest white pleated skirts that I had ever seen in my life, their legs being shown off to their best advantage by being encased by tight fitting white calf-length boots, while the men wore the same overall uniforms but with long trousers also in white.

I stared in sheer disbelief as each person rushed about in a seemingly haphazard manner while blowing, beating or waving huge shiny instruments from which emanated sounds which would have made John Philip Sousa spin rapidly in his grave, sounds that even insane people could not even laughingly describe as music.

Some of the girls, whirling and prancing like drug-besotted dervishes, hurled huge tinselled batons in the air, not always catching them as they crashed down on unsuspecting heads, knocking tall, plumed hats to the ground to be unceremoniously marched on by other equally deranged members of the band, while others waved and shook bright blue and silver pompoms while kicking their legs in the air in a most alarming manner.

Unable to contain myself any longer, I turned to where Nick sat clapping and cheering, a huge grin on his face as he stamped his feet in time to the music.

'What in God's name are they doing?' I shouted, desperately trying to make myself heard above the cacophony of noise rising up from below.

Nick grinned delightedly as he nodded his head enthusiastically in time, exuberantly throwing his arms about while going through the motions of conducting the orchestra below with his half-empty beer bottle.

'That's the base High School Marching Band,' he announced proudly. 'Terrific aren't they? You watch how they march and play in those complicated columns and ranks; you can't really believe what you're watching can you?'

'I sure as hell can't argue with that,' I said. 'That's the truest thing you've said since I got here.'

I shook my head in sheer disbelief as I watched hats being trampled, batons being lost and 'musicians' banging into each other as they lost the plot of the furious performance going on below, my cousin doubling up with laughter at my cynical and unsympathetic comments.

Nick continued to watch, completely oblivious to my grimacing and my cousin's laughter, pretending to play a trombone as he pushed the imaginary instrument's slide in and out while making noises like a horse breaking wind, a look of utter bliss on his face. After several minutes of enthusiastic trombone playing and bottle waving, he leaned towards me, shouting to make himself heard above the noise.

'I don't know why your guards at Buckingham Palace don't do this sort of thing when they do that Trooping the Colour stuff, it's a great crowd pleaser and I think it would look great. It sure beats the hell out of just marching up and down.'

I stared at him in utter horror, thinking briefly that he might just be joking, but the sincere and serious expression on his face told me that this was not the case.

'One of these days I'll tell you why I don't consider that to be one of the greatest ideas you've ever had in your life,' I said. 'Mind you, having said that, I'm pretty damn sure that you won't like either my reasons or the way that I express them.'

Once again, Pam convulsed into fits of uncontrollable laughter, wiping the tears from her eyes before she spoke.

'Come on Nick let's go, enough is enough' she said, trying hard to stop herself from giggling. 'I'm not sure that I can stand much more of this either.'

Gratefully, I followed my cousin's lead as she headed back down towards ground level where, thankfully, the sound was slightly more diffused by the terracing and the canvas sheeting, my thumping head relieved for the slight reduction in the volume.

As Nick headed off for refills from the one of the beer containers, Pam turned around as she heard her name being called.

Strolling through the crowd we saw Marie and Robert Bishop waving in our direction, their son Clifford happily skipping along by their side, one hand firmly holding on to that of his mother while the other held on to a huge cone of pink candyfloss, some of which appeared to be decoratively intertwined with his blonde, almost white hair.

'Hi everyone,' she called. 'Have you all been watching the ball game?'

Pam nodded, a small grimace twisting her lips.

'Yeah, I know what you mean,' Marie answered. 'That marching band didn't exactly light my fire either.'

'Robert loves that sort of stuff,' she said. 'What is it with men and that all that crap? Mind you, he never did grow up anyway so he was in his element; he was standing there banging a pretend drum like his life depended on it.'

Pam laughed, wagging a thumb in Nick's direction.

'It was a trombone with Glenn Miller here, plus we had the noises as well.'

Marie grinned as Pam copied Nick's rapturous example of trombone playing and blowing long-winded raspberries.

'Old "Billy Bob Bishop" there will try and tell you that he just likes a good band, but he's only got to see some seventeen year old in a little old itsy-bitsy skirt waggling her hips and putting on the style and he's there for the duration.'

Bishop feigned a hurt look at her comments.

'How can you say that, woman? You all know that it's just the music I love best.'

'Yeah,' she scoffed. 'I could see that you were sure paying a whole lot of attention to the performance of that waitress from the NCOs' club.'

'Hi, my name is Candy,' she mimicked. 'I'll be your waitress for today, is there anything I can do for you good old boys?'

She curtsied slightly and fluttered her eyelashes as she looked into Bishop's eyes.

'I noticed that you were pretty well enthralled by her musical talent and all those other fine Southern attributes she had on show.'

'Oh come on honey,' he retorted. 'You know I do admire how those cheerleaders can do that sort of stuff.'

Marie snorted and dug her husband in the ribs at his homespun humorous response.

'You want to see some good old-fashioned cheerleading? I'll show you some stuff that you ain't never seen before when I get you home. I'll show you things you can do with a baton that you wouldn't believe.'

Bishop's face fell at Marie's provocative remarks.

'Aw, honey. With all due respect, it just ain't the same without the music.'

I laughed uproariously at their unrehearsed double act as Bishop slipped his hand behind Marie's back to fondly squeeze her bottom.

Returning with three more bottles of Budweiser, Nick greeted the Bishops.

'Hi you guys; what's the joke?'

Still laughing, Pam took two of the bottles from Nick's hand, giving one to me.

'I'll tell you later honey. It's just those two doing what they do best.'

Happily wandering along enjoying the non-stop banter between Bishop and his wife, I felt my hangover becoming a thing of the past as I listened to their light-hearted repartee, slaking my alcohol-induced dehydration with the cold beer.

As we strolled along enjoying the carnival atmosphere of the fairground stalls, I began to feel the sun beating down on my unprotected head, noticing that nearly all of the men were wearing baseball caps or Stetsons while most of the women also wore some sort of hat or sun visor.

Turning to my cousin, I mopped my brow and rolled the ice cold beer bottle across my forehead.

'God, it's hot! If we see a stall that's selling hats I'm going to have to get one, it feels as if my head's on fire. I was going to take off my T-shirt but I think I that would be asking for trouble, I don't want to burn.'

Pam touched the top of my head.

'Yes, you're right, I think that's a good idea about the hat, you are pretty hot. You don't want to end up in bed with sunstroke.'

Grinning, she said, 'Whatever you plan on doing, don't tie knots in the corners of your handkerchief and stick that on your head like our dads used to when we went to the seaside when we were kids. Do you remember that?'

I laughed as I remembered some of the photographs in our family photo albums which showed Pam's dad and my own father displaying their makeshift headgear as Pam and I played happily on the beach at Ramsgate in Kent.

Still smiling as I recalled those blissfully happy days, I winced as I heard her say in a voice loud enough for all to hear. 'I don't think it's a good idea to take off your T-shirt Pete, we don't want another spectacle like the other day when you were parading around in my dressing gown showing off all your assets.'

To my acute embarrassment, Pam began to describe the earlier incident to the Bishops who began to hoot with laughter as she elaborated on how funny and how white my legs had looked as they stuck out of the bottom of her robe, telling them also that if the robe had been any shorter, the bounds of decency would certainly have been crossed.

Listening to Bishop's homespun philosophy on how he had always thought that English people were the leaders when it came to tact and diplomacy, he added that Pam's revelations had shocked him to the core, suggesting in a light-hearted manner that if it was kept within the family in the UK, it was perhaps considered to be OK.

Listening to her husband climbing aboard the bandwagon with his flippant appraisal of the English and their characteristics, Marie, to her eternal credit, instantly sprang to my defence.

'Never you mind him none Pete, he's sure had his moments I can tell you. In fact I'm reminded of a time when we lived down in Texas, a time that I'm good and damn sure he'd just as soon forget about.'

Holding up his hand in protest, Bishop quickly tried to change the subject.

'Now listen woman, I'm sure old Pete here doesn't want to listen to any of that old Texas stuff, anyway that was years ago.'

'You just hush up,' Marie continued. 'I'm sure that Pam and Nick wouldn't mind hearing that you ain't that good old, clued up, smart arse you like to make out all the time, and that you've done some pretty foolish things in the past as well.'

Bishop visibly cringed as he realised what Marie was about to tell us, waving his hand dismissively as if implying that it wasn't really worth listening to anyway.

'Like I said,' she continued. 'We were living down in Texas, way out in the boonies, miles from anywhere and were in bed on this particular night. Anyway, we had this big old house with a long driveway that backed right down on to this country road, and down there every one of them good old boys has a gun or three in the house and a few more in his pick-up just for back up. Believe me, those guys down there really believe that bit in the constitution where it says that everyone has the right to bear arms.'

Bishop groaned, and on the pretext of needing more beer, headed off to a nearby drum to fetch fresh supplies.

'Anyway, like I was saying,' Marie continued. 'We were in bed one night and I heard this noise coming from outside. I woke Robert, who was snoring like he always does and I tell him that I think there's someone trying to break in. He tells me to go back to sleep as it's just an old racoon or something digging in the trash.

'I told him that I wasn't having any of that old racoon crap and he was to get his backside out of bed and go down there and find out what it was all about.

'After a lot more prodding and poking with me telling him that he's supposed to be the man of the house and that he should get down there and find out what's going on, he finally gets his backside out of the bed and heads downstairs.

'After a while, I hear him go outside and then it all goes quiet and I get a mite worried, as them good old boys down there have a bit of a reputation for being, how shall we put it, for getting a bit on the twitchy side when it comes to drinking the odd fifth or two of Jack Daniel's and then doing daft things.

'I got out of bed and looked around, and when I couldn't hear anything, I went downstairs and looked out of the window to see what he was up to. Well, I'm telling you, it gets pretty dark down there out in the country and they don't have no street lamps and stuff like there is in the city.

'I opened the porch door a mite and I'm yelling "Robert, are you alright?"

'Nothing, not a word. I call him again and there's still no answer.'

Despite feeling slightly apprehensive at the possible outcome, I began to smile. Both of them were still here in one piece so I assumed that good old Bob was simply going to emerge from all of this as just the fall guy. Clearly he had beaten a hasty retreat to fetch the beer to avoid being around when the punchline was delivered, so I knew that whatever the outcome, he was going to end up with egg on his face.

After taking a quick drink, Marie carried on with her tale.

'About a year previous to us moving down there, there had been a couple of bad break-ins relatively close to where we were going, so we decided that as we were so isolated we would have some sort of security system with some big arc lights which would also light up the drive when we came home. Anyway, after calling Bob a couple more times and not getting a reply I decided that I'd switch on the lights.

'After I yanked on the switch that turned them on, I looked out of the window and down the drive. There was old Bob lit up like the fairy on a Christmas tree, naked as a jay bird with a twelve gauge shotgun in his hand, racing back up the drive like his arse was on fire. He's a yelling and a running and then all of a sudden he stubs his foot on a big rock or something, he's got nothing on his feet and over he goes. He drops the shotgun and the thing goes off with one almighty bang.'

By this time, we are all in hysterics as the vision of Bishop running back up the drive with no clothes on carrying a shotgun is more than we can stand; also, we are literally convulsed with laughter at the laconic way Marie is telling the story.

'Like I said, there's one hell of a bang and there's good old Bob sitting on the ground holding his busted foot and screaming blue murder, displaying all that he's got to display, which I might add, ain't all that, while every bird that was roosting in the vicinity flies off and leaves little reminders of their hasty departure all over him.'

As Bishop returned holding more beers, he bravely faced up to what he knew was about to come.

'Has she done?' He asked. 'I take it she gave you the whole unabridged story and didn't leave anything out?'

In between bouts of uncontrollable laughter my cousin let him know that we had been given an insight into his most intimate details as she spluttered, 'Bob, whenever I see you from now on I'm going to look at you in a new light.'

Taking a swig from his newly acquired beer, Nick laughed at Pam's unintentional pun in referring to seeing Bishop 'in a new light' by adding, ' It's a good job old Chico wasn't around then, otherwise he may well have got off by sniffing more intimate parts of your anatomy as well as your armpits.'

Bishop wiped a few froths of beer from his mouth before answering.

'Damn fool dog does that as well now. I guess you have to be thankful that the little guy is just a one-eyed midget, at least he can't get you while you're standing up.'

As we walked on, it became clear that several more visits to the bins containing beer were having an effect as Robert and Nick began a friendly but nonsensical North versus South argument on the merits of various foods and NFL football teams. With Bishop loudly proclaiming the benefits to be had from Southern fried food like Creole chicken, black-eyed peas and the Dallas Cowboys; Nick elected to praise New York Italian restaurants for their pastas, and rich sauces and the New England Patriots. It was clear that, despite calls from both Pam and Marie to 'give it a rest', this good-natured argument needed to be settled.

Suddenly Bishop let out a loud shout.

'Well now, look at what we have here. Now we'll just see who's the hunter and who's the hunted. I used to have an old BB gun when I was only six years old and I could out-shoot anyone in the school.'

I looked across to where Bishop was pointing, where an elaborately decorated shooting gallery dressed to look like a scene from Custer's Last Stand carried a huge banner which read, 'Win Your Sweetie a Cupie Doll'.

'Oh no,' Marie Groaned. 'Please tell me that old Davy Crockett here is not aiming to shoot something? The last time he had a rifle in his hand was when he enlisted, he wasn't much good then and I'm damn sure he ain't improved none now.'

With both men eager to take up the challenge, they hurried across to where a man in a large Stetson hat, cowboy shirt and jeans stood holding what looked like a .22 calibre rifle. He smiled as they both placed dollar bills down on the counter, each of them grabbing a rifle as soon as the man counted out six bullets each.

Watching them both making a lot of noise but failing miserably to cover themselves with any sort of glory or even coming close to winning anything, they eventually decided that the sights on the rifles were faulty, this after each having parted with at least five dollars. Studying the paper targets which the man handed them after each attempt, there appeared to be a distinct lack of bullet holes and finally, with great solemnity, they shook hands, earnestly declaring that the whole noisy contest was a well fought draw, each vowing that the next time it would be altogether different.

'Ain't you boys going to keep them targets to show future generations of Bishops and Dumases what their daddies could do with a rifle?' Marie scolded. 'I would have thought that you would like to keep them for posterity?'

Pam and I both laughed as both men muttered something decidedly uncomplimentary as they handed back their targets for the stall holder to dispose of.

As we strolled happily around the showground I was beginning to think that maybe this Parents' Day thing wasn't such a bad idea. I had been treated to free beer, eaten several delicious hot dogs complete with masses of onions, pickles and mustard, and not only that I had been creased up with laughter at the non-stop banter between the two Bishops. Whatever the authorities chose to throw at me with regard to my possible lateness at reporting for duty, I knew in my heart that I was doing the right thing. I felt that this was an important and formative period in my life which I would look back on and cherish, and whatever the future had in store for me, bring it on.

With the scorching sun continuing to beat down on my unprotected head, the idea of tying my handkerchief on to my head for some sort of protection was becoming increasingly more appealing when a shout from Nick offered a remote possibility of my salvation, at the same time helping me to avoid looking the complete idiot.

Spotting a stall inviting participants to pin three individual playing cards with three darts to win, Nick excitedly called out for me to 'get on over there and give it my best shot'. Strolling over, I looked at the prizes which were on offer and saw that they included various types of baseball caps, each one sporting the logo of teams playing in the NFL. Patting me on the back,

Nick hissed in my ear that this was right up my street and that I could easily win some of that 'crap'.

When Nick had been stationed at RAF Chicksands, we had regularly gone to a pub in nearby Shefford called the Sportsman which was owned by a friend of mine named Mike Campbell, someone who not only offered the best kept beer in the area but excellent food as well, a place that had become a regular haunt of the Americans. It was in this pub that newly posted young American servicemen had discovered the intricacies of the English game of darts, many of them considering themselves the equal of the legendary William Tell when it came to throwing the 'English Arrow.'

I have always been blessed with fairly good hand and eye co-ordination and Nick and I had gained a bit of a reputation as the guys who needed to be beaten, and as a result of this we were constantly being challenged to play for beer and sometimes money on the side as well.

Although Nick was no great shakes as a dart player, he could always be relied upon to keep his end up by hurling darts randomly at the board and scoring fairly decent scores, and it was my role in this partnership to not only throw decent scores but to finish off the opposition with the necessary doubles needed to win.

'Come on Pete, step up to the mark and win us some goodies.'

I began to feel slightly embarrassed as Nick went to great lengths to explain to Robert and Marie that him and I were the undisputed champions of Bedfordshire, a claim which was certainly untrue as we were just a couple of guys who won a few beers playing against Americans who thought that they could play a decent game of darts but realistically couldn't, secondly and probably more importantly, our opposition were usually drunk anyway.

While staying with Pam and Nick, I had often found myself as the butt of anti-English jokes of one sort or another at the hands of Bishop and other sundry Americans. Usually these derogatory comments were made by Americans who had never met an Englishman before and who accepted the publicised view of the stiff upper lipped Englishman as epitomised by Jeeves and Wooster as being the norm.

Over the past weeks there had been various Americans who had delighted in making comments in respect of my accent, also in relieving me of money at the poker table, now it was time to redress the balance and I wasn't going to let it pass.

With a whispered, 'Come on Pete, show these Yanks what we're made of,' Pam squeezed my arm as Nick handed over some money for the offered darts.

Despite the amount of beer I had already consumed, I knew that I was still reasonably sober and that there was no way I was going to be left wanting. This was an ideal time to put right all that had gone before and a perfect opportunity to put it to rest. Although Robert and Marie had gone out of their way to be friendly, I felt that even now they wouldn't be disappointed if they saw me fall at the first hurdle.

At school we had learned of the surrender of Cornwallis at Yorktown, the surrender of General John Burgoyne at Saratoga, and last but not least, the ignominy of the Boston Tea Party, and I was now being offered, albeit in a very small way, an opportunity of levelling the score as I accepted the darts that Nick handed to me.

The groan from behind me as my first dart thudded into the board between the ace of spades and the king of hearts did nothing to make me feel that this was going to be the moment of redemption I was praying for.

Undeterred, Nick gave the stallholder more money and presented me with a further three darts, at the same time urging me to concentrate.

My first dart skewered the centre of that same ace of spades; the second dart embedding itself into the centre of the sneering king of hearts while my third dart pinned the ten of diamonds to its backboard.

From somewhere behind, I was conscious of a small cheer as the stallholder declared that 'We have a winner', and would I like to try again.

Offering the stallholder more money, Nick again handed me the three darts that I had previously used, the ace of spades, the king of hearts and the ten of diamonds now bearing witness to my accuracy.

Twelve darts later, those three cards were a vision of their former self as I ripped them apart. To say that I felt like a modern day hero would not be an exaggeration as dart after dart thudded into its target, each successive winning dart being accompanied by a cheer from an enthusiastic gallery that was becoming larger, minute by minute, as more and more people joined to watch this impromptu drama.

To his credit, the stallholder somewhat grudgingly shared the enthusiasm of the crowd of onlookers, while my cousin and my newly acquired fan club greeted each successive dart thudding into its target with loud shouts of 'olé'.

Feeling the euphoria slowly beginning to wear off and the effects of the previously consumed beer beginning to take effect, I reluctantly took the three darts which Nick again thrust into my hand, shaking my head saying that this would be my last throw.

Up until now the stallholder had no inkling that I was not an American, my hair was cut into a crew cut and spiked up with gel and I was wearing fatigue pants that gave the impression that I was indeed an American. Until that moment I had not spoken, but on hearing my English accent the man's face betrayed the fact that he was somewhat surprised and not altogether happy.

'If I had known that you were a limey,' he said. 'I would have called time out on you.'

The derisive term 'limey' and the cumulative effect of the beer that I had consumed, might, at any other time, have triggered me into being more aggressive, but my feeling of 'goodwill to all men' and, of course, not forgetting as well that it was Parents' Day caused me to smile and reply in my best affected English accent,

'And had I known that you were someone whom I believe your fellow Americans describe as a "cracker", I would have probably declined the invitation to play anyway.'

Behind me I could hear cheers and shouts of approval at my contentious remark, and after a shrug of his shoulders, the guy on the stall smiled as he thrust out his hand, 'Yeah, OK buddy, take your pick. You've got six prizes to come. What do you fancy?'

Feeling that I was now master of all I surveyed and couldn't let my fan club down, I grinned as I said, 'I think I might have one last throw. What's the big prize?'

On hearing this, the man's face lit up.

'Well, now we're talking' he said, 'It's that big pink fluffy elephant up there on the top shelf.'

He turned and pointed to an enormous pink elephant that seemed to be smiling at me and begging to be taken to a new home.

The man turned back and laughingly said, 'Listen buddy, you're good but you ain't that good. You have to put three darts into just one card to win that little beauty.'

Feeling that I had just flown the flag for Englishmen the world over, I cockily turned to my cousin and said, 'How do you fancy that big fluffy elephant then? The man here says we can't do it, what do you reckon?'

'Quit while you're ahead Pete, he just wants to see you fail. Don't do it.'

The clapping from the people behind, coupled with shouts of 'go get it limey' and cries of 'you're the man', boosted my confidence as I made my decision.

'I'll take the throw.'

Picking the ripped and torn king of hearts as the card I felt the most comfortable with, I quietly waited as the noise from behind slowly subsided.

Slowly and deliberately, I raised my arm and released the first dart.

With a looping, dipping flight, the first dart thudded into its mark.

Even before the dart had found its mark, the people behind had started to cheer, one down, and two to go.

With the first dart quivering in the playing card, it was starting to dawn on me that if I failed in this quest I was in danger of looking like a bit of a braggart, and with this niggling thought in mind, I launched my second dart towards its target.

Before the dart had even reached half way I knew that at least this one was going to join the first. Offering up a small prayer, I watched as it joined its predecessor, grinning as it buried its point deep into what remained of the king's head. The small crowd behind me were now silent as they revelled in the drama that was beginning to unfold.

Despite the beer I had already consumed, my mouth felt as dry as the sand tray in the bottom of a budgie's cage as I gulped and licked my dry lips.

Why had I been such an idiot and shown off like that? Why hadn't I kept my big mouth shut and gone quietly? I was already a winner, why hadn't I quit while my reputation was still intact?

I looked behind me to where Nick had one arm around my cousin's shoulders, both of their faces telling a different story. Pam, undoubtedly fearing the worst, stood with both hands clasped together beneath her chin as if in prayer, while Nick waved a clenched fist in encouragement as he urged me on.

Turning back, I tried to tell myself that it was only a cuddly toy and what the hell did it matter if I missed anyway. It was only a stupid fairground prize that you could probably buy in the commissary for five or six bucks, but in my heart I knew that it was much more than that, this was all about pride.

It's fair to say that never before or since have I been so nervous. No matter how I tried to dismiss the whole exercise as being totally pointless and trivial, the fear was slowly growing inside me but there was no way that I was going to fail now.

Suddenly, I knew what it must feel like to be the person who has been elected to take the penalty which would decide the result of the Cup Final on Wembley's hallowed turf.

Up until this moment I had been unbearably hot strolling about the fairground but not anymore, it now felt as if the temperature had dropped quite dramatically, my palms were still sweating but the rest of my body was icy cold. Until now, the noise from the marching bands and the kiddies' funfair had echoed around the ground, but apart from the loud beating of my heart, I could hear nothing, there was a silence that prompted my hand to shake even more as I prepared to throw my last dart.

Staring at the playing card in which two darts now bristled, the target looked even smaller, and the more I stared the smaller it became.

Slowly raising my arm and staring intently at the remains of the king's sneering face, I held my breath as I sent the final dart on its way. As if in slow motion, I followed its flight as it arced towards its intended mark.

Rattling against the other two darts which remained in the target, the point of the dart pierced the piece of card and hung at a drunken angle, seemingly only held there by its two predecessors. For what seemed an age, myself, the stallholder and the crowd stood in absolute silence, all staring at the target board waiting for the inevitable, but the dart stayed in.

As one, the crowd behind me roared its approval, rushing forward to rain stinging slaps on my back and shoulders as Nick grabbed me around the neck nearly dragging me to the ground, whooping and shouting while Pam stood staring and shaking her head in disbelief.

Taking the huge pink elephant down from the top shelf, the man smiled and ceremoniously presented it to my cousin.

'Here you go ma'am, I hope you enjoy it. Your guy there deserves it, even if he is a limey.'

Shaking my hand, the stallholder grinned as he graciously said. 'Well done buddy, you've still got six other prizes to come, so choose what you want and get the hell out of here and don't come back, you're going to bankrupt me.'

Still grinning, he turned to retrieve my darts from the target; his grin turning to a look of disbelief on his face as my final dart slowly slipped from the board and fell to the floor.

Accompanied by pats on the back and cries of 'Well done buddy', we pushed our way through the crowd who were still whooping and hollering, each of us wearing or carrying our additional prizes.

Feeling like the fearless Black Knight from Arthurian legend, I had selected a black Los Angeles Raiders baseball cap from the stallholder's huge selection, while Nick and Pam chose St. Louis Cardinals caps. Robert and Marie happily sported identical Dallas Cowboys caps, and Clifford, the remainder of yet another cone of candy floss having been consigned to a nearby trash can, excitedly played with a model of a B52 bomber.

With a decidedly pink face that wasn't the result of being out in the sun too long, Pam laughingly accepted the plaudits of sections of the small crowd as she carried the huge pink fluffy monstrosity through the well-wishers as we made our way back on to the fairground concourse in the direction of other stalls which offered other tantalising delicacies as prizes.

'That sure was some show you put on back there Pete,' Bishop said as he slapped me on the back. 'Nick always reckoned that you two were the dog's cojones back in England when it came to shooting the darts, and for once in his life it seems he wasn't just whistling Dixie. That good old boy with the stall back there got one hell of a shock when he heard you speak, I don't reckon he'd come across any English guys before, his face was a real picture when you accused him of being a cracker.'

I grinned, feeling slightly embarrassed, but at the same time thrilled that I had shown that, from now on, I might not be the butt of too many 'limey' jokes.

'In England we have a saying that says, "You can't always tell a book by its cover." I remember one time when we were playing poker you won a pot with a full house that you dragged out of nowhere and I recall you saying that "not all trappers wore fur hats", so maybe we're not that different after all.'

Amid hoots of laughter and good-humoured comments from some of the people who had obviously overheard my remark, we strolled on towards a narrow piece of open ground, where at one end a steel spike was stuck into the hard ground, and at the other, several fat, red-faced men wearing check shirts and Stetson hats stood with large horseshoes in their hands awaiting their turn to toss the heavy metal shoes at the spike.

'Now here's something us good old Southern boys are good at,' Bishop announced. 'I was practically raised with a horseshoe in my hand and now I'm going to show you soft city folks how it's done.'

A loud groan from Marie told us that she had obviously seen Robert in his hillbilly farmhand guise before, and she left us all in no doubt of what was likely to come next.

'Aw, come on Robert, you just told us how good you were with a rifle and I do believe that old Clifford here could have done better than you, why don't you just quit while you're ahead. With all that beer you boys have just drunk, I doubt you can even see what you're supposed to hit.'

Ignoring Marie's taunts, Bishop joined the small queue of heavily perspiring men and handed over a few cents for the privilege of hurling these cumbersome and heavy horseshoes in the general direction of a spike which stood in splendid isolation some fifteen to twenty yards away.

'Now listen up Pete, here's what you have to do. Just hold the shoe like this, not too tightly mind and aim it at the spike down there at the end.'

Holding the horseshoe by its curved front with the open back of the shoe pointing downwards, he demonstrated a lazy slow underarm swing without actually letting go.

'You need to throw the shoe so the open end here goes around the spike, that's called a ringer. If you hit the spike and it stays leaning against it that also scores; here, I'll show you what I mean.'

I don't know who was the more surprised, Bishop or the man who stood watching nearby, when the horseshoe slipped from his hand and flew sideways, neatly taking the neck off the bottle of beer he was holding, spilling the remainder down the front of his trousers.

I thought that I would wet myself as I howled with laughter watching Bishop attempting to pacify the irate man who stood looking as if he would like to take the shoe and hit him over the head with it. After offering the man the remainder of his horseshoes as some form of recompense and desperately trying to wipe off the man's trousers with his handkerchief, some degree of sanity returned as the man finally calmed down. And with Bishop still offering his apologies, he was led away from the scene of his disaster by Marie; Pam, Nick and I still virtually convulsed with laughter.

Still chuckling, we walked around the rest of the showground until it was finally decided that, before anyone got killed or seriously injured as a result of the two men showing off any further, we would call it a day and head for home, thus ending one of the most enjoyable days that I had spent in my entire life; a day that had been filled with some of the most wonderful and hilarious memories that I would treasure forever.

Granada...

For several days, the niggling thought of returning to England to do my National Service had continually preyed on my mind. I knew that, sooner or later, I would have to accept the fact that I really had no choice; realising that the longer I put off making the decision on when to return, the harder it would become. After hours of quietly sitting alone on the balcony and contemplating what I should do, I came to the conclusion that applying for American citizenship was not a serious option for me at this time, accepting however, that as much as I hated the prospect of what was to come, I needed to get home and face the immediate reality of my future.

It would be wonderful to stay in Spain and continue to enjoy the hospitality of Pam and Nick and to hang out with Robert and Marie, but I knew that it was simply a pipe dream. If I failed to return and face the music pretty soon, I could become listed as a deserter and this was something that I could never let happen. I reasoned that if I failed to return to England and report for duty, my continued absence would mean that, when I next returned home again some time in the future, I risked being arrested and the disgrace of this was something that didn't bear thinking about.

Early one morning after a particularly uneasy night's sleep, I sat pensively staring into a mug of coffee which had gone cold at least twenty minutes earlier. Suddenly, I was startled by Nick's voice breaking into my train of thought.

'What's up buddy boy? You've been a bit quiet for the last few days, is something bothering you?'

I managed a small grin as I replied.

'No, not really,' I answered. 'I was just thinking that if I stayed with you guys for much longer I would be in danger of wearing out my welcome.'

'That's silly,' Pam scolded overhearing our conversation as she walked into the room. 'You know that we love having you and you're welcome to stay for as long as you like.'

'That's kind of you,' I replied, 'but I guess all good things must come to an end.'

'I reckon Mum and Dad must already be thinking that I've emigrated and I'm never coming home, so I really need to start thinking about getting back. On top of that, I'm down to my last few hundred pesetas,' I laughed. 'The only way I can afford to stay here any longer is to win some money from you guys at the poker table and I can't really see that happening in a hurry, can you?'

On hearing of my intention, there was a moment of quiet before my cousin asked the question that I knew would be asked sooner or later.

'When do you have to report for duty, is that anytime soon?'

Shrugging my shoulders, I replied that I wasn't quite sure but there were things I needed to do. As soon as the lie left my lips it stuck in my throat like a fish bone, I certainly had things to do but that particular date was burned into my brain.

'We'll miss you buddy boy,' was Nick's reply. 'It's been great having you here; even the cat is going to miss you.'

I smiled at the thought of my confrontation with the cat, recalling the flea-bitten animal's bedraggled escape. It had finally returned on a more or less permanent basis but every time we made eye contact, it arched its back and beat a hasty retreat to a safe distance where it would sit watching me, poised to make a swift exit if it looked as if I had further intentions which would jeopardise its well-being.

Seeing the sadness in my cousin's face, I tried to be upbeat about the time I had left. Attempting to lighten the mood by saying that now I had been shown the good life, the minute my obvious star-studded and successful career in the air force came to an end, I would be back on the first plane and they would probably never get rid of me.

Accepting a fresh mug of coffee, I mentioned that I had been talking to Paco and he had spoken of Granada, in particular the Alhambra. I added that he had mentioned that if I only ever saw one more glorious testament to Moorish architecture in my life it had to be the Alhambra and the Royal Palace. He also chastised me by saying that, while I was here in Seville, it would be criminal if I wasted such a golden opportunity of not visiting it before my return to England, comments which had set me thinking.

Pam quickly jumped in to endorse what Paco had said.

'We always said that we would visit there as well and we never have. Didn't we buy a book in the commissary which covered the history of Granada when we first got here? What ever happened to that book Nick, it must be about here somewhere?'

Carrying his coffee, Nick got to his feet, leaving the room to return several minutes later, still clutching his coffee in one hand but carrying a small Baedeker type guidebook in the other.

'Is this what you wanted?' he asked, dropping the book down in front of her.

'That's it', she answered, flicking through its pages and suddenly stopping to stab at one of the pages with her finger.

'Here it is, Granada. I remember thinking at the time that we must see it. How far from is it from here Nick?'

'I don't think it's a trip we can do in a day. Here, let me take a look.'

Watching his finger trace a route along what appeared to be a very small map, he finally shook his head.

'It looks like it's over two hundred clicks from here; it's a long haul in a day.'

'Clicks?' I asked curiously. 'What are clicks?'

Pam grinned.

'He means kilometres, it's something they say in the military, don't ask me why, they have a lot of these weird expressions.'

I shrugged.

'I'm not even sure what a kilometre is,' I said. 'I know it's some sort of distance but that's about it, how far is a kilometre anyway, is it more than a mile?'

Nick looked at me in mock horror.

'Come on Pete, you're kidding me right?'

'No, I'm not kidding, why would I want to know what a kilometre is. While your lot were playing cowboys and Indians, we gave the world uncomplicated imperial measurements, so why would I need to know about kilometres?'

Shaking his head in apparent disbelief, Nick put down the book before answering.

'Are you seriously telling me you didn't learn about metric measurements at school?' he asked. 'What in hell do they teach you guys in England these days?'

'Alright you two, let's not start all that old nonsense again,' Pam laughed. 'I don't need any more of that England versus the US crap right now; let's just concentrate on Granada shall we? Can we make it in a day or not?'

Despite my cousin's protestations, I wasn't prepared to let him have the last word and I dug deep into my memory for something I could retaliate with. In a flash of inspiration, the answer came leaping from one the deepest corners of my brain.

'You think you know a lot about that sort of stuff, so maybe you'd like to explain the theory of the rod, pole or perch, that's been around for a good number of years and I'd be interested in the way that measures up to your metric system, or maybe they didn't teach you pretty basic stuff like that at school?'

'Now you are kidding me right?' he snorted. 'What in hell has that got to do with distance, metric or otherwise? That's just some lunatic English fishing crap that you've just dreamed up.'

To this day I don't know how I remembered that a rod, pole or perch was the equivalent of five and a half yards or sixteen and a half feet, but I was pretty confident that he didn't know and I delivered the coup de grâce with a straight face.

'Surely you're not seriously trying to tell me that you didn't learn stuff like that when you went to school? For Pam and I and millions of others like us, that was pretty basic in junior school. You surprise me man, I'm beginning to revise my opinion about you; you've really gone down in my estimation.'

Trying hard not to laugh, I turned my face away as I got up from the table, taking my empty coffee mug back into the kitchen. When I was sure that I couldn't be seen, I punched the air in triumph as I heard Nick say to Pam, 'Is that right what Pete just said or is that just bullshit?'

'Don't involve me in your little mind games, just tell me if we're going or not?'

'I still don't believe him,' Nick muttered, 'he's winding me up. Sure, OK, we'll go. I don't have to check in at work until Friday so we'll find a decent little hotel when we get there and we'll stay over night, it will make a nice trip.'

Pam threw her arms around his neck before walking into the kitchen to where I stood leaning against the sink with a grin on my face, trying desperately not to laugh.

'What was all that rubbish about a rod and whatever else you said? I've no idea what you were talking about; I don't remember learning anything like that at school.'

I kissed her on the cheek as I walked past.

'That's alright cousin, just don't tell him that, that's all.'

* * * *

After having thrown a change of clothes into a small American air force flight bag, we left the bar after a brief chat with Paco and walked the few yards to a slightly wider street where Nick always parked his car. As we got nearer, I commented on the group of four or five children who were gathered at the kerb, each one watching us as we walked towards them, happy smiles on their faces as they recognised who we were.

'These kids always seem happy,' I said. 'I've never noticed any of them begging or making nuisances of themselves when we come out and pick up the car; they always seem genuinely pleased to see us?'

'That's right,' Nick replied, fishing the keys out from a trouser pocket. 'When we first got here I asked Paco if it was safe to leave the car out on the street here. He assured me that it wouldn't be touched and told me that he would have a quiet word with the people who live here just to make sure that they all knew that the car belonged to his guests. Since that time, whenever we go to get the car, we always have this little reception committee to welcome us.'

'When you say that you've never seen them begging around here it's because this is their district, their home patch if you like. The other reason is that they don't beg around here because they wouldn't get anything given to them anyway, everyone here is pretty much in the same boat. Remember when you first arrived and we picked you up from the station and all those kids were begging there?'

I nodded before answering.

'I asked you why you didn't give them anything and Pam said that if we had done so we would have been surrounded by dozens more in minutes.'

'That's right,' he replied. 'Some of the kids from around here go down to the cathedral and the *alcázar* and hang out there. They know that the pickings are going to be richer there so they go for the tourists and such.

'After we'd been living here for a while, we got to know what to do and what not to do. We gave Paco a bunch of stuff from the commissary, just a few goodies for the kids, nothing much, just a few Hershey bars, some gum and stuff like that and he handed it out, since then we've had our own little security squad, they're good kids.'

'They're lovely kids,' Pam added. 'They're always the same, always smiling, always pleased to see you. Like most of the people who live around here, their folks don't have much but they always make sure that the children are well fed and the clothes they wear are clean and not ripped or anything, it's a good place to live.'

As Nick unlocked the car, I ruffled the jet black hair of one youngster who had lost his front teeth, his gummy smile lighting up his face as he reached up to touch my hand.

'Isn't he just the cutest thing you've ever seen?' Pam said with a wistful smile.

'Come on honey, don't you start getting broody on me now,' Nick said with a grin, ' we've got a whole bunch of stuff to do yet before we start thinking about kids.'

As soon as we left the outskirts of the city we began to follow the course of another river, one not as wide as the Guadalquivir but narrower and fairly fast flowing as it meandered through the hot dusty landscape. Soon we were driving through a small Spanish village whose dusty white washed houses and colourful tiled roofs provided homes for people who, by the look of their frayed and poor appearance, scratched a meagre living from the dry arid fields which stretched as far as the eye could see.

As I looked out of the car window, Nick reached down to a pocket in the door and threw me the book he had been looking at before we left.

'Here, make yourself useful, give me the route as we go. I think we stay on this road pretty much until we get there, it's not quite the freeway but it's the main route to Granada. That village we just passed through was Alcala and the river you can see is the Guadaira. The next place we come to should be El Arahal and then Osuna.'

Turning to the appropriate page, I found the villages that Nick had mentioned and traced a route with my finger in the direction of Granada, pausing momentarily at what looked like a fairly large village called Antequera.

'I don't know if anyone fancies it, but there's a small town ahead after we pass through Osuna called Antequera, and it says here that it has some Roman caves and some sort of megalithic monument, it might be somewhere to get some lunch and stretch our legs?'

'How far ahead is that?' Nick asked, glancing at the clock on the dashboard.

'It's about thirty-five or forty minutes drive from where we are now. Perhaps we can find a little *taverna* and get a beer and something to eat. Lunch is on me, and if you want to go exploring afterwards we can take a stroll and have a look at what these caves and the monument are all about, today is going to be my treat.'

There was a laugh from the back as Pam patted the back of my head.

'This boy doesn't care what he spends his money on does he? First it's a beer, then it's lunch, and after all that he wants us to go poking around in some holes in the ground. Thanks for the offer Pete, but I'll stay with the beer and the lunch, you won't get me anywhere near any caves. I have trouble on the subway, so I'm sure as hell not built for clambering about in a bunch of caves thank you very much.'

With a chuckle, Nick lit a cigarette from the lighter on the car's dashboard.

'Well I guess that's it Pete, It doesn't look as if we'll be doing any underground stuff today but I appreciate the thought. If it's all the same to you, we'll just settle for a couple of beers and lunch if the offer is still on.'

I shrugged in an overly exaggerated manner.

'OK, if that's the way you feel, but I've got to say that when I've gone, you're going to be sorry that we didn't get to see those caves. Don't you go writing to me to say that you're sad that you missed out, this was a one-off offer and you blew it.'

Driving into the outskirts of Antequera, we pulled off the dusty road and pulled up outside a small bar, stopping near to a formidable looking hedge of some of the spikiest cactus I had ever seen, beside which, two mangy straw-coloured dogs lay dozing fitfully in its shade.

Having been previously warned that patting any of the painfully thin and forlorn looking dogs that wandered the streets around the city wasn't exactly the smartest thing to do because of the risk of rabies, I stared out of the car window thinking of the best way to stay well clear of them. I needn't have worried as Pam immediately gave the thumbs down to our intended lunch venue.

'No way José, I'm not going in there. Take a look at those four guys sitting at the table by the door, let's get out of here and find somewhere else.'

I looked to where the four men were seated, mentally agreeing that this was definitely not the place for us. The four unshaved and scruffily-dressed men watched as we sat in the car, one of them not taking his eyes from Pam as he began peeling a large raw onion with a long wide bladed knife which he took from the chest pocket of a pair of ragged and grime-stained overalls. As we watched, one of them appeared to say something to the man with the knife who spat in the dust before drawing his thumb along the blade as they stared in our direction. Needing no further urging, Nick turned the key in the ignition and rammed the car into gear, gunning the engine and leaving behind a huge cloud of dust as we bounced back on to the main highway.

'What was that all about?' I gasped, as we gathered speed to put as much distance as we could between us and the four men.

'Obviously they're not big fans of Americans,' Nick said with a frown.

'Some of these country boys out here in the boonies haven't yet seen the light and still hold a grudge about what happened during the civil war. I reckon those guys were part of Franco's fan club who still want to carry on with the struggle.

'Do you remember when I told you that people are still disappearing as a result of what happened in the past? Well, out here in the sticks, I guess there are a few people who reckon they have a few scores to settle, particularly with foreigners like us. If you look at some of the road signs as we go along, you'll notice that some have bullet holes in them. They're not the result of any fighting, those are the equivalent of Don Quixote tilting at windmills, that's what some of the natives do to show that they're not too keen on authority or the new regime.'

As we drove along the almost-deserted highway, I kept checking the map to see how much further we had to go, tracing the route right through to Granada. Looking up, I saw that we had just passed a small village called Loja, near which a road sign stated that we had less than sixty five kilometres to go before we reached our destination.

'We've just passed a sign that said it's only about sixty five kilometres to Granada,' I said, wondering if Nick had also noticed the sign.

'I saw it,' Nick replied, glancing at his watch.

'I think that as we're making pretty good time, we might as well head on through and get some lunch when we get there if that's alright with everyone?'

Scanning the book for information on what we could expect to see when we got there, I began to feel excited, taking me back to when I was a small boy when, in the summer months, Mum and Dad would take me to the seaside. Sometimes we would travel by train, or more often by an alternative mode of transport which was usually referred to as a day trip on a chara. The origin of the expression 'going on a chara' almost certainly came from my grandmother who often used to relate stories of how she and my grandfather would sometimes treat themselves and go out for the day on a far more primitive version of coach travel, a vehicle more familiarly known in those days as a charabanc.

Unaware that I was quietly chuckling out loud as I remembered those blissfully happy days when the sun seemed to shine continually from May until October, I was suddenly brought back to the present by Pam interrupting my train of thought.

'What are you giggling at? You were a thousand miles away just then weren't you?'

'I was just thinking back to when we were kids, when we all used to go to the seaside. We never had much money but we had some wonderful times didn't we?

'I remember that time when we went to the seaside for the day and you wet your knickers on the coach, and when your mum changed you, your dad had to hold up his raincoat so no-one could see what was happening, do you remember?'

'Trust you to remember that. You always were a little snitch and I suppose now you've remembered you'll be telling Paco as well when we get back.'

Nick and I both laughed in unison as he remarked that not much had changed, swearing that my cousin still carried a spare pair in her handbag every time they went out together, just in case.

With a snort of indignation, Pam whacked her husband hard across his shoulders.

'Oh, that's right, just because you've got old sneaky there on your side, don't you start getting too cocky or I might just blow the whistle on some of the little things that you get up to when you think no-one else is around.'

****

I think it fair to say that none of us were prepared for the awe-inspiring sight that greeted us as we drove into the outskirts of Granada.

Rising above us, the warm red brick outer walls of the Alhambra soared upwards into the cloudless blue sky, glowing as if on fire as the sun danced on the ancient ramparts and towers, beyond which the snow-capped peaks of the Sierra Nevada stared down as a magnificent backdrop to this unbelievably beautiful setting. In complete contrast to the soaring grandeur of the ancient walls and towers, the deep gorge of the Rio Darrow plunged dramatically down into the wooded valley below.

In the distance, beyond this precipitous chasm, a cluster of red roofed, white walled houses of the old Albaicin quarter looked out towards the historic Sacromonte cave dwellings. Primitive caves and tunnels carved into the soft rock hundreds of years ago, many of them still remaining occupied to provide homes for some of Granada's proud and defiant gypsy population.

Stepping from the parked car, we each gazed in silence at the steep climb leading towards the Alhambra, a narrow street leading upwards to where an unadorned and sturdy gateway consisting of three stone archways tempted visitors to enter into the cool inviting shade of a seductive leafy oasis nestling beneath the mighty fortress walls.

Deciding to forgo lunch, we slowly climbed the hill and entered through the carved archways into the historic and beautiful fortress. Nick pointed above our heads at three carved images depicting some form of fruit nestling in its attendant branches, the worn and detailed stone carving standing proudly above the gateway.

'Look at that up there; they're pomegranates. I've just realised that the word for a pomegranate in Spanish is *granada*, I guess that's the emblem of the city? I knew they grew pomegranates in Spain but I didn't make the association.'

Once through the arched gateways, we were confronted by a trio of roads, one which veered off to the right, a central one which appeared to run virtually parallel to its neighbour through pine woods and clipped hedges, and the third, a shorter road, at the end of which we could clearly see another small gateway offering access through the outer walls of the Alhambra itself.

Opting for the road on our left, we climbed upwards towards the outer defensive walls of this great fortress, passing a monument dedicated to the Emperor Carlos V before reaching a double arched gateway which, with its high battlements and strategically placed arrow slits, gave an indication of the purpose of its architecture. Through a shimmering heat haze we stared at the great defensive walls, the towering ramparts taking on the appearance of being constructed of solid gold.

Pausing to get our breath in the shade beneath a second smaller arch, I whistled as I read out loud the inscription carved into the stone above our heads.

'Wow, can you believe that? This gateway was constructed by someone named Yusuf I in 1348. That is amazing, no wonder the Moors could hold on to this place for so long before they were finally driven out of Spain. Just imagine how many people were slaughtered trying to capture this place, it's virtually impregnable.'

Just above the dedication to the long deceased Yusuf was another carving which, strangely enough, appeared to be that of the Virgin Mary and the new born baby Jesus, its almost pristine condition suggesting that this was an image which had been added at a much later date.

Puzzling over the significance of a Christian subject being in evidence in such an imposing Muslim stronghold, I was startled by an urgent tugging at my sleeve. Turning around I was confronted by the grizzled figure of a man wearing a sack about his shoulders. Brandishing a broom made from twigs, his role appeared to be that of keeping the paths and patios clear of leaves which occasionally fluttered down from the surrounding trees. Speaking in a lisping Andalucian dialect he pointed to the carvings above our heads, clearly attempting to make himself understood with regard to either the earliest inscription, or that of the image of Mary and the Christ child.

Pam and Nick both listened intently, occasionally interrupting his well-practised dialogue to translate what was being said.

'He says that the original carving was replaced much later by this one and he thinks the original might be housed in the Museum of Fine Arts in Madrid. He also says that he cannot explain why that Christian image comes to be here.'

The old man, although clearly not an official guide, waxed lyrically as he proudly described what we would see as we walked through the ancient palaces and gardens of the Alhambra and the Palacio de Generalife. He explained that he had worked in this beautiful place all his life and loved telling visitors of the joys of what he described as his second home. Finally, we wished the old man goodbye and made our way deeper into the incredible Alcazaba fortress and the unbelievable beauty of the historic Moorish palaces.

Wandering through magnificent piazzas and terraces, no words could possibly do justice to the breathtaking beauty of that incredible place. Detailed carvings and frescos adorning the walls and archways linked one gallery to another, each decorated wall and alcove ablaze with a golden, fiery beauty and highlighted by the sumptuous colours of the intricate tiles and mosaics.

Beautifully carved and sculptured archways led to the unbelievable 'Lookout of Lindaraja', where carved stone embellishments literally dripped from the walls and ceilings like man-made stalactites. Inside, elaborately carved and embellished open arched porticos were cleverly positioned to embrace the soft warm pine-scented breeze offering a cool paradise away from the searing heat outside.

I strolled on my own through rooms adorned with intricately carved arches and pillars to where the Royal Baths and the magnificent spectacle of the Hall of Kings left me spellbound and dazzled by its brilliance, each room and gallery also designed to gather in the soft warm breezes which created further wonderful oases in this amazing structure.

From one of the upper galleries, I gazed down on to the beautiful Court of the Lions where a twelve-sided marble font rested upon the backs of twelve large carved lions. In the centre of this delicately carved marble basin, a small fountain bubbled upwards which, in turn, provided water to each of the lions from whose mouths further fountains cascaded into a shallow trough which then distributed the water throughout the courtyard.

It would be impossible to find a more beautiful place than the one in which I now stood as each room and gallery struggled to outdo the other in both the intricacies of its carved walls and ceilings and the brilliance and magnificence of its tiles. There can be no other structure in the world which illustrates more clearly the desire of man to appease or worship God by dedicating their life's work through the skill of their own two hands and the sweat of their brow than here, be it Arab or Spaniard, Christian or Muslim.

Passing through a small doorway, I followed a winding passageway and emerged outside to find myself in an impressive rectangular courtyard, in the centre of which a bubbling fountain gently distributed its cool waters into a circular stone trough from where it trickled into a crystal clear pool. In the clear water, the porticos and the superb tower of the Emir's palace were reflected in shimmering beauty while shoals of goldfish swam gracefully below the surface, seldom rising to disturb the tranquillity of the scene.

Along each side of the rectangular pool, hedges of myrtle gave off a sweet perfume which hung heavy in the still air, a perfect retreat of peace and solitude, a place which has inspired such towering works as those by Manuel de Falla, Joaquín Rodrigo and the great Spanish poet, Federico García Lorca.

As I stood and closed my eyes, the only sound to disturb this perfect peace was the chirping of cicadas paying their own tribute to this awe-inspiring place, and in that precise moment I knew that it was time to leave. The history and the beauty of Granada and the Alhambra had reached out to touch my heart and I knew that nothing else I ever saw or did would have such an impact; this was my own 'moment of truth' and I knew that the time had come.

Certain in the knowledge that I would return many times throughout the course of my life, I also knew that future visits would be joyful pilgrimages back to the baptismal font of my emergence into manhood.

Idly watching the goldfish in their lazy processions around the pool, I felt a slight touch on my elbow.

'Well, what do you think; it sure is something isn't it?'

I turned to see my cousin standing at my side.

I shook my head.

'I could never have imagined anything so beautiful,' I said. 'When you look at the magnificence of it all, it's hard to believe that people had the skills to construct such a place, and taking into consideration its age and the carnage that took place here, it's a miracle that it's still standing.'

Changing the subject, I looked around.

'Where's tricky Nicky?' I asked. 'Is he on a mission to find the nearest bar or has he slipped off quietly to pray?'

Pam laughed at my character assassination of her husband.

'The second question is certainly a no-no; he's beyond redemption on that score. He's slipped back to the car for the guidebook we brought to see if it mentions a decent hotel where we can have dinner and spend the night, he'll be back in a bit.'

'I saw a couple of places that looked interesting just near where we parked the car,' I remarked.

'I did too,' she said, 'Nick thinks we'd be better off if we stayed somewhere that's recommended in the book.'

As Pam and I strolled around the pool talking, I told her of my decision to leave within the next few days, not mentioning that I was already a week late in reporting to Cardington for my call up.

On hearing my news, her face fell, saying that she would miss me and that it had been a pleasure having me stay with them, adding also that if my call up was due sometime in the future, she was sure that there were lots of things I needed to sort out before I went. Reaching up to give me a light kiss on the cheek, she slid her arm through mine as we walked, stating that any time I fancied coming out to see them wherever in the world they might be I would be more than welcome.

Strolling through the beautiful gardens of the Generalife, we chatted about all the things we had done when we were kids, reminiscing about the Christmases we had enjoyed with our two really close-knit families, and how our respective parents had worked miracles to provide such wonderful times for us together with the multitude of presents we had been fortunate enough to receive in times of such austerity during and after the war.

We laughed as we remembered our mutual grandmother being unable to move away from the table and wetting herself whilst stricken with uncontrollable laughter when I had crunched a stink bomb beneath the table, much to the annoyance of my father who was forced to open all of the sitting room windows in the middle of what can only be described as a freezing blizzard one Boxing Day; our happy reminiscences being interrupted by Nick's return.

'I think I've found us the perfect place to stay for the night,' he said, waving the small guidebook in triumph.

'There's a small family-run hotel in the Paseo del Generalife not a million miles away from where we parked the car,' he said. 'I've checked it out and I'm pretty sure you'll love it. The guy who owns it asked if we wanted dinner and I told him that we did, and he's going to cook traditional paella. Is that OK with you two?'

We both enthusiastically agreed, Pam stating that this would be my first authentic paella during my visit, saying that she knew I wouldn't be disappointed, with this signature dish that this area of Spain was renowned for.

Although we had enjoyed paella on the base, both Pam and Nick had agreed that while, at times it had been alright, it usually lacked the authenticity that can only be brought about by someone who knows exactly what he is doing by using the right ingredients cooked in the traditional way.

'I had a quick peek around the place while I was there and it looks as if the guy has got a few decent bottles of wine as well. I saw a couple of bottles of good Rioja in the rack and, by the amount of dust that was on them, they've been there a few years.'

'Now why am I not surprised that you noticed something like that,' Pam laughed. 'I bet your alcohol antenna was working overtime while you were in there. Let's just hope for his sake that he hasn't hidden the good stuff away for the locals before we get there, I'm sure the last thing he wants to see is you crying your eyes out all over the place.'

With the thought of good food and wine now uppermost in our minds, we fairly skipped through the remainder of the gardens and palaces as we made our way back to the car, each of us looking forward to a bath or shower and the promise of a good dinner. On the way, Pam told Nick of my plans to return home within the next few days, explaining that if by any chance my call up papers had arrived while I'd been away, I obviously needed to get back home as there would be hundreds of things I needed to sort out before I reported for duty.

When we arrived at the hotel, it became immediately obvious that Nick had chosen wisely. As soon as the car rolled up outside, the figure of a small roly-poly man, accompanied by an equally roly-poly lady, appeared beneath the small stone arched doorway, the man coming forward to greet us as we stepped from the car. With his hand outstretched in greeting, he welcomed us to his 'humble home', turning to introduce us to his wife and beckoning us to follow him inside.

Once inside, a delicious smell of freshly baked bread drifted through from another part of the house, filling the stone and oak-beamed room in which we stood with a homely rustic smell, an aroma that boded extremely well for the dinner which would later be cooked for us.

Motioning for us to sit down in the deep comfortable leather armchairs, he turned to be greeted by his wife who had entered carrying a tray of wine glasses, in which a pale golden liquid sparkled in the subdued light.

Speaking in Spanish, she suggested that we might like to try a glass of the local Amontillado sherry before we went to our rooms to freshen up before dinner. I had never tasted sherry before and I was pleasantly surprised by the cold dryness of its taste, and sinking back into the comfort of the armchair, I breathed a deep contented sigh as I stretched out my legs and took in our surroundings.

The room had obviously once been their sitting room before becoming an integral part of the hotel and was decorated quite simply in a traditional Spanish style. There were pictures on the walls and several framed family photographs resting on a solid oak sideboard, its gleaming polished wood shining dully from cast iron and wooden wall lights, and leaning casually against the sideboard was a well used guitar, standing as if its owner had moments before finished playing before leaving it there.

Amongst the photographs, I noticed one which featured a girl dressed in a long flowing flamenco dress, her dark hair dramatically scraped back and held in place by a tall mantilla and in her hands she appeared to be holding a pair of castanets.

Touching my cousin's arm to attract her attention, I nodded discreetly towards the picture of the girl. Getting to her feet, Pam wandered over to take a closer look, as she did so the lady of the house came back into the room.

Seeing my cousin studying the picture, she smiled proudly as she took it down and handed it to her, gratefully touching Pam's hand when she complimented her on her outstanding beauty.

After several minutes during which time there was an abundance of gesticulation and laughing, Pam turned and explained what the lady had been saying.

'I think we may be in for a treat this evening,' she said.

'Señora Aguero has told me that the photograph is of her daughter and she is well known in the area as a dancer, and if we would permit it, together with her son who plays the guitar, they would be very happy to perform for us this evening after dinner.'

'Permit it?' I gasped. 'No wonder Nick said he thought that we would love it here.'

Turning to Nick, I grinned. 'I take back everything I ever said about you man, you've really outdone yourself this time.'

'Thanks a bunch Pete,' he replied. 'I do my best to try to look out for you and that's all the thanks I get. Remind me when we get back home just to call a cab for you when you leave. Old Nick's family taxi service is a thing of the past from now on.'

On hearing Pam's laughter, Señora Aguero looked puzzled, clearly believing that her offer of after dinner entertainment had not been received in the manner in which it had been offered. Sensing her disappointment, Pam took her hand and began to explain that it would be a great honour to see her daughter and son perform, apologising for the laughter and explaining that Nick was an American and that I was English, and because of this there was always an ongoing banter between us, something that could only be appreciated if you spoke English and understood fully what was being said.

Satisfied with the explanation, Señora Aguero once again happily carried on talking, smiling in my direction and saying something that caused both Pam and Nick to laugh uproariously, something which was clearly directed towards me.

Still laughing, they both looked in my direction, my cousin raising her hands almost in supplication as she explained.

'Señora Aguero thinks that you are '*muy guapo*' and asked me if you were married?'

Taken aback, I didn't know how to respond as I felt my face beginning to redden.

'I think madam here may have plans for your future, she told me that her daughter is also single and thinks that you would look very good together.'

'What was that you just said?' I stammered. 'What's *guapo*?'

'*Guapo*?'

'*Guapo* means attractive or handsome. She thinks you are very handsome.'

Immediately, Nick seized on his opportunity.

'Very handsome? I think the old girl needs her eyes testing. You wait till I tell Bishop about this; he's going to give you hell. Mind you, if this daughter is all she's cracked up to be, you could be in there kid, this could be one hell of a place for a wedding. I don't know what your old man is going to make of all this though. He's probably not going to look too kindly on you marrying someone who wasn't born and bred in Luton.'

I looked across to Señora Aguero who had what I thought was an alarmingly maternal look about her, smiling back at me as she nodded in my direction.

To cover my embarrassment and avoid further leg pulling from Nick I hastily finished my drink, putting the empty glass down on to a nearby table before standing up.

'I think I need a bath before dinner,' I said. 'Do you know where our rooms are?'

'Well now, look at this,' Nick joked. 'I reckon our boy here is thinking about getting in the mood for a little romance, I've never seen him this keen on getting himself spruced up before. I should start looking around for a new wedding outfit if I were you Pam; you know what these English guys can be like.'

After being shown to our rooms, I lay on the bed and looked around. Although fairly small, the room was comfortably furnished and with the window open, it was refreshingly cool.

We had been escorted to the first floor of the hotel, which, as I had guessed, was once the family home and although now classified as a hotel, it still managed to retain a warm family atmosphere, and although the bathroom and toilet were at the end of the landing, everything was scrupulously clean and tidy.

I had agreed that Pam and Nick should use the bathroom first, and in the meantime I took out my change of clothes for the evening. Looking at what I had brought with me I began to think of what the evening had in store, glad now that I had bothered to pack the new shirt and trousers that I had recently purchased from the PX.

I knew that in view of what had been said earlier I was bound to be the subject of more pointed comments from Nick, but I was ready for that, deciding that I might well play a few games of my own. I knew that I would be treading a fine line if I pretended to play the amorous tourist to Señora Aguero's daughter, but it might well be worth the risk to put Nick firmly in his place.

Thinking about dinner and what lay beyond, my train of thought was interrupted by a knock on the door.

'Bathroom's free, buddy boy. Better get yourself moving if you want to join us for dinner.'

Acknowledging Nick's wake-up call, I got up from the bed and opened the door, making my way down the hall to the bathroom. Once inside, I took out shampoo from my toilet bag and began to run the bath.

Fortunately there appeared to be no shortage of hot water and, after shaving, I lowered myself into the steaming water, tipping in some liquid smelly bath soap before stretching out in the foaming hot water. Twenty minutes later, I was back in my room and ready to take on whatever the evening had in store, eagerly looking forward to dinner and the impromptu entertainment afterwards.

Dressed and ready to go, I tapped on Pam and Nick's door, breathing in the wonderful aroma of cooking coming from downstairs.

Opening the door, my cousin stood framed in its threshold, stepping back as she beckoned me inside.

I had never seen my cousin in this light before; normally she wore either tight blue jeans and a simple blouse, or a simple cotton dress with a belt around the waist which emphasised her slim waist.

'Wow,' I gasped. 'You look absolutely gorgeous, what did you do with my cousin?'

'Thanks Pete, you sure know how to make a girl feel good. Once in a while I do make an effort.'

I stepped back to look properly at what she was wearing.

Wearing simple, flat, black, slip-on shoes and a figure-hugging black dress with her blonde hair scraped back and held in place with a Spanish-style mantilla, the overall effect was simply stunning.

'Wow,' was all I could say again. 'I've never seen you look more beautiful.'

She took my arm as she stood on tiptoe to lightly kiss me on the cheek.

'Thank you kind sir,' she said, lightly bowing her head in response to my compliment.

'That's the difference between you and O'Henry there, all he could think of to say was, "Is that dress new?".'

She sniffed as she looked at him sitting on the edge of the bed. 'Who was it who said that the age of romance is dead?'

I laughed at Nick's raised eyebrows and outspread hands.

He shrugged, 'I just thought I hadn't seen it before.'

'If I were you Nick, I wouldn't say anything else otherwise you could find yourself sleeping in my room with me.'

Getting up from the bed, Nick took Pam's hand to escort her from the room.

'You're right though Pete, she doesn't scrub up too badly does she?'

Paella and Passion...

Sitting down at a long, solid oak dining table on which the flickering light from two large fat candles cast romantic shadows around the room, I thought back to the palaces of the Alhambra, thinking that this is how it must have been when the Emir and other assorted Caliphs sat down to dine.

An all-consuming feeling of romantic history transformed the whole room as I was swept up with both the ambience of the setting and the aura given off by this ancient building as again I experienced the feeling that I had been here before.

Half expecting scantily veiled serving wenches to appear weighed down with trays of exotic fruits and delicacies, I glanced across at my cousin whose whole countenance seemed to glow in the light from the candles, the whole scene becoming slightly bizarre as I tried to dismiss this overwhelming feeling of déjà vu.

'Are you alright Pete?'

Pam's insistent voice brought me down to earth with a start.

'Sorry, did you say something?' I asked.

'Are you all right?' she asked again.

'Um, yes,' I said.

Leaning across the table, I shook my head as I looked into her face.

'I know this is going to sound daft, but ever since we arrived here I've had this overwhelming feeling that I've been here before. Not recently I mean, but hundreds of years ago, do you get that feeling or is it just me?'

'I know what you mean but it's this place. It's because it's so atmospheric it is just like a journey back into the past.'

I gazed about the room. 'It's weird; everywhere I look I seem to remember being here before, or thinking that I once lived here.'

'When you opened your bedroom door and stood there wearing that dress with the mantilla it shook me, it was as if you and I had known each other in a previous life and that we had both been here before.'

Nick's down-to-earth cynicism brought me back to the present with a jolt.

'Man, you need a drink, all this history is starting to freak you out.'

I looked into my cousin's eyes and saw a flicker of understanding, and although the moment had quickly passed I knew that she had felt it too.

With a brief tap on the door, Señor Aguero appeared carrying a tray, on which a bottle shrouded with years of dust and five large wine glasses were precariously balanced, and placing it down on the table, he produced an old and much used wooden handled corkscrew from a pocket in the front of his striped apron.

After placing a glass in front of each of us, he wiped the dust from the neck of the bottle before slicing off the lead collar covering the cork. Holding the bottle in front of one of the flickering candles to show off its deep red colour, he carefully screwed the corkscrew into the cork, expertly withdrawing it in one easy motion.

As he reverently placed the opened bottle on the table, he spoke quietly to Nick who nodded his approval.

'Señor Aguero wishes us to know that the wine we are about to taste is over twelve years old and is a fine Rioja which was produced from a vineyard in this area. He would also like to say that he considers it to be a great honour that we have chosen to stay with him and his family. He also asks if he might be allowed to bring his wife into the room and that they might also be allowed to drink from this bottle and to raise their glasses in a toast to our continued good health and happiness.'

On hearing his words, I felt moved that these good people had not only taken it upon themselves to welcome us into the heart of their home, not just as paying guests from a different culture, but perhaps as newfound friends as well.

Glancing across at Pam, I saw that she was staring at me with a strange faraway look in her eyes. As our eyes met she smiled, not smiling as someone who was enjoying this moment in time, but as someone who was reliving the past and had enjoyed moments like this in an environment such as this.

With the sudden opening of the door, the spell was broken as Señora Aguero entered the room, smiling broadly as she stood at the side of her husband.

Picking up the bottle of wine Señor Aguero held it against one of the candles, again peering at its contents through the glass before testing its aroma with a loud sniff. Satisfied, he gently poured a small amount into my cousin's glass.

'Señora, *por* favour.'

Raising up her glass, she slowly swirled it around its bowl as if this was something she had done all of her life before raising the glass to her lips.

'*Perfección Señor, muy, muy bien.*'

The little hotelier beamed from ear to ear, delighted that he had chosen my cousin to taste the wine, filling each of our glasses with the remainder from the bottle.

Speaking in his native tongue, Señor Aguero motioned for us to raise our glasses as he proposed the toast which perhaps typifies best the generosity and hospitality of the inhabitants in this wonderful country.

'*Amigos, Mi Casa, Su Casa.*'

Sipping his wine, he placed the half empty glass on the tray before grasping Nick's hand, explaining that he considered it an honour to be able to offer good wine and hospitality and that this bottle of wine was his gift, adding with a wry laugh that he was sorry, but further bottles would have to be paid for.

With a short bow, he took his wife by the arm and practically dragged her from the room, her expression clearly indicating that she would have much preferred to stay and enjoy our company, further adding that he must concentrate on dinner and should we require further wine, it would give his wife great pleasure to serve us.

As the door closed, I raised my glass and thanked Pam and Nick for the wonderful time that we had spent together, adding that I was sorry that the time had come for me to leave, insisting also that dinner and the wine tonight was on me.

Before leaving Seville, I had worked out how much money I had left and how much I would need to get me home, and if I was careful I reckoned that, without indulging in any more sightseeing detours on my way back, I had enough to pay for my accommodation also to treat us all to dinner by way of thanks.

The arrival of dinner not only heralded a visual sensation but a culinary masterpiece which I felt should simply be looked at, admired and photographed, not something to be vandalised by the wanton destruction of eager knives and forks.

Opening the door, Señora Aguero stood to one side to allow her husband entry.

Nothing could have prepared us for the sight of the food that he had lovingly prepared; indeed, a triumphant fanfare of trumpets would not have been out of place as he placed the huge paella pan down on to the table.

The traditional pan in which the paella had been prepared was made of heavy cast iron with carrying handles at each end and was at least two feet in diameter and three inches in depth. In it, basking in a sea of golden rice, chicken, mussels, langoustines and other assorted shell fish, provided the most mouth-watering smells imaginable.

We all stared at this superb masterpiece of traditional Spanish fare he had created, all of us momentarily speechless by his obvious artistry in the kitchen.

'Wow, take a look at that,' Nick gasped, shaking his head.

As we all leaned forward to breathe in the wonderful aromas drifting up from the table, Señora Aguero reappeared carrying a large flat basket containing still warm home-cooked bread, dishes of plump green olives and wedges of creamy goat's cheese, and in addition to this, a large bunch of juicy black grapes perfectly complemented this wonderful display. In an unrehearsed moment of grateful approval, each of us spontaneously placed our hands together in a heartfelt round of applause.

Smiling proudly at seeing our pleasure, he appeared slightly embarrassed by our enthusiastic outburst, bowing slightly before hurriedly taking his wife's hand and ushering her from the room.

An hour later, all that was left of this wonderful meal was the detritus from the delicious clams and mussels, together with the legs and scales from the langoustines, amongst which a few morsels of the yellow rice clung stubbornly to the bottom of the pan. The olives, cheese and bread also bore testament to our appetites with only a few of the grapes remaining.

A soft knock on the door heralded the arrival of Señora Aguero who smiled as she saw the remnants of dinner. Happily, she began to clear the table, obviously pleased that we had devoured practically everything that had been placed before us, laughing with my cousin as Pam complimented her on what was, without doubt, the most delicious meal I had ever had in my entire life.

Reaching across the table for the long-since empty wine bottle, I decided that I would attempt to practise my very hesitant and limited Spanish by asking for another, a phrase that during my stay I had used with moderate success on several occasions.

'Señora Aguero, *por favor, traiga más vino tinto?*'

It was though I had asked for her daughter's hand in marriage as she dropped the almost empty basket back on to the table, smiling from ear to ear as she patted my shoulder before excitedly answering me in Spanish. Nick thumped the table as he laughed at the bewildered look on my face as I looked in desperation across the table for a translation.

Coming to my rescue, Pam explained that Señora Aguero had been delighted that I had attempted to speak to her in Spanish, replying that it would give her the greatest pleasure to serve us with more wine, adding that her surprise was due to me asking so fluently in a language that she understood I did not speak.

Still chuckling, Pam completed the utter destruction of my attempt at appearing worldly by saying, 'Don't worry Pete, I told her that when you asked for more wine you were just exercising virtually your total knowledge of the Spanish language. I also said that she wouldn't get any more surprises like that unless you decided to use the only other phrase you know by maybe ordering coffee. '

Before leaving, our jovial hostess suggested that we would be more comfortable if we retired to the other room where her husband would serve the wine before her son and daughter came to entertain us, something that both Pam and Nick happily agreed to, and with a final flashing smile in my direction, she scurried away.

With a huge satisfied sigh, I flopped down in one of the big leather armchairs in the comfortable sitting room, very much tempted after that wonderful meal, to loosen the belt on my trousers, deciding finally that even if I tried to hide what I had done by pulling out my shirt to cover it, it wasn't quite the right thing to do.

Hearing Nick quietly chuckling to himself, I looked across to see what had amused him and seeing him looking in my direction I knew that once again I was about to be the butt of another of his wisecracks.

'OK, let's have it,' I said wearily, 'let's all share the great man's next earth-shattering and philosophical remarks.'

'I was just thinking Pete, if you play your cards right and Señora Aguero's daughter somehow manages to resist your boyish charms and good looks, you could always chance your luck with her mother, she seems to have taken a shine to you. Be careful though, judging by the expertise the old man used with a knife to carve up that chicken for the paella, you'd do well to keep your hands on your cojones.'

He laughed uproariously at his own bar room style humour.

'Why don't you leave him alone?' Pam said. 'You could take a few lessons from him and try to behave like a gentleman instead of picking on him all the time.'

'That's alright Pam, let him have his fun. He's just some backwoods hic from Presque Isle, Maine who thinks that baseball is a game for men and that just about says it all. The only reason he vaguely recognises the word "gentleman" is because he's seen it written on a toilet door.'

The opening of the door stopped any further banter between us as Señor Aguero stepped to one side to allow entry into the room of his son and daughter.

Carrying a guitar, with his dark handsome face wreathed in a broad smile, a young man not much older than me led his sister by the hand. Standing to one side so as not to take away any of the glory of his sister's entry, he bowed, still lightly holding her fingertips as she stood beside him.

Proudly, Señora Aguero held her daughter's other hand as she carried out the introductions; the only words in her brief speech being recognisable to me were their names, the son, Isidro, and the daughter who she lovingly announced as Catalina.

The photograph I had seen earlier, although cleverly posed to illustrate her outstanding beauty, was a pale facsimile of what now stood before us.

Dressed in a blood-red, figure-hugging dress which flowed out from just below her hips in wide flowing flounces, she smiled, her dazzling white teeth acting to underline her dark sensuous beauty. Her jet black hair was simply scraped back from her face and tied in a ponytail behind her, while large gold-hooped gypsy earrings glowed in the light from the candles which added to the lustrous beauty of her skin.

Her brother was dressed in dramatic contrast, wearing a simple, white-frilled fronted shirt tucked into tight black trousers which clung to his slim waist and hips. A wide black leather belt held in place by a large square silver buckle underlined his lean athletic figure, while on his feet a pair of soft black leather high-heeled boots completed the picture of a young man completely relaxed in his masculinity.

Standing with one foot on the seat of a plain wooden chair, his guitar resting easily across his thigh, his fingers suddenly darted towards the strings, the single reverberating chord acting as an invitation to his sister to begin her participation in a duet of mesmerising and unrestrained passion.

In spellbound delight at this magnificent display of traditional Spanish flamenco music played with such amazing dexterity by Isidro, Catalina's breathtaking and sensuous dance caused the hairs on the back of my neck to stand on end as I soaked up the complexity of the rhythms echoing around the simple splendour of the room.

It is easy to understand how Hemingway wrote the way he did; his was a passion which devoured the soul, his love of a country so alien to his own which transcended his mortality and allowed him to feel great joy but also to suffer the pangs of despair for its people, an overwhelming passion which caused him to take his own life in the way that he did. When reading arguably his most important study of the Spanish psyche contained in *Death in the Afternoon* and also now beginning to understand the passion he must have felt when writing *Fiesta*, a sense of impending tragedy is to my mind clearly evident, something which ultimately led to the termination of his own amazing voyage of discovery.

The thought of Hemingway's untimely end sent a slight shiver down my spine as I was brought back down to earth by the applause and shouts of '*olé*' as both Pam and Nick rose to their feet in appreciation of the magical display we had just witnessed.

Jumping to my feet, I was sorry that I didn't have flowers to throw at the feet of Catalina, instead making do with raising my still half-empty glass in a silent toast to both her beauty and her bewildering skill.

Inclining her head slightly, she acknowledged my tribute with a smile, extending her arm to where her brother stood, beads of perspiration trickling down his face as he too smiled in appreciation of our spontaneous tribute. In a moment they were both gone, Señora Aguero closing the door behind them as they quickly left the room.

'Well, I don't know about you guys,' Nick said as he slumped back down in his chair, 'but I'm pretty damn sure that you will never witness anything better than that.'

I stared at the closed door, unable to think of anything to say as I thought about what we had just witnessed. Nick was right, nothing could possibly compare to what we had just seen as I too flopped down in my chair. Not only had it been spectacular, we had been privileged in watching two of the most accomplished individual performers entertaining us simply because they had thought that we were people who would understand and appreciate the magic in what they did.

Accompanied by cups of strong black coffee, Pam and I waited for some form of self-congratulatory remarks from Nick who would no doubt tell us how resourceful he had been in choosing this place but he remained strangely silent, pensively swirling the coffee around in his cup as he stared into the distance.

With Pam and I both looking at him curiously, he finally spoke, bending forward as he looked at me with an expression on his face that I had never seen before.

'You know what Pete; I just got a feeling of what you meant earlier when you said that you felt that you had been here before.

'It's the damndest thing, but when those two were doing their thing I had the funniest feeling. I don't get swept up with things like that, this is it, the here and now and history is history and there's no way that you could have ever convinced me otherwise, but I just had the weirdest sensation that all of this was in some way familiar.'

I glanced at Pam who had a slight smile on her face.

Never had there been a better moment than now to remind Nick of his previous scepticism and his cynical remarks but, seeing him so vulnerable, I knew that to make any sort of derogatory remark wouldn't be right, this was a moment that would live in his memory for a very long time and I wasn't going to take that away from him.

As we talked, there was a light tap on the door and Señor Aguero entered the room carrying a wooden tray on which stood a bottle of brandy together with five glasses, his wife happily trotting along behind with a huge smile on her face. Placing the tray down on the table, our jovial little host spoke to Pam and Nick asking if they might be allowed to join us, explaining that he and his wife would like to say thank you to us for choosing to stay with them, adding that on behalf of his whole family he would like to take the opportunity of proposing a toast for what they hoped had been an enjoyable stay and that we would grace his 'humble home' again in the near future.

Gratefully accepting their kind offer, the room was soon filled with the sound of laughter, my only regret being that my lack of Spanish meant I couldn't join in with the carefree banter, but nevertheless, I was far from excluded from the conversation as our hosts readily included me by asking questions which Pam happily translated before passing on my answers and comments.

Not wishing to refuse a second glass of the exceedingly fine brandy, it soon became abundantly clear that in coming into contact with the previously enjoyed wine, the effect of both coupled with the amount of food I had previously consumed was beginning to take its toll, so much so that all attempts at stifling my yawns became predictably noticeable.

Commenting on my obvious tiredness, Señora Aguero smiled and reached forward to take my hand, indicating that I appeared ready to call it a day. After thanking them both once again for their superb hospitality, Pam asked that they express our sincere thanks to their son and daughter before we all happily took our leave, ending for me one of the most memorable days of my life.

All Good Things Must Come to an End...

The following morning, after a breakfast of freshly baked rolls, ham and cheese followed by strong black coffee, we reluctantly said goodbye to our hosts before revisiting the Alhambra and the gardens of the Generalife, strolling happily through the scented cypresses as we relived our pleasures of the previous evening, promising that we would again return to visit our generous hosts.

After a leisurely journey back to Seville, we were greeted by Paco who, after bringing bottles of ice-cold beer, sat down with us to enquire about our trip, eagerly questioning us about what we had seen and where we had stayed. As we enlightened him in great detail the delights of both Granada and of our hosts, Paco suddenly announced that while we were away, a letter had arrived from England marked for my attention which he had taken upstairs to the apartment. On hearing this, my heart skipped a beat, that letter could have only come from home and I was pretty sure that they weren't just writing to enquire about the state of my health.

Ordering two more beers and a coffee for my cousin, Nick got to his feet announcing that he would just slip upstairs and collect the mail, venturing the idea that my letter was probably from some adoring female who could no longer stand being parted from me. If only that were true I thought, confident that somebody may well crave my company but equally sure that it wasn't any female I knew of, unless of course you counted someone dressed in RAF blue who desperately needed a shave and would benefit from a much finer line in stockings and footwear.

On his return, Nick studied the envelope addressed to me before handing it over.

'Looks like a Luton postmark buddy, I hope everything is OK at home.'

With all eyes on me, I slipped open the envelope, knowing the moment I saw my father's writing that it wasn't going to be a letter that said 'we hope you're having a nice time'.

Despite him being hundreds of miles away, I could sense from the tone of the letter that my father was not a happy man. As I quickly scanned the first page, the reason for his anger became abundantly clear.

Returning home for lunch one day, he had been sitting with my mother when there had been a knock on the front door. On answering, she had returned to tell him that there were two men at the door who wished to speak to him, adding that initially they had asked to speak to me but she had explained to them that I was abroad on holiday.

Going to the door, the two men had told him that they belonged to a section of the RAF Military Police, proving who they were by showing him their identity cards. They explained that the reason they were there was because I had failed to present myself for National Service at RAF Cardington on the prescribed date.

My father, although angry and embarrassed at having to suffer that sort of indignity, had confirmed that I was indeed on holiday and that he would attempt to contact me, stressing also that he wasn't exactly certain where I was but that he was expecting me to return home some time in the immediate future.

Satisfied with both my father's apology and explanation, they stressed that it was imperative that I returned at the earliest opportunity as my absence was a serious matter, telling him also that if he should hear from me I was to be informed immediately of the situation.

Well that was it, game set and match. If ever there had been the slightest doubt in my mind about the right time to leave, that letter had certainly decided it for me.

Sitting back in my chair, I tried to appear calm, sticking the letter in my shirt pocket and picking up my glass.

Pam was the first to speak.

'Well, is everything alright?' she asked.

'Everything is fine,' I replied.

'It's from home just to say that they send you their regards and that they hope I'm behaving myself,' I lied. 'They also said that there's a letter for me which looks like it might contain my call-up papers so I guess I have to think about leaving.'

' Oh well buddy,' Nick said, ' It's been swell having you, but I guess you knew that it would happen sometime, when do you reckon on going?'

As usual, Pam leaped in to defend any decision I might come to.

'Don't sound as if you're in a hurry to get rid of him,' she said. 'I'm sure that a few more days won't make any difference will it?'

'Nick's right,' I said. 'The longer I stay the harder it's going to get. 'If it's OK with you Nick I'd appreciate a lift to the station tomorrow to see what sort of times the trains leave for Madrid.'

'Sure buddy, no problem, but like Pam says, there's no great rush is there?'

As I looked at my cousin, I knew that staying on and prolonging my visit would be a mistake. I could already sense the feeling of sadness that we were now both feeling as I was reminded of the conversation we had had as we strolled through the gardens of the Alhambra, better to make a quick clean break and let them get back to normal.

Trying to lift the mood, I raised my half empty glass in a toast.

'Thanks for everything you two, but when I get out of the service you can bet that wherever you two are there's going to be no hiding place, I'll be back to haunt you.'

Raising his own glass in acknowledgement, Nick replied in his usual flippant manner.

'I'll drink to that buddy boy, but before we see you again, just make some sort of effort to improve your poker technique. Like I tried to tell you a hundred times, never open the betting with just an ace cause you're always going to get burned.'

'I will be sorry to see you leave Seňor,' Paco said raising his glass. 'It has been a great pleasure for me to have you here, but do not forget what we talked of earlier, there is always a place here with me and my sons when you have done your duty.'

'Thanks Paco, I won't forget, but let's get these two years out of the way first before I think of doing anything else.'

After a final dinner at the NCOs' club with Robert and Marie, followed by a long poker session back at the apartment, I had fallen into bed only to toss and turn until the small hours of the morning, finally drifting off to a troubled and interrupted sleep, thoughts of what was to come spoiling my final night after what had been a truly stimulating and remarkable holiday.

The drive to the station the following morning, accompanied by both my cousin and Nick, was in strict contrast to when I had arrived, attempted light-hearted conversation failing to lift the gloom that surrounded my imminent departure.

Once at the station, I had rechecked the times of the trains together with my tickets, and after a brief kiss and a handshake I had insisted that Pam and Nick leave, not wishing to prolong the time I had left with more awkward goodbyes and meaningless conversation, and sitting alone in my compartment, I waited for the train to leave, staring moodily out of the carriage window. Finally with a shrill blast from the guard's whistle, the train dragged its way out of the station, it too, seemingly reluctant to leave this wonderful place.

Travelling through Spain, I thought back to Jaime and the fight I had seen where he had shown his brilliance, Paco and the bar and Pam and Nick's hospitality and, more recently, the wonders of the Alahmbra and of our hosts there, promising myself that as soon as I had finished my time with the RAF I would return.

The following long journey through France dragged by and I remembered Eric Besancon together with his fellow soldiers, wondering what had been their final destination hoping that the fates had been kind to them all and that they would soon return safely to the bosom of their own respective families, and of course the beautiful Avril and the memory of our very own 'brief encounter'.

At long last, after an uneventful Channel crossing followed by further trains from Dover to London and the final leg of my journey to Luton, I stood filled with trepidation at my own front door, putting down my case on the front doorstep as I fumbled with my key. I was finally home, but what sort of reception would I receive when I stepped over the threshold? I didn't have long to wait to find out.

Calling out 'I'm home', just as if I had just got back from a short trip to the local shops, I dropped my case in the hall just as the sitting room door opened and my mother stood there with a look of amazement on her face. I smiled as she stood there still wearing her apron, it was if I had never been away.

Holding out her hands towards me, she threw her arms around my neck, squeezing me as if I had been away for years. This is looking good I thought, aware at the same time that this greeting wouldn't bear any resemblance to the one my father would give me when he got home. I was also pretty sure that when the shock of suddenly seeing me like this had worn off, this 'welcome home' attitude would also quickly change. I didn't have long to wait.

Stepping back, she placed her hands on her hips, the expression on her face quickly changing as she looked me up and down.

'Where have you been all this time, your father and I expected you home weeks ago, didn't you get your father's letter?'

'Calm down, Mum,' I replied. 'As soon as I got your letter, I packed and came straight home, I've been travelling for the last couple of days and I'm pretty tired, any chance of a cup of tea?'

'I'll give you cup of tea my boy! Two RAF policemen came here looking for you and they said that failing to report for duty was a very serious offence. Your father told them that you were abroad and he didn't know exactly where you were, but he was really angry that he had to tell lies.'

'Sorry Mum,' I replied. 'I planned to come home sooner than this but I couldn't remember the exact date I had to report. I'll get myself sorted out and unpacked and report to Cardington within the next couple of days or so.'

I felt bad at having to be economical with the truth but hoped that my little white lie might ease the situation slightly as far as my mother was concerned, vowing that when my father arrived home I would do what I had sworn to do and behave like a man and take whatever criticisms he might throw at me.

When my father arrived home, I was ready. I had unpacked and given my mother the two wooden bullfighting pictures I had previously purchased and was prepared to accept whatever the outcome might be, but equally ready to stand my ground and express my views in respect of my prolonged absence. Both to his eternal credit and my amazement, he quietly listened to what I had to say before shrugging and telling me that he understood how tempted I must have been to stay on there, finally admitting that had it been him, he would probably have considered doing the same thing.

How Nice of You to Join Us...

Three days after my return, I felt sufficiently recovered after my exhausting journey to consider my next immediate course of action facing up to the fact that I needed to present myself at RAF Cardington as soon as possible rather than to wait until the two gentlemen who had previously called, once again came knocking at the door.

After repacking my small case with the suggested items referred to in the letter I had received informing me of the date of my conscription, I stoically said goodbye to my slightly tearful mother and a dour but proud father, and with infinitely less enthusiasm than I had previously felt when embarking on my great adventure, I set off to catch a bus to where, on this occasion, there was a far greater degree of uncertainty together with a much greater feeling of apprehension.

Staring gloomily out of the window of the bus as it followed its rural path towards Bedford, I looked out across the fields where, in the distance, I could see the two massive hangars which had once housed the airship the R101, completely unaware that I, along with other miserable conscripted individuals, would come to know these two huge structures quite intimately as our progression into service life continued.

All too quickly, I finally found myself standing in front of two very large brick pillars from which heavy wrought iron gates stood open to allow access to a small convoy of lorries, each one bearing the familiar red, white and blue roundels of the RAF, while, behind the driver's cabs, the contents of the trucks were concealed by canvas sheeting. As the vehicles continued their journey towards a cluster of large huts, I watched as a man in an RAF uniform wearing a white-topped cap and a red armband, pulled on a large round counterweight which brought a heavy red and white striped metal pole crashing down across the entrance.

With the sound made by the metal barrier ringing in my ears, I was reminded of the film *Escape from Alcatraz* where convicts were locked away by warders slamming shut the barred metal doors of their cells, the irony of serving my own two year 'sentence' behind this slightly less terrifying type of steel barrier bringing an involuntary smile to my face.

As I watched the lorries disappearing between the rows of huts, the uniformed guard saw me standing there and called out to me.

'Is there something I can help you with?'

Steeling myself for what was to come I walked towards him as he stood with his hands resting on the striped barricade.

'I've come to report for duty,' I answered, taking the letter from my pocket and handing it to him.

Reading the letter then looking back at me, his face took on a far more serious look as he re-read the part which related to the original date of my enlistment.

'I think you had better come with me young man, we've been expecting you, how nice of you to join us, I'll just ring the duty officer and let him know you've arrived, I'm sure he'd like to come and say hello.'

And so began my introduction to the RAF and to the unique humour of non-commissioned officers everywhere. To men like these who had heard every excuse imaginable at least a hundred times, this wry humour was their stock in trade, and all over the world any misdemeanour would incur such derisory witticisms accordingly, together with whatever punishment they saw fit to dole out.